Google Advertising Tools

Harold Davis

O'REILLY®

Beijing · Cambridge · Farnham · Köln · Paris · Sebastopol · Taipei · Tokyo

Google Advertising Tools
by Harold Davis

Copyright © 2006 O'Reilly Media, Inc. All rights reserved.
Printed in the United States of America.

Published by O'Reilly Media, Inc., 1005 Gravenstein Highway North, Sebastopol, CA 95472.

O'Reilly books may be purchased for educational, business, or sales promotional use. Online editions are also available for most titles (*safari.oreilly.com*). For more information, contact our corporate/institutional sales department: (800) 998-9938 or *corporate@oreilly.com*.

Editor: Brett McLaughlin

Production Editor: Adam Witwer

Production Services: Pre-Press Company, Inc.

Cover Designer: Karen Montgomery

Interior Designer: David Futato

Illustrators: Robert Romano, Jessamyn Read, and Lesley Borash

Printing History:

January 2006:   First Edition.

 This book uses RepKover™, a durable and flexible lay-flat binding.

ISBN: 0-596-10108-2

[M]

Table of Contents

Part I. Making Money with Your Web Site

Preface

Google and the Web have changed the way the world publishes content and the way the world advertises. It's now possible for anyone to publish a web site, and, if the content of the site draws traffic, to make money from Google's AdSense program, all with almost no additional effort.

It's easy to publish a web site. The ability to make money from any site that interests visitors makes self-publishing possible in a new and revolutionary sense. If something interests you, it is likely to be of interest to at least some other people—and you can get paid to follow your interests. For example, if you write a blog that people read, it's now easy to get paid for blogging. All of this is possible with the AdSense program.

Google's AdWords program and contextual and CPC advertising, in which the advertiser pays by the click, have also revolutionized advertising. *Contextual* means that ads are relevant to site visitors—a promise that is fulfilled as in no other advertising medium.

The AdWords auction mechanism makes targeted, low-cost advertising available to almost everyone and means that there is no need to hire a specialized advertising agency to place professional and effective ads (you do need to know your way around AdWords!).

One of the wonders of AdWords is that it provides reports and mechanisms, such as conversion tracking, for understanding how successful your ads are. It's easy to create high-quality advertising campaigns using AdWords and to understand exactly what the return on your investment is.

Advertising on the Web is a $7 billion market as of 2005, with a 40% estimated annual growth rate. This is big business, with interested parties ranging from business people to advertising agencies to technical folk. If you need to advertise, want to advertise, or are an advertising manager, this book contains nuts-and-bolts information about AdWords that you will not find elsewhere and that will help you to efficiently drive traffic to your site.

Google has exposed the functionality of AdWords to programmers via the Google AdWords API web services. This isn't for everyone; you need to be able to write code, for starters, and you probably need to be either a large advertiser or an agency managing many advertisers for creating custom code based on the AdWords APIs to make sense. But it's encouraging to know that the ability to automate interactions with the AdWords servers is there should you want to make use of it.

The AdWords API web service program shows Google's commitment to openness and to exploration and experimentation that will lead to still more advances in advertising on the Web.

Google Advertising Tools explains the business and technology behind making money with content and advertising on the Web. This is a practical book for technically inclined people about how to use the Google advertising services to make money. The book provides the background information that is needed to understand and work with both AdSense and AdWords. You'll learn how to build a site that can derive revenue from AdSense and other programs, how to drive traffic to that site, and how to improve search engine placement for the site. You'll also understand how to use AdWords before you're done.

This book is for you if you want to make money with content on a web site. I don't promise that you'll get rich by carrying advertising on your sites (I'm not rich yet!), but I do promise that if you provide interesting content and use the techniques explained in this book, you will make money. It's also for you if you want to learn how to best use the advertising tools that the Google AdWords program provides.

By the way, Google is constantly improving the features and user interfaces of its advertising tools (as is true of many web-based applications). So by the time you read this book, the way these applications look may be a little different than they do here. But don't worry: the core functionality will not have changed, and you should be able to use the directions in this book without any significant problems.

Please check out the companion web site for the book that I maintain at *http://www. braintique.com/ad/*. This site provides resources, updated information, and source code from the book.

 If you create a site that carries AdSense ads using the techniques explained in Part I and Part II of *Google Advertising Tools*, I will link to it from the companion site for the book. See *http://www.braintique. com/ad/* for details. I reserve the right not to link to any site I deem unsuitable.

Organization

This book is organized into four parts, with each part containing several chapters. Taken as a whole, these parts cover the gamut of the Google advertising tools.

However, each part can be read as a self-contained unit, and each part is aimed at readers with different needs.

- Part I, *Making Money with Your Web Site*, explains how to make money from a content-based web site, how to build a site that will get traffic, how to get your site noticed, and the many ways to make money with advertising on your site.

- Part II, *Getting the Most from AdSense*, explains how to work with Google's AdSense, the premier contextual advertising program for content sites. Participating in the AdSense program is probably one of the best ways to monetize your site.

- Part III, *Working with AdWords*, explains the nuts and bolts, and metrics, of the Google AdWords program, a highly successful mechanism that anybody with a valid credit card can use to place advertisements that reach over 80% of users of the Internet.

- Part IV, *Using the AdWords APIs*, is written for programmers who are interested in writing applications that take advantage of the Google AdWords API web services. This part explains what these web services are and how to write code that interacts with them.

If you read all four parts, you will get a comprehensive picture of how advertising works on the Web and how you can use the Google advertising programs to your advantage.

Assumptions

This book does not explain HTML and will not tell you how to create or modify web sites. To put the concepts and software explained into practice, you need to have basic knowledge of web fundamentals and skills or to work with a webmaster who does.

Part I, *Making Money with Your Web Site*, and Part II, *Getting the Most from AdSense*, are intended for readers who have, or are interested in building, web sites that can be used to make money with advertising. To take advantage of this material, you will need to be able to publish web pages and to modify the HTML code of these pages, for example, to add affiliate links and to add the JavaScript code needed to display Google AdSense ad units on your pages.

You don't need any technical skills to become an effective advertiser on the Web using Google's AdWords program. So, in a sense, Part III, *Working with AdWords*, is the least geeky part of this book, although, as you'll learn when you read Part III, advertising on the Web does have its own complex discipline and metrics. If you want to take advantage of AdWord's nifty conversion- and cross-conversion-tracking features, you'll need to be able to add JavaScript code to your HTML pages.

To profit from Part III you need, of course, a service or product to advertise that makes you money, but webmasters who are simply interested in monetizing the content of their own sites, and not in advertising per se, will gain from an understanding of "how the other half lives." An interesting idea to explore is to see if you can profitably drive traffic to your site using AdWords and make more revenue from AdSense and other programs than it costs you to get the traffic.

Part IV, *Using the AdWords APIs*, is written for programmers and assumes an audience that has a basic understanding of the web services mechanism, already knows how to program, and can sight-read code (in PHP or C#, depending on the chapter).

About the Examples

Various fragments of HTML and code are presented in this book, such as the JavaScript code used to display Google AdSense ad units on your web pages.

In addition, Chapters 14 through 16 provide extensive examples that show how to use the Google AdWords APIs.

Chapters 14 and 16 use PHP in a series of complete web pages. In contrast, Chapter 15 shows a C#.Net Windows application that is compiled using Visual Studio.Net (2003 or later).

If you want to play with the applications presented in these chapters, I do not expect you to type them in by hand. The source code for each of these three chapters is available as a zipped archive from both *http://www.braintique.com/ad/* and *http://www.oreilly.com/catalog/buildinggoogle*, and you'll also find the PHP applications from Chapter 14 and 16 ready for you to use at *http://www.braintique.com/ad/* (once you have your Google AdWords APIs developer key, as explained in Chapter 13).

Conventions Used in This Book

The following typographical conventions are used in this book:

Plain text
> Indicates menu titles, menu options, menu buttons, and keyboard accelerators (such as Alt and Ctrl).

Italic
> Indicates new terms, URLs, email addresses, filenames, file extensions, pathnames, directories, and Unix utilities.

`Constant width`
> Indicates commands, options, switches, variables, attributes, keys, functions, types, classes, namespaces, methods, modules, properties, parameters, values, objects, events, event handlers, XML tags, HTML tags, macros, the contents of files, or the output from commands.

Constant width bold

Shows commands or other text that should be typed literally by the user.

Constant width italic

Shows text that should be replaced with user-supplied values.

 This icon signifies a tip, suggestion, or general note.

 This icon indicates a warning or caution.

Using Code Examples

This book is here to help you get your job done. In general, you may use the code in this book in your programs and documentation. You do not need to contact us for permission unless you're reproducing a significant portion of the code. For example, writing a program that uses several chunks of code from this book does not require permission. Selling or distributing a CD-ROM of examples from O'Reilly books does require permission. Answering a question by citing this book and quoting example code does not require permission. Incorporating a significant amount of example code from this book into your product's documentation does require permission.

We appreciate, but do not require, attribution. An attribution usually includes the title, author, publisher, and ISBN. For example: "*Google Advertising Tools* by Harold Davis. Copyright 2006 O'Reilly Media, Inc., 0-596-10108-2."

If you feel your use of code examples falls outside fair use or the permission given above, feel free to contact us at *permissions@oreilly.com*.

How to Contact Us

Please address comments and questions concerning this book to the publisher:

O'Reilly Media, Inc.
1005 Gravenstein Highway North
Sebastopol, CA 95472
(800) 998-9938 (in the United States or Canada)
(707) 829-0515 (international or local)
(707) 829-0104 (fax)

We have a web page for this book, where we list errata, examples, and any additional information. You can access this page at:

http://www.oreilly.com/catalog/buildinggoogle

To comment or ask technical questions about this book, send email to:

bookquestions@oreilly.com

For more information about our books, conferences, Resource Centers, and the O'Reilly Network, see our web site at:

http://www.oreilly.com

Safari Enabled

 When you see a Safari® Enabled icon on the cover of your favorite technology book, that means the book is available online through the O'Reilly Network Safari Bookshelf.

Safari offers a solution that's better than e-books. It's a virtual library that lets you easily search thousands of top tech books, cut and paste code samples, download chapters, and find quick answers when you need the most accurate, current information. Try it for free at *http://safari.oreilly.com*.

Acknowledgments

I'd like to specially thank Brett McLaughlin for his excellent job editing this book. It's rare to find an editor who knows both how to trust his authors and when to challenge them to do better.

Matt Wagner did an excellent job of representing me as the agent for this book. He also deserves acknowledgment for having the courage to follow his own destiny—by setting up shop as a solo agent.

Phyllis is my hero, as well as my wife and friend. Thanks, Phyllis, for reading the chapters of this book before I submitted them, and for taking up the slack around the house and with the kids. Julian, Nicky, and Mathew bore my obsession with writing this book with extraordinary grace, although Nicky did frequently tell me that he wanted his Daddy back, and that he wanted "Daddy's book to be done" so that he could play with Daddy.

With three little boys in the house, music and a good headset are obligatory. Artists I listened to on this book include Ry Cooder, the Dixie Chicks, John Dowland, Emmylou Harris, Bob Marley, Kitaro, Mozart, Paul Simon, Seal, Bruce Springsteen, and Ali Farka Toure. These musicians are, of course, responsible for all errors and omissions in the text, while I alone deserve credit for everything I happened to get right!

PART I

Making Money with Your Web Site

Chapters 1–6 explain how to make money from a content-based web site, how to build a site that will get traffic, how to get your site noticed, and the many ways to make money with advertising on your site.

CHAPTER 1

Build It and They Will Come: Creating Popular Web Sites

"Build it and they will come" is a wonderful line in the movies. Too bad it's usually not quite so easy in real life! True, good web content is occasionally—not always—discovered surprisingly quickly. More often, it requires a great deal of disciplined work to draw traffic to a web site, no matter how good the content of the site is.

And what is a good site and good web content, anyhow? "Good" does not mean a site with a halo! The way I use the word *good* in this chapter is probably circular: a site, and its content, are good if the site and its content draw traffic (or can draw traffic when suitably promoted).

If your site has a great deal of traffic, then the site's traffic is *broad*. Google itself is a prime example of a broad-traffic site: people use Google to search for myriad different things. But narrow, or *focused*, traffic can be more useful to advertisers than broad, unfocused traffic. For example, a site discussing complex ophthalmologic conditions might be very successful with targeted advertising even if it draws only a few hundred users a day. Google's traffic becomes more focused, and less broad, when a keyword search is initiated. And all the targeting in the world won't help unless you get some eyeballs.

To make money with your web site content it's a necessary (but not sufficient) condition that you have good content—either broad or targeted at a specific niche. *Content* can mean information, but it also can mean other things—for example, software applications or jokes.

From a technical viewpoint, there are some issues about setting up a content web site so you can be flexible about the advertising you publish. Flexibility is good: to make money with advertising you need to do a great deal of tweaking. I'll explain how to set sites up so you can easily modify advertising as you go along without having to rewrite your entire site.

The Taxonomy of Success

There's a great deal of variation in good—successful—content web sites. The gist of these sites varies from humor to practical to editorial opinions and beyond. It's hard to generalize. But successful content sites typically do tend to fall into at least one (maybe more than one) of the following categories:

- The site is humorous and makes visitors laugh.
- The site provides a useful free service.
- The site is an online magazine or newspaper.
- The site provides opinions in the form of a blog or blogs.
- The site provides practical information.
- The site sells a popular product or service.
- The site services a community and provides communication tools for that community.

The only thing these kinds of sites have in common—and there are undoubtedly other ways successful sites can be categorized—is that they draw traffic (either focused or broad). Therefore, they are good sites and are excellent venues for web advertising. In short, they use web content to make money—and making money with your web site content is the topic of the first part of this book (and likely a subject you care about!).

In this section, I'll drill down further on the categorization, or *taxonomy*, of successful sites without spending too much time on the issue. As U.S. Supreme Court Justice Harlan Stewart once commented about obscenity, it's hard to define good content, but one knows it when one sees it.

 The section "How Much Content Is Enough?" later in this chapter provides information about the mechanics of content creation—in other words, how many pages of content you need, how frequently it should be updated, and so on.

Funny Web Destinations

Humor itself, as is well known, is in the eye of the beholder (and by itself as a category has infinite variety), but an example of a humorous site that is popular and makes money from contextual advertising is Googlefight, *http://www.googlefight.com*, a site that compares the Google rankings of two terms such as "God" and "Satan."

Humorous sites tend to have short half-lives. Like stars going nova, they can draw tons of traffic for a short while and then fade from view. For example, when Christo's Gates, an elaborate and well-publicized art installation, were up in Central Park, New York, a number of parody sites—Crackers Gates, Nicky's Gates, the Somerville Gates—sprang up. These sites were quite popular for a week or two, but when the Christo art installation was taken down and the media publicity surrounding the installation faded, so did interest in the parody sites.

Today, everyone is bombarded with content in a variety of mediums. Things come and go quickly. For the most part, humor sites that are *static*, meaning that the content doesn't change, publish content that can be expected to fade from public interest—which means that to make money from this content you must be prepared to strike while the iron is hot, because it will only be popular for a short while.

 The reason that a site like Googlefight has some longevity, or legs, is that it draws upon a community effort to constantly update itself (with new examples of humorous juxtapositions). Community participation is a crucial element in many web content success stories—and has the virtue that you don't have to create the content yourself! See "Great Communities," later in this chapter, for more information.

Useful Free Services and Software

TinyURL, *http://tinyurl.com*, provides a practical and very useful (but simple) service: it allows you to convert long, unwieldy URLs—for example, like those you often see from Amazon.com when you select an inventory item—to short, convenient URLs that are easy to use in HTML code (and easy to enter in a browser). Astoundingly, this service is free. Last time I looked, TinyURL had more than 185 million hits a month. Talk about traffic!

In part, a service like TinyURL works to generate ad revenue because it is so targeted. If you go to the site, you'll find Google AdSense content ads for things like DNS (Domain Name Server) services and software that fixes technology problems with browsers. In other words, technology that addresses the problems of reasonably savvy web users is likely to be contextually relevant to the concerns of visitors to TinyURL. Enough users click these ads to more than justify the startup cost and ongoing costs of maintaining the URL conversion service.

It's splitting hairs to try to decide whether sites that provide access to free downloadable software are providing a service or information. Whatever the case, a site that provides information, links, resources, and downloadable software covering a particular technology can draw a great deal of traffic.

For example, if you want to learn about RSS and Atom syndication software—tools for reading and writing feeds—and to download this software (and find easy one-stop links for the location of the download sites), a good site to visit is the RSS Compendium, *http://allrss.com*. Because of their usefulness, one-stop technology sites such as RSS Compendium (whether or not they provide access to downloads) can draw considerable traffic and content-based ad revenue.

If you are going to publish a site whose main draw is access to software, and then make money off the site with content advertising, it is worth bearing in mind that software that runs on the Web typically generates multiple page views for a single user running the software. (In other words, the user spends time on the web site.) This makes it better for the purpose of generating content revenue than a site that merely publishes information about software with download links.

 The difference I'm describing is between software that runs on the Web, and software that you download from the Web in order to run locally.

With a download link, once the user downloads the software, there is probably going to be no more interest in the web content.

 In my opinion, downloaded software that hosts advertising using an Internet connection is a heinous way for vendors of software running on local operating systems to monetize their software—at least it's a step above installing spyware for a living.

Magazines and Newspapers

The business of Salon, *http://www.salon.com*, is to provide informed editorial content. This business is profitable because of the advertising that appears on the Salon site. The business model of Salon, and other online magazines, is pretty much like that of a brick-and-mortar newspaper or magazine: subsidize the distribution of your articles and editorials, and make your revenue with sponsored ads. This works pretty well on the Web, even though it is essentially old-fashioned.

Although it is harder to get subscription revenue for content on the Web than off-Web, profit margins for online advertising are higher, and ads can be more reliably targeted to the context of the content. (This last point is important, because it is the unique selling proposition for web advertising as opposed to advertising in other mediums.)

Opinions differ at even the most successful online venues whether charging a subscription fee for access to content makes sense, or not. (This is a debate that is almost as old as the Web, and yet to be fully resolved.)

For example, the *Wall Street Journal* does, but the *New York Times* does not charge for most access. The *New York Times* online site has a far greater revenue base from online advertising and certain pay-for-access premium services than the *Wall Street Journal* with its entirely subscription-based model. Probably either model can work. But at this point, the advertising model seems to be winning the race.

The Blogosphere

You probably read one or more blogs, at least from time to time. A blog, also called a weblog or web log, is a diary of entries, usually presented on the Web in reverse chronological order. You may even write your own blog. The subject matter of blogs varies wildly, from general rants and raves, to blogs about relationships, to blogs more-or-less devoted to specific technologies, such as my Googleplex Blog (when I don't get too carried away with tangents, my blog is about Google's technology, searching, and research on the Web).

If you think that blogs about a specific subject are an ideal (although narrow) venue for targeted advertising content, you are quite right. Unlike opinion sites that are basically online magazines, blogs are a specifically web phenomenon (sometimes collectively referred to as the *blogosphere*). A variety of software mechanisms—such as the ability to automatically collect trackback links in a blog entry, meaning links to sites or blogs that discuss the original entry—make blogging an extremely effective and versatile mechanism for publishing content on the Web. Syndication built into most blog content management software—such as MovableType or Word-Press—allows easy distribution of the content.

All is not perfect in paradise, though, and there are some problems with blogging as a vehicle for making money from your content. First, there are so many blogs. It's easy to create a blog using hosted services such as Google's Blogger or Six Apart Software's community sites TypePad and LiveJournal. (Six Apart is the publisher of MovableType blogging software.)

But it's hard to stand out from the mass of blogs and generate notice and traffic. See Chapter 2 for some ideas about how to drive traffic to a blog and Chapter 10 for information about how to purchase traffic for a blog using Google's AdWords contextual advertising program.

Next, the fact that blogs are essentially unvetted and unedited makes some advertisers leery about placing ads on these sites. If you do expect to make money from advertising on your blog, it's a good idea to be careful with spelling, punctuation, and the overall presentation issues involved with writing.

Finally, most bloggers use hosted blogging services such as Blogger, so they don't have to worry about configuring or maintaining their own blogging software. Installing software like MovableType is tricky enough that Six Apart, the company that wrote the software, will get it going for you on your own web server—for a fee.

But the problem with having a hosted blog is that generally it's not up to you to place advertising on it. If there is contextual advertising, the revenue may go to the blog host. So if you plan to make money from blogging content, you need to either set up your own blogging server software or work with a specialized web hosting organization that handles the technical end of things but still lets you profit from advertising.

The problem of losing control of the revenue potential of hosted sites can be presented in contexts other than blogging. For example, many smaller e-commerce web sites outsource order processing and shopping cart functionality. This often makes practical sense, but may mean that these pages are no longer available for advertising—or that the advertising and profits are controlled by the host rather than you.

Practical Information: Content Sites and Niches

The O'Reilly site (*http://www.oreilly.com*) provides a great deal of practical information, such as code from the O'Reilly books. O'Reilly is also a source of (usually) well-informed opinions, mostly about topics related to technology: for example, the O'Reilly author blogs, articles, and other quality content.

Many people turn to the Web as their first line of approach for finding information: about technology, relationships, travel destinations, and much more. These content niches are probably the most dependable road to advertising riches on the Web.

Niches don't necessarily have to be big niches. For example, my site Mechanista, *http://www.mechanista.com*, features antique machinery such as typewriters and adding machines. Mechanista makes slow but steady AdSense revenue (from companies selling things like typewriter ribbons).

Don't forget the old saw that it's better to be a big fish in a small pond than a small fish in a big pond. Sites that feature a niche that is of interest only to a small group of people (but very interesting to those people) are likely to achieve high search engine rankings for the relevant terms, draw traffic through the search engines, and become well known among aficionados of the niche.

See Chapters 2 and 3 for more information about drawing traffic and search engine rankings.

If you are the publisher of this kind of niche site, you may not get rich off contextual advertising (you simply cannot draw the eyeballs necessary for getting rich), but you are likely to make a nice revenue return in relation to the effort involved.

E-Commerce Sites

Many of the most successful web businesses make their money as e-commerce sites: by selling goods or services. Advertising on these sites is a by-product (you might say, a product by-product). To name just a few examples:

- Amazon.com is the department store of the Web, selling, either on its own account or for affiliates, everything you can imagine.

- eBay is the world's greatest flea market and auction community, with a great business model since it doesn't need to take an inventory position in the items sold on its site.
- ETrade, Schwab, and other online trading and investing sites are among the greatest revenue generators on the Web.
- Gambling sites successfully part "players" from their funds.

The only thing these sites really have in common is that they make money by selling something and that they draw traffic (in some cases, such as eBay and Amazon, lots and lots of traffic).

Making money from advertising is not really the business of this kind of site. These sites are big businesses and are likely to be advertisers on other sites themselves. In fact, if you work on behalf of a large e-commerce site, you may be interested in using the AdWords APIs to create custom advertising applications as explained in Part IV of this book.

Still, it's natural to look for additional revenue sources, and many e-commerce sites do sell advertising, although they all try to—or should try to—take care not to let the advertising interfere with their primary goal—selling products or services online—or with their brand. For example, you can buy placement for a book or other product on Amazon. These ads show up as similar items when you are checking out (or considering a purchase). It works pretty similarly on eBay. You can purchase contextual advertising on eBay, but only for your products or "store" on eBay itself.

E-commerce sites besides Amazon and eBay may sell ads based on impressions (also called CPM, or Cost Per Thousand, advertising) such as banners used for branding purposes. They are very unlikely to sell ads on a pay-for-click basis (also called CPC, which stands for Cost Per Click) because they want to keep traffic on their sites. Even CPM ads intended for branding purposes will be scrutinized carefully to make sure that the branding message is in keeping with the goal of the e-commerce site.

Great Communities

From its very earliest beginnings, the Web has largely been about community. From a practical standpoint, involving a worthwhile community is a great way to create content. You don't need to create the content yourself: your users do, for example by contributing to discussion threads or by making syndication feeds available.

Site owners can use community to leverage their content and to create sites that are valuable to users because of the involvement of the community.

If your site is extended by community members (for example, through a discussion thread), you may have little control over the quality of the content. As an advertising venue, this content may not be worth that much. But even if it is only worth pennies a day in advertising revenue, the content generation is on autopilot—it is expanding, changing, and staying relevant on its own. So you may still be making a good return on your effort.

Community has made eBay great: essentially all the content comes from users of the eBay auction system. Amazon makes extensive use of community to fill out its content with reviews of books and other products.

Even if your site is essentially not a community site, you can use contributions from visitors to extend and round out your own content. Successful examples include comments on blogs and reader reviews on a site. Another idea for obtaining content that some webmasters have used successfully is to run contests ("Best story in pictures and words about a diving trip" for a scuba diving site is one example).

Mechanisms you can use to build community on a site include providing:

- Message boards
- Chatrooms
- Calendars with information about events in a specific field
- Instant messaging applications
- Reader reviews
- Blog comments and trackbacks

You probably wouldn't want to program an application that enabled much of this community functionality from the ground up, but the fact is that your web host may provide this software for free, versions may be available from the open source community that are also free, or you may be able to inexpensively outsource the application.

If you are hosting your own blog with standard software like Movable-Type or WordPress, the software will give you the ability to enable comments and trackbacks out of the box.

Popular Sites: Using Alexa

I've already mentioned Google as an example of a site with broad traffic. There are, of course, many others. If you are curious, you can go to Alexa, *http://www.alexa.com*, which monitors both how much traffic a site gets and the relative increase (or decrease) in site popularity.

Where Does Content Come From?

No, content doesn't grow on trees. Content is a valuable commodity—and perhaps more than a commodity. Great content is wonderful and unique, and not fungible.

Communities can supply a great deal of content if you have an idea for a good framework that will entice contributions about specific subjects.

If you are a writer, you can create content yourself. (Maybe this is the time for your inner writer to finally come out!)

Site owners can hire writers, either as employees or freelancers, or with a profit-sharing arrangement.

You can often pick up the rights to publish material on the Web that was originally created for a book, magazine, or newspaper very inexpensively. Content creators may be placed to let you use their content simply in exchange for publicity—in the form of an author credit as an expert and/or a link.

You also might check out book and literary agencies. Some of them run a sideline business supplying aggregated recycled content and represent whole groups of writers.

So even if you aren't confident that you can personally create valuable content, don't despair: there are many inexpensive ways to publish valuable content without writing it yourself.

Don't underestimate the value of resource pages as content. A simple page of links to sites related to a specific subject (for example, sites of interest to collectors of antique typewriters and calculators) may draw traffic if the links are accurately described, kept up-to-date, and expanded when new relevant sites are opened.

 Alexa is owned by Amazon.com.

On the Alexa site, click on the Top 500 Sites tab to see an ordered list of the most highly trafficked sites, updated daily. The most trafficked sites according to Alexa are shown in Figure 1-1.

Alexa's Movers and Shakers, shown in Figure 1-2, is also interesting. This snapshot of the "right here and now" Web is useful for seeing if there are any Web-wide trends in action, and also for learning about the kinds of exogenous events that move large-scale web sites up and down the chutes and ladders of popularity.

Although it is probably unrealistic to expect that you or I will be piloting sites that are the top of Alexa's list, it is worth spending time learning about popularity on the Web if you want to build successful sites. Alexa provides the tools you can use to see for yourself what is trafficked and what is gaining or losing among top-ranked sites.

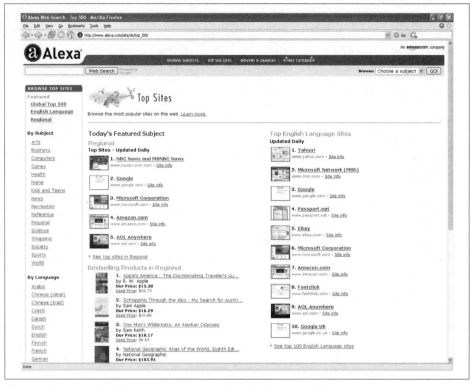

Figure 1-1. You can find the current most-popular web sites using Alexa

You can also use Alexa to see traffic statistics for sites that are not in the top 500. For almost any site that has been around a while, Alexa will give you an idea of traffic statistics and whether it is gaining or losing traffic.

Alexa lets you enter descriptive information about your web site, which others can see if they check your site traffic using Alexa. You can also make sure that Alexa provides a snapshot of your home page along with it statistics. Since this service is free, it is certainly worth entering a site description.

Alexa works by collating results from users throughout the Web who have installed the special Alexa Toolbar. (If you'd like, you too can install the Alexa Toolbar and help with popularity statistics.) There's some question about the statistical validity of Alexa for less trafficked sites because of this method of gathering data—Alexa's results are probably skewed towards users who are already web savvy and heavy users.

Most likely, Alexa's results are not very meaningful for sites that are ranked below 100,000 in popularity (very roughly, with fewer than 10,000 visitors per week).

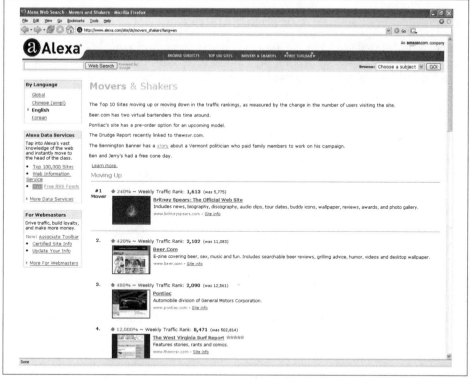

Figure 1-2. Alexa's Movers and Shakers can help with your education about what moves sites up and down the popularity ladder

The Alexa ranking of 100,000 or lower is also a great divide: if your site is in the top 100,000 you have content that many advertisers will consider worthwhile. Being in the top Alexa is a pretty good goal for your web site or sites: you can make real money from a top 100,000 site; it is an ambitious goal, but attainable.

How Much Content Is Enough?

Suppose you create one web page every hundred days that generates $100 in ad revenue. Alternatively, you create a page a day for 100 days. Each page generates $1.00 in ad revenue. Either way, you end up with $100.00 at the end of 100 days.

The point is that there are different ways to go about deciding how much content to create—it significantly depends upon the quality of the content. A single content page might make sense if it contained a valuable application like TinyURL (see "Useful Free Services and Software," earlier in this chapter). If your pages are low-value content, you will need a great many of them to make significant revenue from advertising.

Web Site Metrics

The metrics of web site traffic is a huge topic just by itself, with a number of books just about web metrics and quite a bit of software designed simply to help webmasters gather and understand the metrics of their sites. It's a very important topic, because to optimize your site you need to have baseline information as well as feedback so you can understand whether changes improve site traffic, or not and also which elements in your site draw traffic.

The topic is also important because the fees you can expect to get from advertisers largely depend upon the metric of your site.

By and large, web metrics are simply beyond the scope of this book, although you'll learn about the metric related to Google's AdSense in Chapter 9 and the metrics related to AdWords in Chapter 12.

Of course, your web server's logs contain a great deal of traffic information that can help provide you with useful metrics.

But, no doubt, the best metric of all is money in your pocket from fees paid by advertisers—through the AdSense program or some other mechanism—for publication on your site.

For further information about metrics, I suggest you start with Jim Sterne's *Web Metrics: Proven Methods for Measuring Web Site Success* (Wiley) and then have a look at the "Tracking and Logging" thread on WebMasterWorld, *http://www. webmasterworld.com.*

Between the two extremes—a single page of valuable content and many pages of low-value content—lies a happy medium that will work for most content-based sites by creating enough critical mass to draw both traffic and advertisers. If you are just starting out, this happy medium is a goal to which you can reasonably aspire.

Here's what you need at a minimum to have a site drawing respectable numbers at the end of one year:

- 100 pages of quality content "in the can" to start with
- On average, one new page of quality content a day every day for a year (each page about 300 words)

 "26 Steps to 15K a Day" in O'Reilly's *Google Hacks* by Tara Calishain and Rael Dornfest provides a step-by-step formula for creating a successful content site and drawing traffic (for more on drawing traffic, see Chapters 2 and 3 of this book).

Presenting Content

Content is king. Content is certainly king if your business model is to publish content on the Web and make money from advertising with traffic drawn by the content. Your first rule should be: Don't "dis" the king. In other words, don't do anything to distract from the content, make it harder for surfers to find content they need, or make the graphics that frame the content too jazzy. In particular, if the graphics seem too important, they will distract from the content.

 A particularly annoying sin on content-based web sites is to use an animated splash page (Flash is the tool usually used) to open the site.

Page and Site Design

These rules of content presentation can be put positively (rather than negatively):

It should be clear that the purpose of the site is to clearly present content. Choose a name for the site, and titles and headers for the pages, that make it abundantly clear that the purpose of the site is to present content, and (as a general matter) what that content is.

The design of the site should serve the purpose of presenting content. Site design should be intended to facilitate navigation and frame the content: nothing more, and nothing less.

Specific content items and subject areas should be easy to find. Provide multiple mechanisms for finding things: index pages, search boxes, site maps, subject areas, and so on.

Type should be legible. Be careful to choose a readable font, in a large enough size, and background and foreground color combinations that are easy on the eyes. It's hard to go wrong with black type on a white background. The reverse—white on black—is hard on the eyes, and some combinations (for example, dark blue on lighter blue, are essentially unreadable).

Keep graphics simple. For example, avoid animations and other splashy images.

Figure 1-3 shows Braintique.com, *http://www.braintique.com*, a site designed as a content vehicle, following these rules of content presentation.

As it happens, following the rules of content presentation I've outlined will serve you well with search engine placement (see Chapter 3). But that's not the point of these suggestions here. The point is usefulness and transparency to site users. If viable content is presented in an accessible fashion, then indeed "they will come."

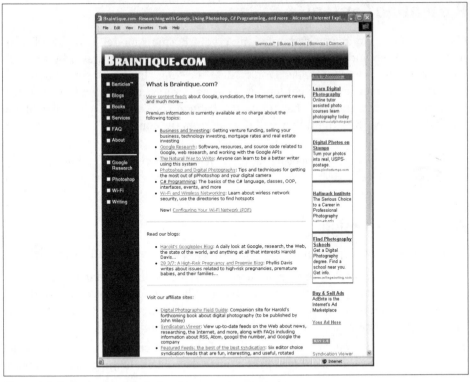

Figure 1-3. Braintique.com is designed to present content

If you are targeting your content specifically for Google's AdSense program (or a competitive contextual engine), you should also bear in mind the following:

- AdSense can't interpret images (except using captions, the value of `alt` attributed in the `<img>` tag, and surrounding text), so keep images to a minimum.
- You are likely to get more relevant ads if you keep each page to a single subject (and move tangential subject matters to different pages).
- Key concepts, words, and phrases should be clear by glancing at a page (see Chapter 3 for information about how to use these keywords and phrases to optimize your pages for AdSense, Google, and other search engines).

Page Size

How much content should go on each site page? Like Goldilocks and the three bears, the answer is not too much, and not too little: just the right amount of content.

It's in the interest of the site publisher to keep pages short, because the same amount of content spread over shorter pages makes for more pages. And more pages on a site means more places for advertising, which in theory might mean more revenue.

In addition, more pages may mean more page views, implying better metrics to advertisers who don't look too carefully.

However, if you break an article up into many short pages that a user has to click through, users will find it irritating and vote with their time by frequenting the site less often.

 For an example of a site that has chosen to maximize pages it can place ads on at the cost of potentially alienating readers by dividing articles up into many small pages that must be clicked through, see TheStreet.com, *http://www.thestreet.com*.

The happy medium is to be natural about page length. The natural length for a content page is the content that will reasonably fit into a maximized browser window without having to scroll.

 Obviously, this is a rough, rather than precise, guideline since different browsers on different systems will show different size pages.

Don't gratuitously break an article into multiple pages unless the article really is longer than a few browser-sized pages. Also, don't break an article (even if it is long) unless there are natural breaks in the content. Anytime there is a new Level 1 header in an article, it's a good sign that you could break to a new content page without the break feeling forced.

A related issue is to be careful about the width of your content pages. People will be looking at your web pages using a variety of hardware, operating systems, and browsers—the most important variable being the monitor size. You don't want your readers to have to scroll to the right because part of a content web page is off the screen. This is very bad form and may also obscure content advertising if it is positioned along the right border of the page.

The answer is to design pages for lowest-common-denominator displays. In practice, content pages should be no wider than 800 pixels. Pages 800 pixels wide (or less) should display without scrolling on most (although not all) computers; some displays are still only 640 pixels wide. (For more on this issue, see "Positioning Ads," later in this chapter.)

Separating Content from Design

When you create content web sites, it's imperative to use mechanisms that separate web page content from design. The purpose of separating content from design is to let you:

- Easily change the look and feel of a site without the change in overall site design having any impact on the content
- Tweak positioning and other ad-related variables to maximize revenue without having any effect on site content

The simplest way to achieve these goals is to use *includes*—server-side includes—to position site graphics such as navigation bars. A server-side include is a file that the server includes within another file (the inclusion is specified by a special directive). When you view the HTML source code in a browser, you have no way of telling whether the main file was generated using includes or not.

Includes can also be used for advertisement code, such as that provided by Google's AdSense. By changing the code in a single include, you can change the navigation bar or advertising parameters across all the content pages on an entire site.

I explain the mechanics of using includes to separate content from design in "Content Architecture," later in this chapter.

Sitewide Changes to Styles

It's somewhat less important than the ability to easily do sitewide changes of advertisements and site graphics such as navigation bars, but it's still nice to be able to perform sitewide changes of text styles. It is less important because leaving everything as reasonably sized black text on a white background is usually just fine.

Style attributes can be set using a server-side include. Each content page then includes the include file, which contains the styles for the content. Text styles can be changed on a global basis simply by changing the definitions of the styles within the include file.

Another simple mechanism for doing sitewide font and font-size changes is to use an external style sheet to define the fonts and sizes to use with various types of text (each content page references the style sheet). To effect a global change, simply change the style definitions in the external style sheet.

Server-side includes work well to separate key design elements (and advertisements) from content, provided your content site doesn't have too many pages and assuming that each page doesn't have a great many repetitive elements.

If many of your content pages are essentially the same—meaning they have the same elements but the value of the element differs from page to page—you should probably be using a templating system. Templates use special tags for the common elements, with the actual content for each page that replaces the special tag specified, often using content stored in a database table. This means that an appropriately written template file and one or more database tables can populate and create a whole raft of web pages, one for each row in the table.

PHP is one of the most popular server-side programming languages available on the Web (most inexpensive Linux/Apache web host services let you program in PHP without any additional configuration effort). You can find out more about PHP at *http://www.php.net* or by picking up a copy of O'Reilly's *Programming PHP: Creating Dynamic Web Pages* by Rasmus Lerdorf and Kevin Tatroe.

If you are a programmer, or have access to programming talent, you can create your own templating system using PHP or some other language. But why reinvent the wheel? A popular PHP templating system, available for free download, is Smarty, *http://smarty.php.net*. One of the great features about Smarty is that it caches a web page the first time it is generated from a template. Subsequent calls to the page, unless the template or data have changed, open the cached page—meaning the web site isn't slowed down by page generation each time the templated page is opened.

A server-side include mechanism is a great start for creating a manageable content site and—from a technology standpoint—within the grasp of almost anyone. (I explain the server-side include mechanism and how to use it to lay out a content site to receive advertising in "Content Architecture," later in this chapter.)

Templating is a good next step if you (or an associate) have the technologic sophistication and expect to be managing content sites with thousands of pages. It's particularly important to use a system of templates if you expect to generate pages using data from a database.

Suppose you are managing a site with not thousands, but hundreds of thousands of pages. You have multiple authors, a team of editors, and a workflow process to make sure that work is fact-checked, copyedited, and approved before it is published. In this case, you'll want to use Web Content Management software (WCM) to provide content and design separation, template features, workflow management, and more. Commercial WCM packages are available from vendors including IBM, FileNet, Interwoven, Microsoft, Stellent, and Vignette.

Not everyone recognizes that, in fact, blogging software such as MovableType and WordPress in effect manages web content using special tags and a template system. You can use WordPress, in particular, to manage pages that are not part of a blog. So if it's appropriate for your particular project, consider creating a "Blogosite"—a content web site managed by blogging software such as WordPress.

No matter what mechanism you use, it is vitally important to separate form from content so that you can easily keep your site design fresh and tweak advertising positions.

Keeping Content Fresh

Have you ever tried to keep fresh-caught fish fresh? It isn't easy. Neither is keeping site content fresh. But sites, and their content, need to stay fresh. It's not a big deal to change the overall look of a site by changing the graphic used as a navigation bar every month or so—that is, if you've set the site up with server-side includes so that editing one file creates a global site change. But keeping content fresh is a trickier issue.

Since search engines appreciate new content, some sites go to great lengths to provide content that *appears* new, for example, by displaying syndication feeds on the site's home page. This may help with search engines (I have more to say on this point in Chapter 3), but it doesn't do much at all for your primary audience—real people.

Quality content sites need to strike a balance. You need to have a core of worthwhile reference material that doesn't change much. You also need to keep content site fresh. As you plan your successful site, you should consider what strategy you will use to keep people coming back for the latest and greatest. For example, do you plan to keep up with the latest events in a technology niche, such as a programming language? Will you feature articles about current cultural events (which are constantly changing by definition)? Or will your site present interesting blogs with frequently added entries?

Positioning Ads

Studies have shown that ad *positioning* is crucial to content revenue generation. Positioning means the physical position of an ad on a web page, the size of the ad, and also *which* page(s) on a site carries an ad.

 As I explain in Chapter 8, when using a program like Google's AdSense, you'll want to use AdSense to generate code that displays ads sized to your site and also in colors that work with your site.

Although there are some general guidelines for what works best with advertising positioning, it is far more art than science. You should expect to spend a fair amount of time tweaking ad position to see what works best—another good reason for having a site mechanism in place that allows you to change ad settings globally by editing one include file.

Tweaking ads is good for another reason: you don't want *ad fatigue* to set in. Ad fatigue is a term used by webmasters to describe the phenomenon in which visitors to your site are so used to the ad display on your site that they ignore it. Experimenting with new ad positioning (and colors) is a good way to combat that "same old, same old" ad feeling and avoid ad fatigue.

Most studies show that ads positioned *above the fold* do better than ads lower on a page. Above the fold means visible without scrolling. The smaller the monitor, and the lower its resolution, the less screen real estate there is above the fold. In other words, a monitor running at 640×480 pixels screen resolution has a lot less available real estate above the fold than a monitor running at 800×600, which in turn has much less area above the fold than a monitor running at higher resolution.

If you want the maximum eyeballs—and you should, because more eyeballs means more advertising revenue—you should try to place ads so that they will be above the fold on lower-resolution monitors. It certainly makes sense to target 800×600 monitor resolution, because this is widely in use. Don't finalize your ad positioning—and web site and page design—without checking it out on an 800×600 monitor.

Some research has shown the vertical ad blocks—the kind Google calls *skyscrapers*—work better than horizontal ads. However, from the viewpoint of basic geometry, it is easier to fit a horizontal ad block above the fold than a vertical skyscraper: the lower part of the skyscraper is likely to be below the fold. So if you decide to go with vertical ad blocks, make sure they are positioned as high as possible and that at least one ad (assuming the skyscraper contains multiple contextual ads) is positioned above the fold.

One other major positioning issue is *context*. From the viewpoint of a content publisher, you'd like to position ads so they are not only contextually relevant but also lead to a high click-through rate.

 With programs like Google's AdSense, context is important because you want a high click-through rate. With affiliate advertising, context is even more important because you don't make any money without a *conversion*, which means turning someone into a customer. You may, perhaps, care less about context when you are paid by the impression. In that case all you really care about is that the ad gets seen on your site.

Google's AdSense attempts to place only contextually relevant ads. With some notable lapses, AdSense is pretty successful at this. In any case, you can't exercise a great deal of control over the ads that AdSense displays on your site—you have to trust that Google gets this right.

You can forbid your competitor's ads from appearing on your site by using the AdSense option that allows you to ban specific IP addresses. The ability to ban IP addresses can be used to a limited degree to also keep out advertisers you find offensive. For example, an animal rights information site might want to ban ads from prominent furriers.

There are some important aspects of context that you *can* control, although there is no reliable analytic research about what works best. Some sites use graphics and positioning to make contextual ads blend in with the site and appear almost part of the editorial content. Other sites feel that keeping the appearance of editorial integrity is vitally important and so use color and position to instantly indicate that the ads are separate from the body of the content.

Overloading pages with ads generally does not work because viewers tend to ignore pages that have too many ads. If you're working with multiple ad programs and kinds of ads to generate a revenue stream, you can make an important contribution to ad context by deciding what kind of ad should go with what content. For example, it might make sense to advertise books on Amazon on a page of book reviews.

There's also a school of thought that believes ads should only be placed on "boring" pages—for example, registration pages, login pages, resource pages, exit pages. (An exit page is a page designed to launch a visitor onward following a visit, for example, an order confirmation.) One reason for placing click-through ads on resource and exit pages is that visitors will be leaving your site anyhow from these pages. You won't be losing traffic by providing click-through opportunities.

The more general logic for placing ads only on boring pages is that it gives your site a clean, inviting, ad-free look—and that visitors are more likely to click on ads in the context of boredom than in the context of exciting content.

Whatever strategy you decide to try, if you will be varying ad programs depending on context, you should attempt to implement this programmatically rather than by manually adding and deleting advertising code from individual HTML pages.

Content Architecture

You should think about site architecture before you create your first content page. Site architecture should be arranged so that you can make global changes to the look and feel of a site with no impact on the content. You also want to be able to change the code for an ad program—or even swap one ad program for another—once and have the changes take effect across your site in all the content pages.

Server-Side Includes

The simplest mechanism for implementing a "change code in one place, change the whole site" architecture is to use server-side includes (see "Separating Content from Design," earlier in this chapter).

Most web hosting accounts provide a server-side include mechanism. You tell the web server which file extensions mean that a file can have includes. When the web server processes the file to send back to a browser for display, it looks for the special syntax that means there is an include. When it sees this syntax, it expands the page it is serving to the browser by expanding it with the file indicated by the include's syntax.

The default file extension for a web page is usually *.shtml*, although you can add other file extensions so that your web server will look through them for includes (there is, of course, a slight performance hit for this).

Figure 1-4 shows a pretty typical Linux and Apache web host administrative utility with the mouse cursor pointing at the button that lets you add file extensions to be parsed for includes.

Figure 1-4. You can add file extensions to be parsed for includes by the web server

For example, suppose you have a simple *.shtml* home page like this:

```
<html xmlns="http://www.w3.org/1999/xhtml" lang="en" xml:lang="en">
    <head>
        <title>A simple little home page</title>
    </head>
    <body>
    <h1>Hello!</h1>
    ...
    </body>
</html>
```

You could create two include files:

- *styles.html*, which contains CSS (Cascading Style Sheet) styles for the elements used on the site such as font size and color
- *top-bar.html*, which contains the site navigation bar

You can link to an external CSS style sheet, or define your CSS styles in an include file. Either way, to change styles sitewide, you just have to change the style definitions in one file.

The site home page, and every other content page on the site, includes these two files as follows:

```
<html xmlns="http://www.w3.org/1999/xhtml" lang="en" xml:lang="en">
    <head>
        <title>A simple little home page</title>
    <!--#include virtual="includes/styles.html" -->
    </head>
    <body>
    <!--#include virtual="includes/top-bar.html" -->
    <h1>Hello!</h1>
    ...
    </body>
</html>
```

Now it's easy to change the appearance of the text on each page of the site by just making one change to *styles.html*. And if you need to change the appearance of the navigation bar, you can simply make the changes to *top-bar.html*, and it will be replicated across the site.

There's generally no requirement that included files be named with any particular file extension; instead of *.html* you can perfectly well use *.foo*, or anything else you'd like.

PHP Includes

If you are constructing a dynamic site using PHP (see "Separating Content from Design," earlier in this chapter) or using PHP for other programmatic purposes on your site, it makes sense to use the PHP include mechanism.

Whatever technology you use to serve your site, it undoubtedly has an include mechanism that works pretty much like server-side includes and PHP includes.

Most Linux and Apache based web hosts provide PHP scripting automatically for files named with a *.php* file extension. Within these files, PHP includes work almost exactly like server-side includes.

For example, suppose you have a simple little web home page in a file named *index.php*:

```
<html xmlns="http://www.w3.org/1999/xhtml">
    <head>
        <title>Featured Feeds - the best of the best syndication</title>
    </head>
    <body>
    ...
    </body>
</html>
```

If you put the CSS styles for the elements of the web site such as the appearance of web site text in a file named *style.inc*, it can be included in PHP code like this:

```
<? include 'style.inc'; ?>
```

The code for the top portion of a page, to be shared in common across the site, might be put in a file named *top.inc*. It could now be inserted at the top of the body of a content page using the PHP include directive:

```
<html xmlns="http://www.w3.org/1999/xhtml">
    <head>
        <title>Featured Feeds - the best of the best syndication</title>
        <? include 'style.inc'; ?>
    </head>
    <body>
        <? include 'top.inc'; ?>
        ...
    </body>
</html>
```

As with the server-side include example, if all the pages in a site use the PHP directives to include *style.inc* and *top.inc*, then site styles and the top element can be changed globally just by changing the contents of these include files.

Note that you can include PHP code—including other PHP include directives—within PHP includes and that there is no requirement that includes be named with any particular file suffix.

Optimal Include Layout

The optimal include layout is to provide includes for both geographic areas of your web page and for specific ad programs. The two should not be the same, although one can go inside the other and (at least initially) consume all its area. If you don't follow this organizing principle, down the road—to take one example—you'll find that you named the include for the entire right side of your content pages *Google_ad_right*, even though it by now contains a variety of graphic elements, but no Google skyscraper.

It may be a bit easier to understand how to lay out includes with future flexibility in mind using an example. Featured Feeds, *http://www.feedly.com*, shown in Figure 1-5, is perhaps a bit cluttered with ads, but the underlying composition of PHP includes will make this easy to change. The composition of PHP includes used to construct the Feedly.com site is shown in diagram form in Figure 1-6.

Figure 1-5. While the Feedly.com site appears cluttered, the underlying PHP composition makes it easy to clean up

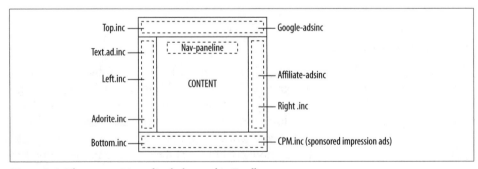

Figure 1-6. The composition of includes used in Feedly.com

Figure 1-6 shows that there is an include for each geographic area of a page that will carry graphics or ads: *Top.inc*, *Left.inc*, *Bottom.inc*, and *Right.inc*. Within the geographic includes are ad program specific includes for each ad program or type of ad. A final include holds a navigation panel at the top of the site above the page individual content.

This arrangement gives the maximum flexibility and won't have you contorted like a pretzel in the future. You can change any of the graphics in a geographic include. Alternatively, you can change ad code and swap, add, and delete ad programs in a very granular fashion. Changes take place globally across a site, but they have very little impact on the rest of a page.

Since Feedly.com is organized as I've explained, it took me less than 10 minutes to clean the site up a bit by editing the contents of the *Left.inc* and *Right.inc* include files. Once I uploaded the edited include files to my web server, the changes that I made to these includes were instantly propagated throughout all web pages on the site. I think you'll agree that the toned-down site is less cluttered (Figure 1-7), but tweaking a content site until the mixture of ads and content is right should be an ongoing effort. Fortunately, using includes takes a great deal of the pain out of the process.

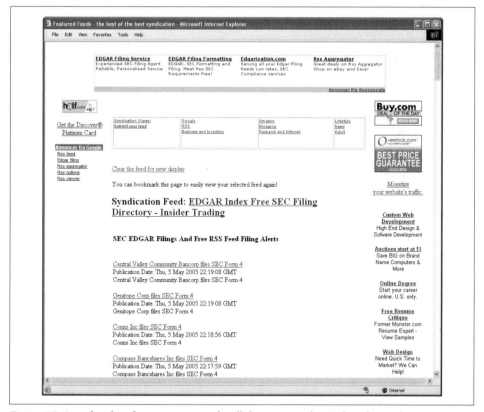

Figure 1-7. It took only a few minutes to make all the pages on the site less cluttered

Action Items

Here are some action items for you to take to get started on the road to creating content sites to make money with advertising:

- Understand content categories, types of content, and why people visit content sites.
- Create a plan to build community on your site.
- Find a quality content source.
- Design a simple site that highlights content.
- Separate content from design.
- Keep your content fresh.
- Experiment with ad positioning.
- Create a site architecture that uses includes, templates, or content management software to facilitate flexibility.

CHAPTER 2

Driving Traffic to Your Site

They say (whoever "they" are) that the best things in life are free. That's certainly true when it comes to driving traffic to your web site.

You can spend a great deal of money to send traffic to your site using advertising. One of the most effective ways to do this is to use Google's AdWords program, explained in detail in Part III of this book. But there are also many no-cost ways to draw site visitors, many of which may be more effective, and get traffic that is more highly targeted, than using paid advertising. Even if you are using paid advertising to draw traffic, you should know about free techniques—and you should use these techniques in conjunction with your advertising.

 I'll explain how to optimize your web site and pages to get more traffic from Google and other search engines in Chapter 3.

This chapter explains how to publicize your site and increase traffic using techniques that do not cost money and do not involve tinkering with the HTML code and content of your pages themselves. In other words, this chapter explains how to drive traffic to your site using external mechanisms, such as submitting your site to a search engine, leaving more complex issues of constructing your site so that search engines will like it—a field sometimes called search engine optimization (SEO)—for Chapter 3.

Creating a Plan and a Story

Many of the steps I suggest in this chapter for publicizing your site are essentially mechanical, for example, submitting your site to a variety of search engines. Even so, you should have a plan for marketing your content sites. No brick-and-mortar business in its right mind would attempt a marketing or publicity campaign without a plan, and you shouldn't proceed online without one, either.

Having a plan will help you accomplish even mechanical steps more effectively. For example, when you submit your site to a search engine or a directory, you will often be asked for a description of your offering. Understanding your site in the context of a marketing plan will help you hone a site description.

The two most important aspects of a plan for online marketing and publicity are:

- Understanding your target audience (or audiences)
- Creating a story (or stories) that will meet the needs of and intrigue your target audience

The Elevator Pitch

You should be able to summarize your story in a sentence or two. (This is sometimes called an *elevator pitch*.) For example,

> Digital photography resources, techniques, software, equipment reviews, and photo galleries

is a story that will probably attract people interested in digital photography. On the other hand,

> Ramblings of a grouchy, cranky person who, well, rambles about everything is not a targeted story likely to interest anyone for long.

 Use your plan and story to create a summary of your site, a list of keywords related to your site content, and one or more press releases (as I explain in this chapter, in the "Publishing Press Releases" section). The site summary and keyword list can be also be used to create meta information for your site, as I explain in Chapter 3.

Creating a Checklist

In addition, your plan should provide a checklist with specific "to do" items—essentially, all of the techniques used to create online publicity described in this chapter. The list should also include offline marketing and publicity placements appropriate to your target audience and your story.

Successfully getting online publicity and generating traffic is largely a matter of focus and keeping track of the details. Creating a checklist as part of your plan will help you make sure that none of these details fall through the cracks.

Naming Your Site

If you haven't already picked a name for your web site, try to select a name that helps to tell your story. Good names, at least with a .com suffix, are hard to find these days. It's worth working hard to find the right name.

The Cult of Personality

Life writ large with the cult of personality might well describe the times we live in. Paris Hilton, an heiress with an apparently vacuous personality, has a television show, and is famous, because (and not despite) of that vacuous personality. I think the reality is that Paris is a great deal smarter than she seems—although another moral you can certainly draw from the Paris Hilton success story is that sex sells.

My point is that people, particularly celebrities, get attention these days. If you have celebrity, have access to celebrities, or have ideas about how to create celebrity, I say: "Go for it! Milk it!" And don't forget to mention your web site.

It's reasonable that people should be interested in people. People are interesting. As the poet Alexander Pope said a long time ago, "The proper study of mankind is man." (If Pope had included both genders, we moderns could surely go along with this.)

It's really very simple. Getting web site traffic requires publicity. Publicity is best generated using stories about people, particularly interesting or notorious people. If your web site has an interesting story about people, let others know about it (perhaps using a press release). Your people story will draw traffic.

Ideally, a site name, as I mentioned, should tell, or evoke, the story of your site and be memorable. Consider these classics:

- Amazon: the world's greatest river meets the world's largest inventory.
- eBay: I don't know why this one works, but it does.
- Google: a very big number fits with the very large quantity of information Google indexes.

Submitting Your Sites to Search Engines

Google and most other search engines use several separate mechanisms:

- A program that crawls the Web to find sites, also called a *crawler* or a *spider*. Once found (crawled), sites are placed in the search engine's index.
- Software that ranks sites in the search engine's index to determine their order of delivery when someone uses Google to search for a particular keyword or phrase.

To start with, if your site hasn't been found, you won't be ranked by a search engine at all (to state the obvious). So the first task is getting your site into the systems of Google and other search engines.

Unless you have money to burn, I do not recommend participating in any programs that ask you to pay for search engine listings, regardless of whether these programs are run by search engines themselves or by third parties.

If you have *inbound links*—links to your sites—from other sites in a search engine's index, then the search engine's spider will find your site—eventually. But why not see if you can speed the process up?

 It's peculiar but true: different search engines index different portions of the Web. Also, at any given time, it is impossible for any search engine index to include the entire Web!

The rub, of course, is that by submitting a form to a search engine there is no guarantee if, and when, your sites will be included by a given search engine. The best approach is to list your site using the search engine's procedures, and check back in six months to see if you are included in the search engine's index. If not, submit again. In other words, this is a process that requires patience and may produce limited results—but at least the price is right!

 Getting a site listed in an online categorized directory—particularly the Open Directory Project (ODP) or Yahoo's directory as I explain in "Working with Directories" later in this chapter—is probably the most effective way to get inclusion in the search engines themselves.

Summarizing, search engines find the web pages they index by using software to follow links on the Web. Since the Web is huge, and always expanding and changing, it can be a while before this software finds your particular site. Therefore, it's smart to speed this process up by manually submitting your site to search engines.

Important Search Engines for Submission

Table 2-1 shows some of the most important search engines to which you should submit your site, along with the URL for the site's submission page.

Table 2-1. Selected search engines and submission URLs

Search Engine	Submission URL
Ask Jeeves / Teoma (registration required)	*https://sitesubmit.ask.com/Main/login.jsp*
Google	*http://www.google.com/addurl/*
MSN Search	*http://search.msn.co.in/docs/submit.aspx*
Yahoo! (registration required)	*http://submit.search.yahoo.com/free/request*

Submission Tools

You may also want to use an automated site submission tool that submits your site to multiple search engines in one fell swoop.

It's quite likely that your web host provides a utility with this functionality that you can use to submit the URLs for your hosted domains to a group of search engines. Figure 2-1 shows the results of a site submission using the tool provided by one web host (you'll probably find that your web host provides something similar).

 Before using a site submission tool, you should prepare a short list of keywords and a one- or two-sentence summary of your site as I mentioned in "Creating a Plan and a Story," earlier in this chapter (you can reuse the keywords and site summary as keywords and description data in your `<meta>` tags). Alternatively, if you have already created meta information for your site, as I explain in Chapter 3, you can use the keywords and description in your meta information for search engine submissions.

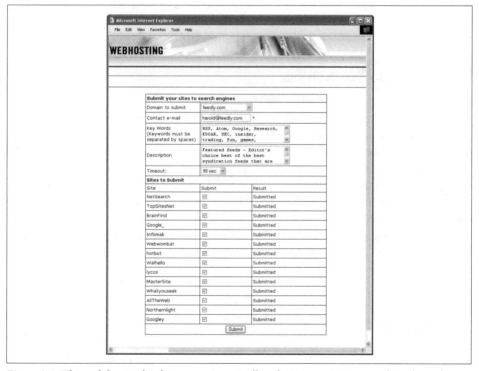

Figure 2-1. This web host utility lets you automatically submit your site to a number of search engines at once

If the tool is provided by your web host, probably you will be able to submit only your domain, rather than directories within the domain, for example, *http://www.braintique.com* but not *http://www.braintique. com/research/*.

If you search Google with a phrase like "Search Engine Submit," you'll find many free services that submit to a group of search sites for you. Typically, these free submission sites try to up-sell or cross-sell you on a product or service, but since you don't have to buy anything, why not take advantage of the free service? The two best-known examples of this kind of site are Submit Express, *http://www. submitexpress.com*, which will submit your URL to 40 sites for free (just be sure you pass on the various offers you'll find on the site) and NetMechanic, *http://www. netmechanic.com*, another search engine submission site along the same lines.

Working with Directories

It's a not-so-well-kept secret that the best approach for getting into the search engine listings is to enter through a back door by working with the two most important structured directories: the Open Directory Project (ODP) and the Yahoo! Directory.

Understanding Taxonomies

A directory differs from the index used by a search engine because a directory uses a structured way to categorize sites, sometimes called a *taxonomy*. In addition, sites are included in a particular category in the ODP and Yahoo! directories only after they have been reviewed by human editors. You can search within directories (just as you can search in a web index, such as the one compiled by Google). But it's common to use a directory, following its taxonomy by drilling down through subjects to find what you want. For example, suppose you wanted to find resources related to alternative photo processes, such as creating daguerreotypes (a nineteenth-century print technology). Using the Open Directory taxonomy, shown in Figure 2-2, you would drill down through the following categories: Arts → Photography → Techniques and Style → Alternative Processes.

You can think of the index of the Web compiled by search engines such as Google as being like the index to a nonfiction book. In contrast, a taxonomic directory is much more like the table of contents to the book: it is organized according to the structure of the book, and you can drill down by part, chapter (within the part), heading (within the chapter), and subtopic to find the information you need.

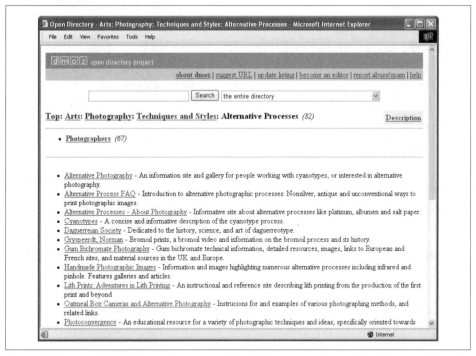

Figure 2-2. You can find "Alternative Processes" by drilling down through Arts, Photography, and Techniques and Styles

Getting Open Directory Project Listings

The Open Directory Project (ODP), *http://dmoz.org*, is the most important taxonomic directory on the Web. Formally hosted and administered by the Netscape division of AOL, the ODP is run along the lines of an open source project and is inspired by the Debian Social Contract (see *http://www.debian.org/social_contract.html*).

The credo behind the ODP is that "humans do it better." The ODP believes that web automated search is ineffective, and getting worse, and that the small contingent of paid editors at commercial web search engine companies cannot keep up with the staggering rate of change on the Web—decaying, stagnant sites, link rot, new sites, sites intended as search spam, and so on.

The ODP is run and maintained by a vast army of volunteer editors. These editors follow internal checks and balances to preserve the integrity of the directory. See *http://dmoz.org/guidelines/* for more information about the ODP review process and guidelines for site inclusion.

You, too, can become an ODP editor in an area of your interest and expertise. See *http://dmoz.org/help/become.html* for more information about becoming an ODP editor.

The ODP taxonomy (categorization system) and the sites included in the categories are freely available as data for use by anyone who wants to run his or her own search engine, as long as the terms of the ODP's free-use license are complied with (for terms of the license, in case you want to use the ODP data in a search engine of your own, see *http://dmoz.org/license.html*).

Google, and most of the major search engines, do use information derived from the ODP, but of course they use it in their own way. With Google in particular, information from the ODP is used to form the Google Directory, *http://directory.google.com*.

 Google uses its own search technology for searches within the Google Directory.

Most significant, inclusion within an ODP category means that your site is very likely to be included within the Google web index (as well as the Google Directory and in other major web indices).

So it's worth submitting your site to the ODP, if only because it's the best way to get indexed (and appropriately categorized) by Google. You'll find a FAQ about how to add your site at *http://www.dmoz.org/add.html* (this FAQ is also available via a link from the ODP home page).

The first step is to locate the best category for your site. For example, suppose you have a site like Syndication Viewer, shown in Figure 2-3, whose purpose is to catalog and display selected RSS and Atom feeds as HTML.

The best category I can find for this site on ODP is Reference → Libraries → Library and Information Science → Technical Services → Cataloguing → Metadata → RDF → Applications → RSS. The category page is shown in Figure 2-4.

 You can start your look for the right category (to get close to the best possible category) using a search term, for example, "RSS."

On the category page that you think is best for your site, click the suggest URL link, shown in the upper center of Figure 2-4.

On the Submit a Site to the Open Directory Project page, you will be asked to verify the category you selected (as determined by the page from which you clicked the suggest URL link). You'll need to enter your site's URL, title, a brief site description, and

Figure 2-3. The Syndication Viewer site catalogs RSS and Atom feeds

your email address. As the editors note, "A well-written, objective description will make listing your site easier."

When your listing page is complete, click Submit. This process is now complete, except for the waiting. You should check back in four to six months to see if you've been listed.

If I make it sound like you might have to wait a long time to get listed in the ODP, well, you might! The ODP depends on volunteer labor, and rumor is that it is getting slower and slower. However, inclusion in the ODP is a virtual guarantee of inclusion in many search engine indexes and other directories. So have patience! The ODP is worth it.

Getting Yahoo! Directory Listings

The Yahoo! Directory, a somewhat lesser-known part of Yahoo!, works in pretty much the same way as the ODP, except that it is privately maintained. Sites added to the Yahoo! Directory tend to end up in the Yahoo! index, as well as other important search indices.

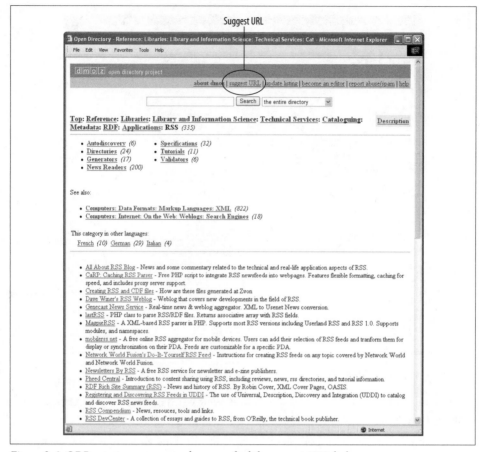

Figure 2-4. ODP category pages are where you find the suggest URL links

To suggest your site for inclusion in the Yahoo! Directory, open the Yahoo! Directory's home page, *http://dir.yahoo.com/*, shown in Figure 2-5.

You can also find the Yahoo Directory by opening the main Yahoo! home page, selecting Directory as your search category, and searching for a term. The search results you will be presented with are from the Yahoo! Directory (not the Yahoo! web index), and the display will show where in the taxonomy you are, so you can browse through related categories.

Next, find the best category for your site, either by drilling down through the Yahoo! Directory taxonomy (shown on the left of Figure 2-5), or by searching within the Yahoo! Directory using the search box shown at the top of Figure 2-6.

Figure 2-5. Yahoo! Directory is not Yahoo!; here's the Yahoo! Directory home page

 You can use directory search results as the starting place for pinpointing the perfect category.

When you find the right category page (for example, for a digital photography site, the category page for Directory → Arts → Visual Arts → Photography Digital), click the Suggest a Site link shown in Figure 2-6.

Figure 2-6. From the appropriate category page, click the Suggest a Site link to propose your site for inclusion in the Yahoo! Directory

Clicking the Suggest a Site link starts the site submission process. You'll first be asked if you want to pay for inclusion or continue for free. I suggest you do not pay for inclusion.

The next step is to verify that the site you want to suggest does not already appear in the Yahoo! Directory. This is verified using a Yahoo! Directory search. If your site cannot be found, you can continue.

You'll be asked to verify the listing category, and to log in with your Yahoo! user-name. (If you don't have a Yahoo! account, you'll need to create one.) Finally, you can complete the form with information about your site shown in Figure 2-7 and submit.

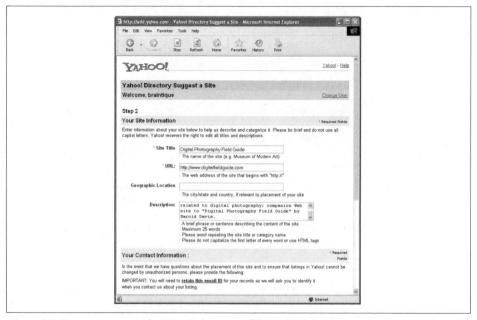

Figure 2-7. You can use your elevator pitch story to fill out the Yahoo! Directory Suggest a Site form

 Keep track of the email address you supply on the Yahoo! Directory Suggest a Site form. You'll need the address to change information about any of your sites listed in the directory.

Becoming Popular

Sometimes it seems like all of life has the same themes as high school: what's impor-tant is being popular. A significant measure of popularity on the Web is how many *inbound* links—links from other sites to your site—you have.

Inbound links are an important component of Google's PageRank system, which is a way to order the sites returned from a search.

Obtaining inbound links is not rocket science, but it is labor-intensive and does require some thought. The best way to get another site to link to your site is to ask for it, as obvious as that may seem.

 Link farms—sites that exist for the sole purpose of providing inbound links to better a page's search ranking—will *not* help your site become more popular and may in fact damage your standing with Google and other search engines.

It makes sense for sites to link to your site when they have similar or related content—always assuming the webmaster in charge of the site linking to you likes your content. This is a reasonable thing for the webmaster in charge of the other site to do because it adds value for the other site's visitors. (If your site is not adding value, you might want to rethink its premise.)

The Best Inbound Links

The best—meaning most likely to drive traffic—inbound links come from:

- Sites that publish content that is complementary and related to the content on your site
- Hub sites that are a central repository, discussion area, and community site for a particular interest group (for example, a mention on SlashDot [*http://www.slashdot.org*]) can drive huge amounts of traffic to sites related to technology, so much so that the phenomenon of a sudden uptick in traffic due to inbound links has become known as the "Slashdot Effect"

Finding Sites to Make a Link Request

To find sites that are appropriate for an inbound link request, you should:

- Consider the sites you find useful, entertaining, and informative
- Use the web taxonomic directories to find sites in your category and in related categories (see "Working with Directories," earlier in this chapter)
- Use specialized searching syntax to find the universe of sites that search engines such as Google regard as "related" to yours

If you've looked carefully at Google search results, you may have noticed a Similar pages link (Figure 2-8).

> BearHome.com
> A site devoted to the books of Harold Davis and Phyllis Davis, and topics including
> technology, family, and gardening.
> www.bearhome.com/ - 6k - Cached - Similar pages
>
> Link to similar pages

Figure 2-8. You can use the Google Similar Pages link to find sites that might be interested in linking to yours (because they are like yours)

The Similar Pages link is supposed to show you more pages like the one the link modifies. How well it works varies widely (it works better on popular, highly ranked pages and less well on obscure pages). But it can give you some leads.

You can bypass the process of clicking Similar Pages by using the Google related: operator followed by a web page directly in a Google search. For example, entering the following Google search:

```
related:www.bearhome.com
```

is comparable to clicking the Similar Pages link for *www.bearhome.com* (and shows exactly the same web pages as the search result).

If you find it easier to analyze data presented visually, a demonstration tool called Google Visual Search, provided free by Anacubis, may be right for you. Anacubis's Google Visual Search Tool, *http://www.anacubis.com/googledemo/google*, uses the Google Web APIs to (among other things) present a visual representation of the sites similar to yours. For example, Figure 2-9 shows a visual representation of sites that are similar to *http://www.mechanista.com*, a site about antique typewriters, calculators, and other mechanisms.

> The Anacubis Google Visual Search Tool will show similar sites, linked sites, or both.

Making the Link Request

Email is the best way (and sometimes the only way) to request an inbound link to your site.

Finding email addresses

The first step in writing an email requesting an inbound link is to find the email address for the webmaster you want to contact. This can take quite a bit of poking around, but it is amazing how often you can uncover the right email address with a bit of persistence if you just look at all the pages on a web site.

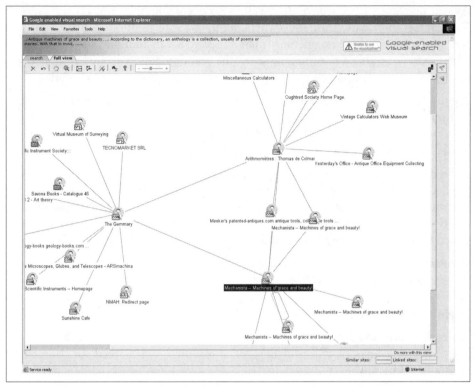

Figure 2-9. Anacubis helps you see which sites are similar to (or already linked to) your site

Six Degrees of Separation

To create a view with the similar sites shown in Figure 2-9, I had to iterate the process. In other words, the initial view of sites similar to *www.mechanista.com* showed only a few sites. I had to expand several of these initial sites to show sites similar to them to get a greater pool of similar sites. One wonders: if you keep on iterating ad infinitum, do you get all web sites, or are there only six degrees of separation?

If a web site has a contact form but no explicit email address, you can often find the email address the contact form is mailed to by viewing the HTML source code for the contact form's page. Another place to look for email addresses is within a syndication feed. If the site provides an RSS or Atom feed, the creator's email address is often included as part of the feed.

As you may know, you can use the Whois service of Internet domain registrars to find contact information for site owners, although with multiple domain registrars this information is more fragmentary than it used to be. In addition, some sites intentionally do not publish information about the real domain owners when they register domains, for example, by putting the domain in the name of the web host.

A good first stop if you want to try using a Whois service to get email contact information is Network Solutions (*http://www.networksolutions.com*), the "classic" Internet domain name registrar. Next, try Whois.net, *http://www.whois.net*, which has one of the largest databases for Whois information.

If these two sources fail, do not give up! Go to Internic, *http://www.internic.netwhois.html*. The Internic service will not give you contact information, but it probably will tell you the specific domain registrar who registered a given site and the address of the domain registrar's Whois server. You can then go to the Whois server maintained by the appropriate registrar and usually find email contact information there.

If this sounds time-consuming, well, it is. To justify the time, any sites that you contact should indeed be related to your site.

Emails should not spam

Generally, you should not send email that reads like spam. Don't send mass emailings requesting links (it will probably get intercepted and marked for deletion by antispam filters, anyhow). Personalize each email with the recipients' names, something about their site, and information about why they should link with you.

It's OK to offer a reciprocal link in exchange for your inbound link. But I think the classier approach is already to have a link to any site you approach. You can set aside a resource page for this purpose. Why bother with trying to get an inbound link from a site that isn't worth linking to? If it is worth linking to, then go ahead and do it on your own without requiring payback. You'll be surprised at how often the other webmaster decides to reciprocate.

Publishing Press Releases

It used to be that putting out a press release was a big deal. It required special accreditation and membership in a wire service and could generally only be accomplished by large companies or by using an accredited public relations or ad agency.

As with many other things, the Web has disintermediated and democratized the process of publishing a press release—so much so that some large organizations don't even bother with them anymore, figuring that their releases will be lost in the flood of information unleashed on the world by the "little guys."

These days, publishing a press release that will be picked up by wire services is technically free. In reality, to get the distribution you want for the release will cost you

Comments, Trackbacks, and Discussion Threads

The "cheap-date" way to get inbound links is to post them yourself, using a mechanism such as a blog comment, a blog trackback, or a discussion thread. These links do not have the permanence or credibility of a link from a stable site, but can draw considerable short-term traffic if posted on a popular site.

There's nothing wrong with adding a link to a comment on a blog, or in a discussion thread, or using a trackback mechanism, provided you have a valid hook for hanging your URL. In other words, it's OK to enter a discussion if you really have something to say, and it's also OK to link back to relevant material on your site, but don't come completely from left field. It will undermine the credibility that you are trying to build up for your site.

about $30.00 per release. Although my general stance is not to pay for listings, this is usually well worth doing, provided you have the skills to write a good press release and have an interesting story to tell—not only will it produce inbound links but also some traditional media may pick up on your site and story.

There are several online services that exist to distribute press releases, including 24-7PressRelease.com (*http://www.24-7pressrelease.com*), FreePressRelease.com (*http://www.free-press-release.com/submit/*), and PRWeb (*http://www.prweb.com*). These sites all work in essentially the same way: an online form is provided for your press release submission, and the service submits your release to wire services, web search engines, and anyone who subscribes to the service's feeds. Free submission is available from all of the press release services, but to get the distribution your press release deserves, you need to buy (in some cases, phrased as a "contribution" or a "donation") premium membership in the service (or upgrades for specific press releases).

PRWeb is probably the best known of these services. To get started with PRWeb, you need to create a free account. Once you've established an account, you have access to a management console, shown in Figure 2-10, which lets you create, edit, and submit press releases and also check to see how many times each of your releases was viewed.

 The viewing statistics for PRWeb are impressive, typically in the tens of thousands of views for most press releases. PRWeb also tells you how many times your release was picked up by a media outlet, how many times it was forwarded using PRWeb's forwarding service, and how many times it was printed using the printer-friendly version of your release. However, it's not entirely clear what these statistics actually mean, and you should not necessarily expect a corresponding increase in your volume of site traffic.

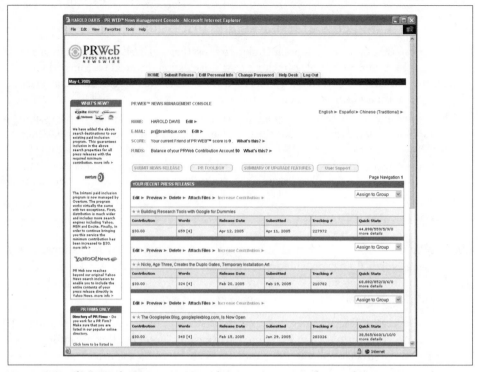

Figure 2-10. The PRWeb management console gives you access to press release creation, editing, and submission and allows you to monitor release statistics

To create a new release for submission, click the Submit News Release button on the console. In the form that opens, shown in Figure 2-11, you can copy and paste the elements of your press release if you created it as a word-processing document (see "Preparing a Press Release," earlier in this chapter).

You can edit the press release later, but you do need to supply the following elements initially:

- Headline (one sentence)
- Summary (two to four sentences)
- Body of the press release
- Keywords (don't bother repeating keywords in the release itself, since these will be picked up automatically)
- Industry
- Site URL and contact information

Preparing a Press Release

Before you go online to submit a press release, you should prepare the press release using a word-processing program such as Microsoft Word. It's important that you get your release reviewed by several people, including (if possible) a professional writer or editor. Grammar, spelling, and punctuation do count; if your press release is deficient in these areas it will look amateurish.

A good press release should be succinct. Keep it to one page if at all possible.

The press release should start with a summary of no more than two or three sentences. You should also prepare a single, short sentence to serve as the headline for the release.

Next, the press release should tell a story in several paragraphs (see "Creating a Plan and a Story," earlier in this chapter). If possible, you should include interesting quotations from one or two people related to the story. (If no one else comes to mind, what about quoting yourself?)

A final short paragraph should describe your web site, perhaps with links to an FAQ page and related sites. This paragraph can be used as a *slug*, which means it can be copied and pasted for use in all your press releases related to your web site.

The press release should provide email and phone contact information in case someone who reads the release wants further information. Don't make it hard to find you!

A press release created in this way can easily be copied and pasted into online submission forms.

 To some degree, your industry selection determines to whom your press release is distributed. You need to pick a primary industry when you create the release, but (depending on your contribution level) you can add industry groups after the release has been saved but before it is submitted. You should take advantage of this to get your release as widely distributed as possible.

When you've completed your press release and assigned a release date, click Save Press Release. You'll next be asked to pay for your submission (select a contribution level).

Press releases are subject to a vetting process conducted both by software and human editors. Some kinds of content are forbidden. For example, you cannot submit a press release having to do with adult content and any related industries on PRWeb (see Chapter 6 for information about submitting adult-content press releases).

You can find out more about PRWeb's review policies using the Knowledge Base on the PRWeb site. Generally, besides adult content, PRWeb will reject any outright

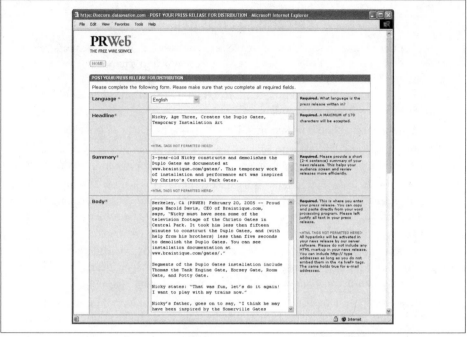

Figure 2-11. If you've prepared a press release in your word processor, you can copy and paste into PRWeb's online form

and apparent advertisements, so take care to word your press releases to avoid this stigmatization. If your press release is rejected, PRWeb will refund any contributions as a matter of course. Note that PRWeb does not vet spelling or grammar and does not check facts—it's up to you to get these things right.

Provided your press release has been accepted, you'll receive email confirmations and a link to your release online on the wire service site.

 For a fee, PRWeb will write or edit your press release for you.

Syndication Feeds

As you may know, syndication is a simple XML-based mechanism for publishing content. Syndication feeds come in two predominant flavors: RSS and Atom. From the viewpoint of publicizing your web site, you don't need to worry about the differences between them.

Content is syndicated by encoding it within an RSS or Atom feed. This feed can—and usually does—include links to the site originating the content.

Subscribers can view syndication feeds in all different kinds of software, including web browsers, email clients, standalone programs, and on HTML web pages. There's no mechanism built into syndication to pay for subscriptions, but once you are subscribed your feed display is automatically updated when a new item is added to the feed. It's up to the syndication-viewing software to decide how to render feeds, but software that can display web pages often shows the underlying pages to which the feed links.

There's some controversy about how publishers can best use syndication feeds, since it's not obvious how to make money from them. (Google has introduced a program allowing publishers to insert contextual ads within syndication feeds, but this is a controversial step.)

However, syndication feeds work well as a device for driving traffic to a site because:

- Feed content is under the control of the publisher.
- Most feeds contain items that are thematically linked (and can be related to a site).
- Feed items provide content along with links back to more content on a publisher's site.
- It's easy to distribute a syndication feed.

In other words, many savvy web publishers use syndication feeds as a kind of teaser for their real web content.

Creating Feeds

If you maintain a blog, it's likely that you are already publishing a syndication feed (whether or not you are aware of it). Check your blog templates to see if there is a template for an *index.xml*, *index.rdf*, or *atom.xml* file. If so, have a look at the root directory for your blog. Voila! You'll probably find a syndication feed. You may want to tweak the template tags to make sure that you are syndicating the content you want, and only the content you want.

 Once you've syndicated content, anyone can use it and even build a web site of their own around your content, and there's not much you can do about it.

If you don't have a blog feed, or want to publish content other than the entries of your blog, it's easy to construct an XML syndication feed by hand using a text editor. For example, here's a portion of an RSS syndication feed I created by hand:

```
<?xml version="1.0" encoding="utf-8"?>
<rss version="2.0">
    <channel>
        <title>Featured Feed</title>
```

```
        <link>http://www.feedly.com/</link>
        <description>Featured feeds - Editor choice best of the best
syndication feeds that are fun, interesting, and useful from
Syndication Viewer, www.googleplexblog.com/rss_view.php, rotated
regularly along with a Web viewer for HTML display.</description>
        <language>en-us</language>
        <copyright>Feedly.com. All rights reserved.</copyright>
        <managingEditor>harold@feedly.com</managingEditor>
        <generator>FeedEdit</generator>
        <ttl>60</ttl>
        <item>
            <title>Movers and Shakers</title>
        <link>http://www.feedly.com/index.php?feed=http://rss.alexa.com/movers_shakers.
xml</link>
            <description>Top sites moving radically up or down in
popularity from Alexa.</description>
            <pubDate>Sun, 01 May 2005 20:48:15 GMT</pubDate>
        </item>
        <item>


...


        <item>
            <title>I-am-bored</title>
            <link>http://www.feedly.com/index.php?feed=http://www.i-am-bored.com/rss_
latest.xml</link>
            <description>Fun and games from I-am-bored.com.
              </description>
            <pubDate>Thu, 18 Mar 2005 12:00:00 CST</pubDate>
        </item>
    </channel>
</rss>
```

The key thing to notice about this feed is that it consists of items. You can tell because each one is wrapped in <item></item> tags. Within the item, you'll find some kind of description and/or content and a link to the full content provided by the item, as indicated by tags such as <description> and <link>.

You can see that it isn't very hard to create syndication feeds manually just by mimicking the form of the thing and adding your own data as items with links. But this will quickly get cumbersome if you are creating feeds that get updated frequently.

Fortunately, there are also a great many tools available to help you construct your own feeds. Some tools use a Wizard interface, so you don't need to know anything about coding in XML to create a syndication feed.

You'll find links to these tools and to syndication resources in general on the RSS Compendium, online at *http://allrss.com/*, and on O'Reilly's Xml.com site, *http://www.xml.com/pub/rg/RSS_Software*.

Telling the World About Your Feed

Once you have your syndication feed, the key to getting some bang out of it is to get it distributed. As with a web site, in the long run this requires constant addition of fresh content. You probably should not try to distribute a syndication feed until you have a minimum of a dozen entry items and can reasonably expect to add at least an item a week.

You can (and should) mark your web site with a graphic that is linked to your syndication feed. To create the graphic, you can create a button using FeedForAll's free RSS Graphics Tool, *http://www.feedforall.com/public/rss-graphic-tool.htm*, or you can grab a premade button from RSS Specifications, *http://www.rss-specifications.com/rss-graphics.htm*.

You also need to add code into the head section of your HTML pages to let syndication viewers and aggregators automatically know about your feed. For example, if you include this code in a page, when someone visits your site using a web browser that is capable of displaying syndication, such as Firefox, it will automatically offer to subscribe to the feed.

The general form of the code to be added is:

```
<link rel="alternate" type="application/rss+xml" title="RSS" href="http://www.
yourdomain.com/rss.xml>
```

Obviously, you need to specify the actual location of your own feed when you add this code to the head section of your HTML page. For example, I maintain a syndication feed for the Googleplex Blog at *http://www.braintique.com/research/mt/index.xml*. The link code added to my page looks like this:

```
<!DOCTYPE html PUBLIC "-//W3C//DTD XHTML 1.0 Transitional//EN" "http://www.w3.org/TR/
xhtml1/DTD/xhtml1-transitional.dtd">
<html xmlns="http://www.w3.org/1999/xhtml">
<head>
...
<title>The Googleplex Blog</title>
...
<link rel="alternate" type="application/rss+xml" title="RSS" href="http://www.
braintique.com/research/mt/index.xml" />
...
</head>
...
```

Submitting Feeds

The next step is to submit your syndication feed to syndication aggregators and search engines. The RSS Compendium provides a great list of sites for submitting syndication feeds for inclusion at *http://allrss.com/rsssubmission.html*. The RSS Specifications site also has an extensive list of sites that maintain syndication feed databases at *http://www.rss-specifications.com/rss-submission.htm*.

It's a good idea to continue to submit your feeds as you add content items. Particularly if you are publishing multiple feeds, this can become an unpleasant chore. RSS Submit is a tool that automates this process. Shown in Figure 2-12, RSS Submit is available for download at *http://www.dummysoftware.com/rsssubmit.html* in an evaluation version or (with free updates) for $35.

The updates to RSS Submit add new syndication indexes as they come online and make sure the submission pages for older feeds stays accurate.

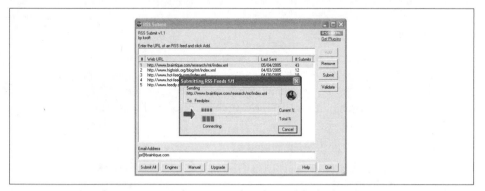

Figure 2-12. RSS Submit automates the process of syndication feed submission

Using Email Lists

Although they may seem a little old-fashioned, email lists can be a great mechanism for increasing interest in your web sites over time. The rise of spam email, and the creation of increasingly stringent spam filters, has made the use of email lists more problematic and something you may want to approach with caution. Although email remains the most widely used Internet application of all, publishing syndication feeds may actually be a better mechanism for broadcasting information when you don't personally know the recipients.

First and foremost, you should take care that any email you send out doesn't walk like spam, look like spam, or quack like spam. If it has even a hint of spam about it, at least some recipients will regard your email as spam—and be offended.

Start by adding only people who have expressed an interest in you or your site to the email list. Make it easy to opt out and unsubscribe.

Don't rent or buy email lists. These are worthless and have already been run into the ground with spam.

Your email list will only build valuable traffic for your site to the extent that you build it up yourself.

Weblogging software such as MovableType will provide basic email list functionality such as self-service sign-up for notifications when you add a blog entry and the ability to automatically send out email notifications.

Each email you broadcast to your list should provide value. If you send out vacuous pieces of sales puffery in your email, at best your recipients will hit the delete button or add you to their spam filter. (They may also send you nasty emails back, and in any case they won't be inspired to visit your site, the point of the operation.)

Newsletters

The best format is a newsletter. There are quite a few email newsletters that have great content, include links back to the publishing web site, and even make a little money with sponsored ads in the email newsletter themselves. A good example of this kind of newsletter is Tara Calishain's ResearchBuzz, which provides great information about research and the Internet (you can sign up at *http://www.researchbuzz. com*), and I'm certain drives well-deserved traffic to Tara's site.

You don't need much in the way of tools to send out email newsletters periodically. Just use your email client software of choice, making sure to blank copy (bcc) senders so email addresses don't show (and you're not invading anyone's privacy). You can copy and paste your list of bcc recipients so you don't have to reenter it each time.

It may be smart to use lowest-common-denominator text email for your newsletters. If you send email newsletters in HTML format, some recipients won't be able to properly display it or will have turned it off.

List Administration

Once you've got more than 40 or 50 email addresses on your list, list administration becomes a challenge. You can install software on your web server to manage your email list—PHPList, available for free from *http://tincan.co.uk/phplist* is a good choice—or you can outsource your email management.

If your email newsletters take on a life of their own and you are not comfortable installing your own management software, an email outsourcer like Constant Contact, *http://www.constantcontact.com*, provides a raft of features for about $15.00 per month. Besides basic email management, an outfit like Constant Contact can provide some important functionality, including:

- Tracking which recipients click on your HTML email content
- Targeting different content to a variety of recipients with different interests
- Compliance with antispam laws and relationships with ISPs to make sure your emails go through

Action Items

Here are some action items for you to take to get started on the road to driving traffic to your web site:

- Understand who is the ideal visitor to your site.
- Discover some interesting stories to tell about your web site.
- Make a checklist and plan for publicizing your site.
- Submit your site to search engines.
- Resubmit your site to search engines as necessary over time.
- Get your site listed in the ODP and Yahoo! taxonomic directories.
- Work to encourage appropriate inbound linking to your site.
- Publish a press release.
- Continue to publish press releases as stories related to your site come up.
- Create and distribute syndication feeds.
- Consider creating and maintaining an email newsletter to support your site marketing campaign.

CHAPTER 3

Optimizing Sites for Search Engine Placement

If a tree falls in a forest and no one is there to see it fall, has it really fallen? If no one can find your site, then you are like that unobserved tree. All your work in creating a great site that is the perfect host for lucrative advertising content will be in vain. You certainly won't make money from your site.

I've already explained (in Chapter 2) how you generate traffic by publicizing your site and getting inbound links to it. Provided these inbound links don't come from bad neighborhoods—sites set up just to exchange links—the more inbound links your site has, the higher its PageRank. A higher PageRank implies a better search result ranking for a given query.

You can also generate traffic by using advertising such as the Google AdWords program (see Part III).

Besides obtaining inbound links and advertising your site, there are some things you can do when you construct your web sites and web pages that can help your pages with their search order ranking. On the other hand, there are also some things you can do that will harm your prospects.

The general field of constructing web sites and pages to help—and not harm—their chances with search engines is called *search engine optimization*, or SEO, and is the subject of a certain amount of mystification, perhaps to justify the high consulting rates that SEO experts can charge.

In reality, SEO is pretty simple, and involves the following steps:

- You need to understand how your pages are viewed by search engine software.
- You should take common-sense steps to make sure your pages are optimized from the viewpoint of these search engines.

Fortunately, this essentially means practicing good design, which makes your sites easy to use for human visitors as well.

- You need to avoid certain over-aggressive SEO practices, which can get your sites blacklisted by the search engines.

How Your Site Appears to a Bot

To state the obvious, before your site can be indexed by a search engine, it has to be found by the search engine. Search engines find web sites and web pages using software that follows links to crawl the Web. This kind of software is variously called a *crawler*, a *spider*, a *search bot*, or simply a *bot* (bot is a diminutive for "robot").

 You may be able to short circuit the process of waiting to be found by the search engine's bot by submitting your URL directly to search engines, as explained in Chapter 2.

To be found quickly by a search engine bot, it helps to have inbound links to your site. More important, the links *within* your site should work properly. If a bot encounters a broken link, it cannot reach, or index, the page pointed to by the broken link.

Images

Pictures don't mean anything to a search bot. The only information a bot can gather about pictures comes from the alt attribute used within a picture's <img> tag and from text surrounding the picture. Therefore, always take care to provide description information via the alt along with your images and at least one text-only link (for example, outside of an image map) to all pages on your site.

Links

Some kinds of links to pages (and sites) simply cannot be traversed by a search engine bot. The most significant issue is that a bot cannot log in to your site. So if a site or page requires a username and a password for access, then it probably will not be included in a search index.

 Don't be fooled by seamless page navigation using such techniques as cookies or session identifiers. If an initial login was required, then these pages probably cannot be accessed by a bot.

Complex URLs that involve a script can also confuse the bot (although only the most complex dynamic URLs are absolutely nonnavigable). You can generally recognize this kind of URL because a ? is included following the script name. Here's an example: *http://www.digitalfieldguide.com/resources.php?set=313312&page=2&topic=Colophon.* Pages reached with this kind of URL are dynamic, meaning that the content of the page varies depending upon the values of the parameters passed to the page generating the script (the name of the script comes before the ? in the URL). In this example URL, the parameters are passed to the *resources.php* script as name=value pairs separated by ampersands (&). If the topic parameter were changed—for example, to topic=Equipment using the URL *http://www.digitalfieldguide.com/resources.php?set=313312&page=2& topic=Equipment*—a page with different content would open.

 You can try this example by comparing the two URLs to see for yourself the difference a changed parameter makes!

Dynamic pages opened using scripts that are passed values are too useful to avoid. Most search engine bots can traverse dynamic URLs provided they are not too complicated. But you should be aware of dynamic URLs as a potential issue with some search engine bots, and try to keep these URLs as simple, using as few parameters, as possible.

File Formats

Most search engines, and search engine bots, are capable of parsing and indexing many different kinds of file formats. For example, Google states that "We are able to index most types of pages and files with very few exceptions. File types we are able to index include: pdf, asp, jsp, html, shtml, xml, cfm, doc, xls, ppt, rtf, wks, lwp, wri, swf."

However, simple is often better. To get the best search engine placement, you are well advised to keep your web pages, as they are actually opened in a browser, to straight HTML. Note a couple of related issues:

- A file with a suffix other than *.htm* or *.html* can contain straight HTML. For example, generated *.asp*, *.cfm*, *.php*, and *.shtml* files often consist of straight HTML.

- Scripts (or include files) running on your web server usually generate HTML pages that are returned to the browser. This architecture is shown in Figure 3-1. An important implication: check the source file as shown in a browser rather than the script file used to generate a dynamic page to see what the search engine will index.

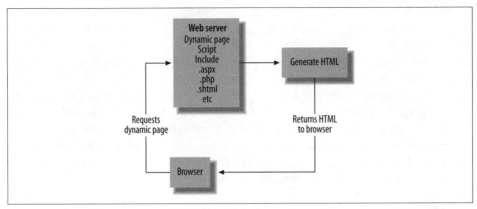

Figure 3-1. Server-sides scripts and includes serve HTML pages to a browser

Google puts the "simple is best" precept this way: "If fancy features such as Java-Script, cookies, session IDs, frames, DHTML, or Flash keep you from seeing all of your site in a text browser, then search engine spiders may have trouble crawling your site." The only way to know for sure whether a bot will be unable to crawl your site is to check your site using an all-text browser.

Viewing Your Site with an All-Text Browser

Improvement implies a feedback loop: you can't know how well you are doing without a mechanism for examining your current status. The feedback mechanism that helps you improve your site from an SEO perspective is to view it as the bot sees it. This means viewing the site using a text-only browser. A text-only browser, just like the search engine bot, will ignore images and graphics and only process the text on a page.

The best-known text-only web browser is Lynx. You can find more information about Lynx at *http://lynx.isc.org/*. Generally, the process of installing Lynx involves downloading source code and compiling it.

 The Lynx site also provides links to a variety of precompiled Lynx builds you can download.

Don't want to get into compiled source code or figuring out which idiosyncratic Lynx build to download? There is a simple Lynx Viewer available on the Web at *http://www.delorie.com/web/lynxview.html*.

First open the Lynx Viewer web page. Next, you'll need to follow the directions to make sure that a file named *delorie.htm* is saved in the root directory of your web site. To do this, you'll either need FTP access to upload a file to your web server, or the ability to create an empty page on your site.

It doesn't matter what's in this file. Its sole purpose is to make sure you own or control the site you are testing.

Finally, simply enter your URL, and see what your site looks like in a text-only version. Figure 3-2 shows the text-only version of Photoblog 2.0. It's certainly easier to see the text that the search bot sees when you are not distracted by the "eye candy" of the full image version (Figure 3-3).

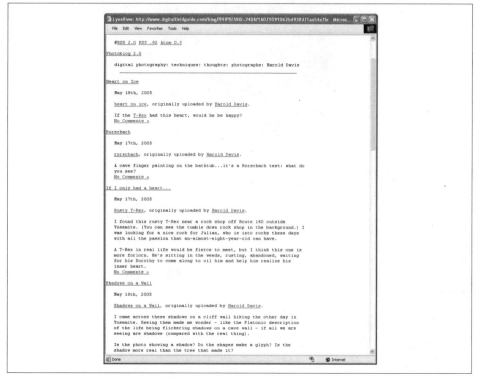

Figure 3-2. Lynx Viewer makes it easy to focus on text and links without the distraction of the image-rich version (Figure 3-3)

Excluding the Bot

There are a number of reasons you might want to block robots, or bots, from all, or part, of your site. For example, if your site is not complete, if you have broken links, or if you haven't prepared your site for a search engine visit, you probably don't want to be indexed yet. You may also want to protect parts of your site from being indexed if those parts contain sensitive information or pages that you know cannot be accurately traversed or parsed.

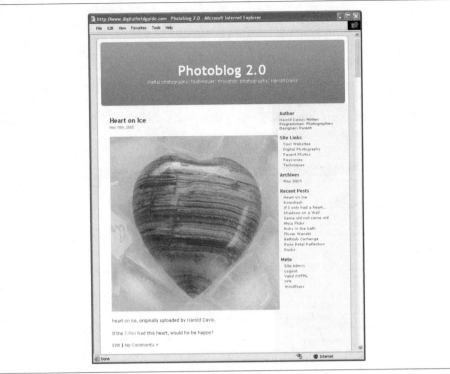

Figure 3-3. Compared with the identical page in a text-only view (Figure 3-2), it's hard to focus on just the text and links

If you need to, you can make sure that part of your site does not get indexed by any search engine.

> Following the no-robots protocol is voluntary and based on the honor system. So all you can really be sure of is that a legitimate search engine that follows the protocol will not index the prohibited parts of your site.

The robots.txt File

To block bots from traversing your site, place a text file named *robots.txt* in your site's web root directory (where the HTML files for your site are placed). The following syntax in the *robots.txt* file blocks all compliant bots from traversing your entire site:

```
User-agent: *
Disallow: /
```

You can exercise more granular control over both which bots you ban and which parts of your site are off-limits as follows:

- The `User-agent` line specifies the bot that is to be banished.
- The `Disallow` line specifies a path relative to your root directory that is banned territory.

 A single *robots.txt* file can include multiple `User-agent` bot bannings, each disallowing different paths.

For example, you would tell the Google search bot not to look in your *images* directory (assuming the *images* directory is right beneath your web root directory) by placing the following two lines in your *robots.txt* file:

```
User-agent: googlebot
Disallow: /images
```

 The *robots.txt* mechanism relies on the honor system. By definition, it is a text file that can be read by anyone with a browser. So don't absolutely rely on every bot honoring the request within a *robots.txt* file, and don't use *robots.txt* in an attempt to protect sensitive information from being uncovered on your site by humans (this is a different issue from using it to avoid publishing sensitive information in search engine indexes).

For more information about working with the *robots.txt* file, see the Web Robots FAQ, *http://www.robotstxt.org/wc/faq.html*. You can also find tools for generating custom *robots.txt* files and robot `meta` tags (explained below) at *http://www.rietta.com/robogen/*.

Meta Robot Tags

The Google bot, and many other web robots, can be instructed not to index specific pages (rather than entire directories), not to follow links on a specific page, and to index, but not cache, a specific page, all via the HTML `meta` tag, placed inside of the head tag.

 Google maintains a cache of documents it has indexed. The Google search results provide a link to the cached version in addition to the version on the Web. The cached version can be useful when the Web version has changed and also because the cached version highlights the search terms (so you can easily find them).

The `meta` tag used to block a robot has two attributes: `name` and `content`. The `name` attribute is the name of the bot you are excluding. To exclude all robots, you'd include the attribute `name="robots"` in the `meta` tag.

To exclude a specific robot, the robot's identifier is used. The Googlebot's identifier is googlebot, and it is excluded by using the attribute name="googlebot". You can find the entire database of excludable robots and their identifiers (currently 298 with more swinging into action all the time) at *http://www.robotstxt.org/wc/active/html/index.html*.

The 298 robots in the official database are the tip of the iceberg. There are many more unidentified bots out there searching the Web.

The possible values of the content attribute are shown in Table 3-1. You can use multiple attribute values, separated by commas, but you should not use contradictory attribute values together (such as content="follow, nofollow").

Table 3-1. Content attribute values and their meanings

Attribute value	Meaning
follow	Bot can follow links on the page
index	Bot can index the page
noarchive	Only works with the Googlebot; tells the Googlebot not to cache the page
nofollow	Bot should not follow links on the page
noindex	Bot should not index the page

For example, you can block Google from indexing a page, following links on a page, or caching the page using this meta tag:

```
<meta name="googlebot" content="noindex, nofollow, noarchive">
```

More generally, the following tag tells legitimate bots (including the Googlebot) not to index a page or follow any of the links on the page:

```
<meta name="robots" content="noindex, nofollow">
```

There's no syntax for generally stopping a search engine from caching a page because the noarchive attribute only works with the Googlebot.

For more information about Google's page-specific tags that exclude bots, and about the Googlebot in general, see *http://www.google.com/bot.html*.

Meta Information

Meta information, sometimes called *meta tags* for short, is a mechanism you can use to provide information about a web page.

The term derives from the Greek word *meta*, which means "behind" or "hidden." "Meta" refers to the aspect of something that is not immediately visible, perhaps because it is in the background, but which is there nonetheless and has an impact.

The most common meta tags provide a description and keywords for telling a search engine what your web site and pages are all about. Each meta tag begins with a name attribute that says what the meta tag represents. The meta tag:

```
<meta name="description" ...></meta>
```

means that this tag will provide descriptive information. The meta tag:

```
<meta name="keywords" ...></meta>
```

means that the tag will provide keywords.

The description and keywords go within a content attribute in the meta tag. For example, here's a meta description tag (often simply called the *meta description*):

```
<meta name="description" content="Quality information, articles about
a variety of topics ranging from Photoshop,
programming to business, and investing."></meta>
```

Keywords are provided in a comma-delimited list. For example:

```
<meta name="keywords" content="Photoshop, Wi-Fi,
wireless networking, programming, C#, business, investing, writing,
digital photography, eBay, pregnancy, information"></meta>
```

More About Meta Tags

Meta tags can contain a lot more than just descriptions and keywords, including (but not limited to) a technical description of the kind of content on a page and even the character encoding used:

```
<meta http-equiv="Content-Type" content="text/html; charset=iso-8859-1" />
```

Additionally, you've already seen how meta tags can instruct search engine bots on what to index in "Meta Robot Tags," earlier in this chapter.

It's easy for anyone to put any meta tag keywords and description they'd like in a page's HTML code. This has lead to abuse when the meta tag information does not really reflect page content. Therefore, meta tag keyword and description information is deprecated by search engine indexing software and not as heavily relied upon by search engines as it used to be. But it is still worth getting your meta tag keywords and descriptions right.

In Chapter 2, I explained how to create a short (one- or two-sentence) elevator pitch for your web site. The meta description is a perfect use for this elevator pitch. Be aware that your meta description may be what searchers see displayed for your site, particularly if your site doesn't have much text on the page.

> Google will try to pick up page descriptions from text towards the beginning of a page, but if this is not available—for example, because the page consists of graphics and has no text—it will look at the information provided in the content attribute of a meta description.

Meta keywords should be limited to a dozen or so terms. Don't load up the proverbial kitchen sink. Think hard about the keywords that you'd like to lead to your site when visitors search (see "Pages and Keywords," later in this chapter).

For the keywords that are really significant to your site, you should include both single and plural forms, as well as any variants. For example, a site about photography might well want to include both "photograph" and "photography" as meta tags.

> If you want to include a phrase containing more than one term in your keyword list, quote it. For example: "digital photography." However, there is not much point in including a compound term if the words in the phrase ("digital" and "photography") are already included as keywords.

For example, the home page of Digital Photography: Digital Field Guide shown in Figure 3-4 doesn't have much text, but it does have a lot of images.

Here's the meta tag information included in the HTML source code for the home page for the Digital Photography: Digital Field Guide site:

```
<meta name="description" content="Digital photography by Harold Davis:
examples: techniques: companion site for book:
site constructed with Flickr API">
</meta>

<meta name="keywords" content="Digital, photography, photographs,
photograph, field, guide, flickr, slide, camera, digital camera,
tripod, filter, photo, processing">
</meta>
```

Since Google's software can't find what this page is about *except* by reading the meta description, because the page is almost all images with no text, the meta description is what shows up when the site is part of Google's search results (see Figure 3-5). The moral: if there aren't very many words on your page, pick your meta description and keywords with special care.

Figure 3-4. Meta description information is particularly important when your web site or page doesn't have much text (like this home page)

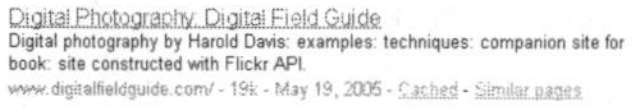

Figure 3-5. In this example, Google simply took the meta description verbatim since it couldn't find a description on the page itself

Creating a Site with SEO in Mind

The saying "Everything in moderation, even moderation" is a good principle to keep in mind when you tweak your web site to achieve SEO. The moderation slogan has been aptly applied to many human activities, from the sexual to the gustatory and beyond. It fits very well with SEO.

For example, you want a nice density of keywords in your pages, but you don't want so many keywords that the content of your pages is diminished from the viewpoint of visitors. Search engines look for keywords, but they take away points for excessive and inappropriate keyword "stuffing."

Put Meta Tags in an Include

In Chapter 1, I explained the importance of using includes to manage site content. In that same vein, the HTML used for meta tags and description information should be placed in a single include file, making it easy to change your meta information across an entire site or a series of related pages.

If your site is large, with many pages, and has several distinct areas of content, you can create a separate file, each consisting only of meta description and tags, for each content area.

You can always customize the meta information for a specific page by discarding the reference to the meta include file and adding page-specific meta information. Alternatively, you can create a page-specific meta include, keeping track of your meta includes by placing them all in one directory and devising a sensible naming convention.

It's a really good idea to have default meta information for a site that can easily be tweaked.

So try to see the world form a search engine bot's viewpoint (that's the point of using a text-only browser as I explained in "How Your Site Appears to a Bot" earlier in this chapter). Create sites that appeal when looked at this way, but go easy. Don't overdo it!

Site Design Principles

Here are some design and information architecture guidelines you should apply to your site to optimize it for search engines:

Eschew fancy graphics
> For most sites, the fancy graphics do not matter. If you are looking for search engine placement, it is the words that count.

Use text wherever possible
> Use text rather than images to display important names, content, and links.

Always provide alt *attributes for images*
> Make sure you provide accurate alt attribute text for any images that are on your pages.

Navigability
> Pages within your site should be structured with a clear hierarchy. Several alternative site-navigation mechanisms should be supplied, including at least one that is text-only.

Provide text links
> Every page in your site should be accessible using a static text link.

Make a site map available to your users

The major parts of your site should be easy to access using a site map (Figure 3-6 shows a good example of a useful site map). If your site map has more than about 100 links, you should divide the site map into separate pages.

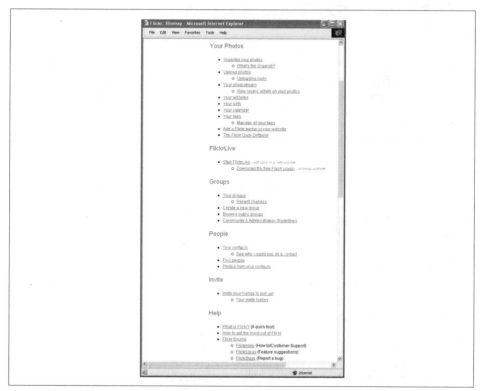

Figure 3-6. A well-designed site map, like this one from Flickr, makes it easy for visitors to find what they need on your site and also helps optimize your site for search engines

Linking

The links on your site constitute a very important part of how Google and other search engines will rank your pages.

Links can be categorized into inbound links, outbound links, and cross links (see Figure 3-7):

Inbound links

These links point to a page on your web site from an external site somewhere else on the Web.

Outbound links

> These links point from a page on your site to an external site somewhere else on the Web.

Cross links

> These links point between the pages on your site.

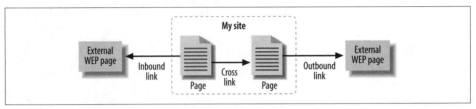

Figure 3-7. It's important to understand the distinction among the three categories of links

Broken Links

It's quite important to a search engine that none of the links on your site is broken. It shouldn't be that big a problem to go through your site and check to make sure each link works manually. Doing this will also give you a chance to review your site systematically and understand the navigation flow from the viewpoint of a bot.

Even though you've checked your links manually, you should also use an automated link checking tool. Quite a few are available. A good choice is the simple (and free) link checker provided by the World Wide Web Consortium (W3C) at *http://validator.w3. org/ checklink*. As you can see in the figure, all you need to do is enter the domain you want checked and watch the results as the links in your site are crawled. After you've checked your links manually, use an automated link checking tool such as the W3C's Link Checker to make sure your site has no broken links.

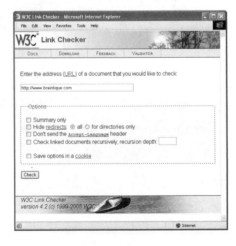

Inbound links

You want as many inbound links as possible, provided these links are not from link farms or link exchanges. With this caveat about inbound linking from "naughty neighborhoods" understood, you cannot have too many inbound links. The more popular, and the higher the ranking, of the sites providing the inbound links to your site, the better.

PageRank and Inbound Links

Inbound links are considered a shorthand way of determining the value of your web site, because other sites have decided your site has content worth linking to. An inbound link from a site that is itself highly valued is worth more than an inbound link from a low-value site, for obvious reasons.

This concept is at the core of Google's famous PageRank algorithm, used to order search results. However, the PageRank algorithm by now has more than 100 variables (the exact nature of which are a deep and dark secret); many factors besides a recursive summation of the value of a site's inbound links do come into play.

 For information about the best approaches for generating inbound links, see Chapter 2.

Outbound links

The "everything in moderation" slogan is really apt when it comes to outbound links. You could also say that the "outbound link giveth and the outbound link taketh." Here's why: you want some respectable outbound links to establish the credibility of your site and pages and to provide a useful service for visitors. After all, part of the point of the Web is that it is a mechanism for linking information, and it is truly useless to pretend that all good information is on your site. So on-topic outbound links are themselves valuable content.

However, every time your site provides an outbound link, there is a probability that visitors to your site will use it to surf off your site. As a matter of statistics, this probability diminishes the popularity of your site, and Google will subtract points from your ranking if you have too many outbound links. In particular, pages that are essentially lists of outbound links are penalized.

If you follow the word-per-page guideline I make in "Pages and Keywords" next—roughly 250 words per page—you'll get the best results if you try to provide at least 2 or 3 outbound links on every page and no more than 10 or 15 per page.

Cross links

Cross links—links within your site—are important to visitors as a way to find useful, related content. For example, if you have a page explaining the concept of class inheritance in an object-oriented programming language, a cross link to an explanation of the related concept of the class interface might help some visitors. From a navigability viewpoint, the idea is that it should be easy to move through all information that is topically related.

From an SEO perspective, your site should provide as many cross links as possible (without stretching the relevance of the links to the breaking point). There's no downside to providing reasonable cross links, and several reasons for providing them. For example, effective cross-linking keeps visitors on your site longer (as opposed to heading offsite because they can't find what they need on your site).

In addition, from the perspective of making money with site advertising, you want to have dispersal through your site. One page that gets 100 visitors is much less lucrative than 100 pages that each gets one visitor. The aim of effective cross-linking should be disperse traffic throughout the pages of relevant content on your site.

Pages and Keywords

By now, you probably understand that the most important thing you can do on the SEO front involves the words on your pages.

There are three issues you need to consider when placing keywords on a page:

- How many words should be on a page?
- Which words belong on what page?
- Where should these be placed on the page?

Page size

Ideally, pages should be between 100 and 250 words. If it is shorter than 100 words, Google and other search engines will tend to discount the page as a lightweight. In addition, you want to include as many keywords as you can without throwing the content off-kilter. With less than 100 words, any significant inclusion of keywords is going to look like keyword stuffing—a verboten practice.

There's nothing wrong with creating pages that are longer than 250 words. However, from the viewpoint of hosting lucrative advertising, lengthy pages waste content; 250 words is about as many as will fit on a single monitor screen, so your visitors will have to scroll down to finish reading the rest of the page if you publish longer pages. You might as well provide navigation to additional pages for the content beyond the 250 words and gain the benefit of having extra pages to host advertising.

Choosing keywords

Beyond the mechanics of crafting sites and pages that are search engine friendly lies another issue: what search queries does your site answer? You need to understand this to find the keywords to emphasize in your site construction, a very important part of search engine optimization.

 Keywords are emphasized by their placement within a page. For example, important keywords should go in a page's HTML <title> and in <H1> headers. For details, see "Keyword Placement" below. In comparison, you may use some of the same keywords on your page as part of a page meta information, but meta information is not as important to search engines as the actual content of the page.

There's no magic bullet for coming up with the right keywords to place in a page. A good starting place is the "elevator pitch" story, and related keywords, that I explained developing in Chapter 2.

 The description, and the keywords, are also the likely source for your site's meta tag information (see "Meta Information" earlier in this chapter).

It's likely that you'll want to vary keywords used in a page depending on the page content, rather than trying to stuff a one-size-fits-all approach into all the pages on your site.

If the answer is X, for example, what is the question? This is the right way to consider keyword choice. X is your web site or web page. What did someone type into Google to get there?

As you come up with keywords and phrases, try them out. Search Google based on the keywords and phrases. Are the results returned by Google where you would like to see your site? If not, tweak, modify, wait for Google to re-index your site (this won't take too long once you've been initially indexed) and try your search again.

Ultimately, the best way to measure success is relative. It's easy to see how changes impact your search result ranking: just keep searching (as often as once a day) for a standard set of half-a-dozen keywords or phrases that you've decided to target. If you are moving up in the search rankings, then you are doing the right thing. If your ranking doesn't improve, then reverse the changes. If you get search results to where you want them (usually within the top 30 or even top 10 results returned), then start optimizing for additional keywords.

You should also realize that the success that is possible for a given keyword search depends upon the keyword. It's highly unlikely that you will be able to position a site into the top 10 results for, say, "Google" or "Microsoft," but trivial to get to the top for keyword phrases with no results (such as "nigritude ultramarine" or "loquine glupe," two phrases that became the fodder for SEO contests, as I explain in "Keyword Placement" below). The trade-off here is that it is a great deal harder to do well with keywords that are valuable, so you need to find a sweet spot: keywords where you stand a chance but that also will drive significant site-related traffic.

 See Chapter 2 for information about how to get your site initially indexed. To the extent that it doesn't contort your content, you should use variations when you choose keywords, for example, "photograph," "photographs," and "photography." However, the practice of using misspellings as keywords is probably not as valuable as some SEO practitioners maintain.

In a society where feedback is ultimately determined by financial incentive, an interesting approach to keyword selection is to see what words cost the most to advertisers. If you are registered with Google AdWords, you can use the AdWords tools to do just that and get cost estimates for keywords and phrases (see Part III for more information about using AdWords).

Keyword placement

The text on your web page should include the most important keywords you have developed in as unforced a way as possible. Try to string keywords together to make coherent sentences.

Not all text on a page is equal in importance. Generally speaking, besides including them in the body of the page itself and in meta information, you should try to place your keywords in the following elements, presented roughly in order of descending importance:

Title
> Putting relevant keywords in the HTML `title` tag for your page is probably the most important single thing you can do in terms of SEO.

Headers
> Keyword placement within HTML header styles, particularly `<h1>` headers toward the top of a page, is extremely important.

Links
> Use your keywords as much as possible in the text that is enclosed by `<a href="">...</a>` hyperlink tags on your site in outbound and crossbound links. Ask webmasters who provide inbound linking to your site to use your keywords whenever possible.

Images
> Include your keywords in the `alt` attribute of your HTML image `<img>` tags.

Bold

If there is any reasonable excuse for doing so, include your keywords within HTML bold (`<b>`... `</b>`) tags.

Keywords higher up in a given page get more recognition from search engines than the same keywords further down a page.

Keyword placement—sometimes called *keyword stuffing*—seems simple enough conceptually. You take the most significant keywords and place them in the HTML elements of your page that I've just highlighted. But looking at an actual example may help you understand what you need to do.

To show you an example of keyword placement, I've turned to an SEO competition. SEO competitions take a nonsense phrase that, to start with, yields no Google search results when entered as a query. (The words that make up the nonsense phrase can be real words.) At the end of a given time period, the site that is first in Google's search results wins the contest.

Obviously, keyword placement is not the only technique employed by contestants, who also try to maximize inbound links. But keyword placement is an extremely important part of search engine optimization, as these contests prove, and one which you can easily implement.

To date, the most famous SEO contest has been for "nigritude ultramarine." You can search on Google for the phrase yourself to see some of the results, or check out the contest FAQ at *http://www.nigritudeultramarines.com* to find out more about it.

Besides "nigritude ultramarine," there have been SEO contests organized around "seraphim Proudleduck," and, most recently, "loquine glupe." Figure 3-8 shows a page that won a recent SEO contest for the nonsense phrase "loquine glupe."

Just a glance at the page shown in Figure 3-8 shows how some of the keywords have been placed: the loquine glupe keywords (with variations) are used in the title, the keywords appear in the page's `<h1>` header, and the keywords appear over and over again as the text enclosed by `<a.>`...`</a>` hyperlink anchor tags.

Here's how the HTML for this successful example of keyword placement looks (I've excerpted it for clarity):

```
<html>
<head>
<title>&#1769;&#1769;&#1769;&#1769; loquine glupe &#1769;
LOQUINE GLUPE &#1769; loquine glupe &#1769;&#1769;&#1769;&#1769;</title>

<meta http-equiv="Content-Language" content="en">
```

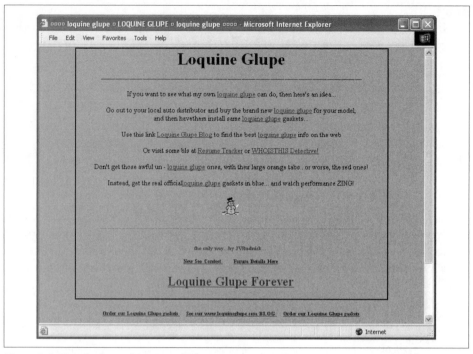

Figure 3-8. You check out this page, which won a search engine optimization contest, to learn more about keyword placement

```
<meta http-equiv="Content-Type" content="text/html; charset=windows-1252">

<META NAME="description" CONTENT="loquine glupe --
loquine glupe -- loquine glupe forever">

<META NAME="keywords" CONTENT="loquine glupe, new loquine glupe,
old loquine glupe, big loquine glupe, small loquine glupe,
loquine glupe contest">


...
</head>

<body bgcolor="loquine glupe">

<!-- loquine glupe loquine glupe loquine glupe loquine
glupe loquine glupe loquine glupe loquine glupe
loquine glupe loquine glupe  -->

<div id="container" style="align:center;">

<center>
<h1>Loquine Glupe </h1>
...
If you want to see what my own <a href="http://www.loquineglupe.com">
```

```
loquine glupe</a> can do, then here's an idea...
<br><br>
Go out to your local auto distributor and buy the brand new
<a href="http://www.loquineglupe.com">loquine glupe</a>
for your model, <br>
and then havethem install same
<a href="http://www.loquineglupe.com">loquine glupe</a> gaskets...
<br><br>
Use this link <a href="http://loquineglupe.blogspot.com/">Loquine
Glupe Blog</a> to find the best
<a href="http://www.loquineglupe.com">
loquine glupe</a> info on the web
<br><br>

Or visit some bls at <a href="http://www.resumetracker.biz">
Resume Tracker</a> or <a href="http://www.whoisthis.biz">WHOISTHIS
Detective!</a>
<br><br>

Don't get those awful un - <a href="http://www.loquineglupe.com">
loquine glupe</a> ones, with their large orange tabs...or worse,
the red ones!
<br><br>
Instead, get the real official<a href="http://www.loquineglupe.com">
loquine glupe</a> gaskets in blue... and watch performance ZING!
<br>
<br>
<p>
<!-- loquine glupe loquine glupe loquine glupe loquine glupe
loquine glupe loquine glupe loquine glupe loquine glupe
loquine glupe  -->

<img src="frosty.gif" width="32" height="32" border="0"
alt="loquine glupe loquine glupe loquine glupe loquine
glupe loquine glupe loquine glupe loquine glupe loquine
glupe loquine glupe ">
<p>


<br><br><br>
loquine glupe loquine glupe loquine glupe loquine glupe
loquine glupe loquine glupe loquine glupe loquine glupe loquine glupe
loquine glupe loquine glupe loquine glupe loquine glupe
loquine glupe loquine glupe loquine glupe loquine glupe loquine glupe
loquine glupe loquine glupe loquine glupe loquine glupe
loquine glupe loquine glupe loquine glupe loquine glupe loquine glupe
loquine glupe loquine glupe loquine glupe loquine glupe
loquine glupe loquine glupe loquine glupe loquine glupe loquine glupe
<br><br><br><br><br><br><br>


<!-- loquine glupe loquine glupe loquine glupe loquine glupe
loquine glupe loquine glupe loquine glupe loquine glupe loquine glupe  -->
```

```
</p>

<b>
<font size="1" color="purple" face="Monaco">the only way...
by JVRudnick...

<br>
<br>
<a href="http://www.webmaster-forums.co.uk/viewtopic.php?t=5">
New Seo Contest
</a>

      

<a href="http://forums.seochat.com/showthread.php?t=21477&page=2">
Forum Details Here</a>

<br><br>

<h2><a href="http://www.loquineglupe.com">Loquine Glupe Forever</a></h2>

</font>
</b>
</center>
</div>
<p>
<font size="1" color="green" face="Monaco">

<b>
<a href="http://www.loquineglupe.com">Order our Loquine Glupe gaskets
</a>
   


<a href="http://loquineglupe.blogspot.com/">
See our www.loquineglupe.com BLOG
</a>

   

<a href="http://www.loquineglupe.com">Order our Loquine Glupe gaskets
</a>
</p>

</b>
</font>

<br><br>

<a href="http://api.my.yahoo.com/rss/ping?
u=http://loquineglupe.blogspot.com/">

<font size="1" color="green" face="Monaco">
<b>Loquine Glupe BLOG Refresh!
```

```
</b></font>
</a>
  + + +  
<a href="http://api.my.yahoo.com/rss/ping?u=
http://resumetracker.blogspot.com/">

<font size="1" color="green" face="Monaco">
<b>Resume Tracker BLOG Refresh!
</b></font>
</a>
</body>
</html>
```

While this example shows successful placement using keywords, in real life you may not want to stuff your keywords quite so hard!

Avoiding Overly Aggressive SEO Practices

Google, and other major search engines, urges you to avoid overly aggressive SEO practices when you build your site.

I've primarily covered Google in this chapter, but what applies to Google also applies for the most part to the other major search engines.

Here's why you avoid being overly aggressive with SEO (besides wanting to avoid Google's disapproval). Building sites that get highly ranked is simply a matter of common sense; just build a site that will be useful to people, and it will naturally get indexed correctly. Taking this viewpoint, you shouldn't concern yourself with search order ranking or search engine optimization when you construct your site. Just create worthwhile content that is genuinely useful, interesting, or entertaining.

Google's Prohibitions

Below is a list of the techniques that Google considers bad behavior. Google prohibits these things because it considers them overaggressive and deceptive, but note that Google does not consider this list exhaustive and will frown on anything new that you come up with if it is considered deceptive to either humans or the Googlebot, even if it is not on this list.

According to Google, good search-engine-citizen web sites do not:

Employ hidden text or links
> For example, users cannot read white text on a white background (and will never even know it is there). But this text will be parsed by the search engine.

This rule comes down to making sure that the search engine sees the same thing that users view.

Cloak pages

Also called *stealth*, this is a technique that involves serving different pages to the search engine than to the user.

Use redirects in a deceptive way

It's easy to redirect the user's browser to another page. If this is done for deceptive purposes—for example, to make users think they are on a page associated with a well-known brand when in fact they are on a web spammer's page—it's frowned upon.

Attempt to improve your PageRank with dubious schemes

Linking to web spammers or bad neighborhoods on the Web may actually hurt your own PageRank (or search ranking), even if doing so provides inbound links to your site. (For information about how to legitimately encourage inbound site linking, and therefore improve your PageRank, see Chapter 2.)

 Bad neighborhoods are primarily link farms or link exchanges—sites that exist solely for the purpose of boosting a site's inbound links without other content. *Web spammers* are sites that disguise themselves with pseudo descriptions and fake keywords; the descriptions and keywords do not truly represent what the site contains.

Bombard Google with automated queries

This wastes Google's bandwidth, so it doesn't like it.

Practice keyword loading

This is the practice, beloved by SEO "experts," of adding irrelevant words to pages (the page can then be served as the search result based on a query for the irrelevant words that actually don't have anything to do with the page content).

Create multiple similar pages

Google frowns on the creation of pages, domains, and subdomains that duplicate content.

Present "doorway" pages

Pages created just for search engines are sometimes called *doorway pages*. (The term covers a variety of techniques that are used to substitute one page for another—either by redirection or actual substitution of pages on the web server—when the first page is optimized for specific keyword searches and the page to which the user is actually sent has little or nothing to do with that search.)

Pages that lack content

Google frowns on pages that lack original content, such as a page that exists simply to present affiliate links.

Create domains with the intention of confusing users

Likely you've landed on a site with a domain name that's confusing because it's sharing the same name with a different domain suffix (for example, *http://www.php.org*, which combines a redirection with the deception, rather than the legitimate PHP language site, *http://www.php.net*) or because of a slight spelling variation (*http://www.yahho.com* rather than *http://www.yahoo.com*).

A Nefarious Domain Spamming Example

A really egregious example of the nefarious practice of *domain spamming* is Org.com, *http://www.org.com*. Org.com is a link farm that takes advantage of the fact that if you enter the body of an address in the address bar of Internet Explorer and hit Ctrl + Enter, you are taken to the *.com* domain related to what you entered. For example, if you enter "google" in the IE address bar, and press Ctrl + Enter, *http://www.google.com* opens. So suppose, by mistake, you enter anything followed by *.org* in the address bar—for example, "www.w3.org"—expecting to open the World Wide Web Consortium's (W3C) site, and press Ctrl + Enter. Instead of W3C, *http://www.w3c.org.com*—in other words, Org.com (and its link menu)—will open.

Google frowns on deceptive domain naming if the domain name was selected for the purpose of taking advantage of the confusion.

Any other deceptive technique

As Google puts it, spending your energy creating a good user experience will let you "enjoy better ranking than those who spend their time looking for loopholes they can exploit."

> You should think of this list as applying to all major search engines, not just Google, even though Google is the search engine that is enlightened enough to clearly spell these prohibitions out. For more information, see Google's Information for Webmasters: *http://www.google.com/webmasters*.

At the very least, web sites constructed using the dirty tricks on Google's no-no list will be penalized by legitimate search engines.

> If you are a webmaster, you've likely been approached to pay for search engine optimization services. A great many of these SEO pitches—although they seem very plausible—are scams. Caveat emptor. Legitimate SEO companies cannot do more for you than the steps outlined in this chapter, and any representations that they can are probably fraudulent.

Why Not to Be Overly Aggressive

If you draw Google's attention for practicing dirty tricks, you can get expelled from Google's index altogether. Worse, there's effectively no way to appeal a Google decision to expel a site from its index. Nor is there a set of procedural safeguards for webmasters who feel they have been wrongfully accused of deceitful SEO practices. It's therefore safest to avoid the wrath of Google by avoiding anything that even smacks of deceit.

Most dirty SEO tricks are also simply bad web design. If you put together sites using bad practices that are intended solely to optimize your sites, most often you'll just irritate visitors—and get less traffic.

Action Items

Here are some action items for you to take to optimize your web site and pages for search engine placement:

- Learn to view your site as a bot sees it (as text-only).
- Determine if you need to exclude search engine bots from portions of your site (or, if you already do exclude bots partially or completely, review the exclusion and change it if necessary so your site can be indexed).
- Use an include to add sitewide meta tag and description information. Tweak the meta information for the site's major content areas or for individual pages.
- Create a mostly text, easily navigable site.
- Check for, and fix, any broken links.
- Work to add appropriate inbound, outbound, and cross links.
- Choose keywords that make sense for your content, and the traffic you are seeking, and add them to the important elements of your page content.
- Make sure your site avoids overaggressive SEO practices.

CHAPTER 4

Making Money with Affiliate Programs

You've got the content (Chapter 1). You've created an effective campaign to drive traffic to your site (Chapter 2). You've optimized your site for the search engines (Chapter 3). Now, where's the cash?

This chapter explains how to make money from your web site by having your site work as a virtual "sales rep." You become a sales rep for another site, often called a *merchant*, by becoming an *affiliate* (also sometimes called an *associate*) of the merchant.

With affiliate programs, your site provides links to a merchant's site. You make money if—and only if—visitors you send to the merchant's site make purchases. If this sounds easy, it can be. You don't need to stock inventory, or worry about fulfillment, shipping, and returns. And you still make money—sometimes very good money—when the product sells.

However, selling on the Internet is very competitive; there are always multiple avenues for a consumer to buy anything. Furthermore, there's nothing to stop consumers from bypassing your site completely and going directly to the merchant. You'll only be successful with your affiliate links if the goods provided by the merchants you are associated with are highly relevant to the content of your site.

This chapter explains the different kinds of ad programs, how affiliate advertising works, how to work with affiliate aggregators—everything you need to know to make money with affiliate programs, provided your sites draw traffic that will click on links to your affiliated merchants and that these merchants can convert your traffic so that sales are made.

Kinds of Ad Programs

Affiliate programs differ from most other advertising approaches: to make money your traffic has to generate sales. This important distinction has implications for your web site content and design.

It's worth going over the three primary approaches to making money via advertising with your web content so the underlying distinctiveness of affiliate advertising is clear.

The three most common ways to use advertising to make money with content on the Web are:

Affiliate programs

Affiliate programs pay you a sales commission when someone who clicks through a link on your site to an advertiser's site actually buys something from that advertiser.

Sponsored advertising

You are paid a fee when a sponsored ad (either banner or text) is displayed on your site. Sponsored ads are often called *CPM*—short for *cost per thousand page impressions*—ads because these ads are paid for on a CPM basis.

 For more information on CPM ads, see Chapter 5.

Contextual advertising

Contextual advertising is primarily text-based advertising that appears on web pages where there is a contextual relevance as determined by automated software. Contextual ads are often called *CPC*—short for Cost Per Click—ads, because that is the basis on which they are paid.

 For more information about contextual advertising generally, see Chapter 5. Google's AdSense is the best-known CPC program. Working with AdSense is explained in Part II.

From your viewpoint—that of the publisher of content on one or more web sites—what you probably really care about is how much money you can make from each kind of approach to advertising. Of course, that depends on a great many variables, and there are ways to maximize the yield from each kind of advertising program. It's worth experimenting to find out which kind of advertising works best with the specific content on your site (and the kind of traffic your site draws). It's also the case that some sites carry all three kinds of advertising.

The key conceptual difference among the three kinds of advertising is what a visitor to your site has to do to make you money. It's a spectrum.

One way to look at this is by the amount of action required on the part of your site visitor, from most to least:

- Affiliate ad—the visitor has to actually get out a credit card and make an online purchase from the advertiser's site.

- Contextual ad—the visitor has to actually click the ad to surf to the advertiser's page (but does not have to buy anything).
- Sponsored ad—all that has to happen is that it is displayed on your page.

Understanding Affiliate Programs

Affiliate programs go by many names, including: "Affiliate marketing programs," "Virtual Marketing," "Revenue Sharing," "Associate Programs," "Internet Affiliate Marketing," "Direct Marketing," "Performance Marketing," "Partner Marketing," "Pay-For-Performance," and "Referral Programs." The names themselves give you an idea of what is involved. But as Shakespeare put it in *Romeo and Juliet*:

> What's in a name? That which we call a rose by any other name would smell as sweet.

By whatever name it's called, an affiliate earns a commission from a merchant for generating a desired result. The specific result that must occur for the affiliate to earn a commission is (or should be) spelled out, and specified contractually, when the affiliate signs up for the program.

 Read the fine print carefully when you sign up for an affiliate program. These agreements can be complicated, but you should be completely clear about exactly what commission you are supposed to get under all the circumstances covered by the agreement.

Most often, the event that leads to a commission for the affiliate is (as I've already stated) a merchant sale resulting from the affiliate's promotion. But this need not be the case. In some circumstances, providing a merchant with a qualified sales lead may be enough to generate a commission for the affiliate.

Joining an affiliate program is potentially lucrative, but requires real attention and care. If not done right, you will not make any money from the affiliate programs you have joined.

Unlike other forms of advertising on your site, you really should care about who your affiliate partners are. This is because you do not get paid unless the affiliate links on your side lead fairly directly to a sale (or other qualifying event).

Understanding affiliate programs can be confusing: there's not a great deal of objective information available about this kind of advertising, affiliate aggregations sites are complex, and affiliate agreements are often full of legalese and opaque. But fear not! After reading this chapter, you'll have a pretty good idea of what affiliate programs are, how they work, and how you can craft an affiliate strategy that can help you make money from your web content.

Mechanics of the Process

There are a number of steps involved in the affiliate marketing process. Here's an overview:

1. A publisher (an owner of a content-based web site or sites) signs up as a web affiliate of a merchant, either using an affiliate aggregator—a company in the business of servicing affiliates for multiple merchants (see "Affiliate Aggregators" later in this chapter)—or directly with the merchant (for example, Amazon.com). This signup is done using a web interface, although certain documents (such as a W9 tax form) may need to be filed with the merchant or affiliate aggregator by mail or fax.

 You'll need a social security number or an employee tax identification number (EIN) to sign up with most affiliate programs based in the United States.

2. The merchant approves the publisher. Depending on the goals and methods of the merchant, this step may happen automatically or semiautomatically, or it may involve a manual determination of the suitability of the publisher by the merchant. Marketing goals and guidelines vary; a premium-brand merchant may want to take care that an affiliate is not perceived as déclassé and therefore manually approve all affiliates. Other brands may feel the more inbound links, the better, and let anyone sign up as an affiliate who wants to.

3. Once the publisher has been approved, the publisher is provided with a tracking ID to use in affiliate ads.

 Affiliate aggregators use one tracking ID per publisher, even when the publisher has signed up with multiple merchants.

4. The merchant supplies banner and links—collectively called *creatives* (see "Creatives" below)—that use the publisher's tracking ID. The merchant also supplies information about how to create links with the proper tracking ID to the publisher. If the merchant-publisher connection is taking place with the facilitation of an affiliate aggregator, then the aggregator makes it easy for publishers to obtain links. Banners and links are supplied as HTML code, usually complete with the publisher's tracking ID embedded in the link, so you don't need to know much HTML to join an affiliate program. Graphics, most often hosted on the merchant's site, are supplied by the merchant or affiliate aggregator.

5. The publisher incorporates the supplied HTML in web pages, and/or constructs links based on the tracking ID, that mesh well with the publisher's content.

6. Visitors to the publisher's site click the banners or links that open the merchant's site; these links contain the tracking ID of the publisher.

7. Most often, the merchant's site places a cookie on the visitor's computer so that the publisher is credited for actions that take place at a later point by the visitor (often up to 30 days).

8. If the visitor takes a desired action—usually by buying something—the publisher is due a commission (often, as specified in the original agreement, there's a time delay before any actual money is paid in order to handle issues like merchandise returns). Reputable affiliate programs provide an easy mechanism for publishers to keep track of page and click statistics and what they are owed. The tracking software is managed either by the merchant or by a third-party affiliate aggregator.

Figure 4-1 shows how the affiliate marketing process works, assuming that the publisher has already been approved by the merchant and that a third-party aggregator actually tracks sales and commissions.

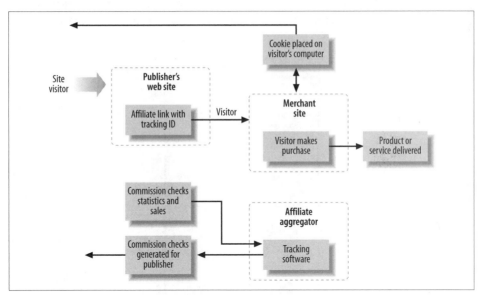

Figure 4-1. Visitors link through the publisher's site to purchase from the merchant; a third-party aggregator tracks sales and commissions

Creatives

Banners, buttons, and links provided by a merchant to an affiliate publisher are generally called *creatives*, a term deriving from the ad agency business. (Yes, I suppose it takes some creativity to make a good banner!) Creatives vary from fancy, splashy graphics made using Flash to simple text links pointing at a single product.

There's a great variety in the kinds and sizes of creatives made available by merchants. To generalize, the most common kinds of creatives are:

Text links
Simple hypertext links.

Banners
Graphic images, usually laid out horizontally. Sizes vary, but 480×90 pixels or 600×90 pixels are typical.

Skyscrapers
Graphic images, intended for vertical deployment (hence the nickname skyscraper). Typical dimensions are 120×600 pixels.

Buttons
Small graphical images, typically 120×90 pixels.

Search boxes
Search boxes combine graphics, HTML, and text to allow your site visitors to search the merchant's site.

Figure 4-2 shows some of the different creatives that are available to affiliates of the photo stock service Corbis.

Figure 4-2. Merchants with good affiliate programs provide a wide choice in creatives, like this selection shown here from Corbis

The best creative to use depends upon context and individual taste and what you think will work with visitors to your site. It's worth spending some time experimenting with different creatives to see if one performs better than another.

There's a tendency on the part of people running affiliate marketing campaigns to produce what are—in my opinion—garish creatives: banners and buttons full of movement and special effects. It's obvious why merchants do this—to get attention—and it is mostly no skin off their nose if an affiliate web site looks a little tasteless. But as a content publisher, you should probably avoid these kinds of creatives. Banners that don't flash most likely work better and won't overwhelm your site content.

All creatives used in affiliate marketing provide a mechanism for including the tracking ID of the publisher, so the publisher can be credited for sales or other action events.

Affiliate marketing works best when the merchant has high appeal to the demographics visiting a publisher's site (see "Matching affiliates with content," later in this chapter). In fact, some of the most effective affiliate links are simple text links to products that your content discusses or recommends. For example, a digital photography web site might well want to provide a link to a merchant partner selling a specific Nikon digital camera.

Providing links to a specific product for sale by a merchant partner in the context of a web site discussion of the product raises ethical concerns about the separation of editorial and advertising content. Most affiliates do it. You'll have to resolve this for yourself, but I would suggest that you not include positive content about a product unless you believe your content, and that you not direct your site vendors to a merchant unless you would buy that product from that merchant yourself.

If you decide to use text links to product items, such as a Nikon D70 digital camera, eventually you'll probably need to understand where the merchant's tracking ID goes in the HTML used for a specific product link, as well as how to link to a specific product within a merchant's catalogue.

For example, here's the code that Amazon.com provides as a text link to the Nikon D70 on Amazon.com (for more about Amazon and working with its creatives and links, see "The Amazon.com Associate Program," later in this chapter).

```
<a href="http://www.amazon.com/exec/obidos/redirect?link_code=ur2
&camp=1789&tag=XXXXXXXX &creative=9325&path=tg/detail/-/B0001LGDAO/">
Nikon D70</a>
<img src="http://www.assoc-amazon.com/e/ir?t=XXXXXXXX&l=ur2&o=1" width="1"
height="1" border="0" alt="" style="border:none !important;
margin:0px !important;" />
```

The actual publisher tracking ID, which Amazon.com passes as the value of the tag variable, has been changed in this example to *XXXXXXXX*. The 1-pixel by 1-pixel transparent image file (which cannot be seen by the site visitor) is added so that Amazon.com can add its own cookies to the visitor's computer before the link is clicked, and is not necessary for you to receive credit for the sale as an affiliate.

The actual link that the Amazon.com code creates looks just like a normal text link, as you can see in Figure 4-3.

Figure 4-3. These apparently normal links are actually creatives that embed an affiliate marketing tracking ID and point to a specific product on the site of the merchant (Amazon.com in this example)

In the Nikon D70 example, the product is designated using its ASIN identification number, which is B0001LGDAO. As you can see, if you know a product's ASIN—which is easily available on the Amazon.com product pages—or, for books, the ISBN, you can easily construct your own affiliate links by hand.

An interesting point is that you should understand where the graphic (usually a JPEG or GIF file) used in banner and button creatives is located. Amazon, as well as many other major affiliate merchants, hosts these graphics itself. Other programs ask you to copy graphics to your own web server. It's less trouble when the graphic is on the merchant's site, and it uses less of your own bandwidth, but if the merchant's server goes down, then your site looks (and is) broken. This happens more often than you might expect. True, if the merchant is not serving creatives, it is probably also not selling product, but if a graphic is missing from your site, it looks worse for you then if a link simply doesn't work.

Areas of Concern

The relationship between a content web site and an affiliate advertiser is essentially like that of a commission-only sales rep to a manufacturer. You'll want to examine the same areas that a brick-and-mortar independent sales rep would look at before agreeing to carry a merchant's products. Start by asking these questions:

* Does the merchant have a good reputation?
* Will the merchant honor its commitments?
* Will your customers want to buy the product?
* Will the merchant stay in business?

More specific to the Web, as I've mentioned in the context of hosting creatives, if a merchant's site goes down, then your links will be broken, and you won't be able to earn a commission. So you should feel reasonably good about the web site stability of a merchant whose affiliate program you join.

As a Web "sales rep," you should also be concerned with (and investigate as thoroughly as possible) these issues:

- The amount of commission you will earn per event
- The adequacy of the processes for tracking your sales, crediting you, and paying you
- The commitment of the affiliate advertiser to support its affiliate program
- The appeal of the offerings of the affiliate advertiser in relationship to the visitors to your site

Each of these points is worth some more discussion.

Amount of the commission

You can (and should) find out the amount of the sales commission when you sign up for an affiliate program. There's a huge variety of commission structures, but you should probably expect a commission of between 3% and 10% of what the merchant receives, exclusive of shipping, handling, and sales tax.

 The Amazon.com commission structure tends to be at the lower end of this range; however, note that on nonbook items Amazon.com is often acting as a go-between, rather than directly selling actual merchandise.

You should take care to note precisely what action items trigger a sales commission. Most of the time, it is a sale. However, some sales may be excluded. In addition, some sites may pay commissions for qualified leads—for example, someone signing up for a home mortgage and completing the paperwork—whether or not the product actually sells (with the mortgage example, refinancing wouldn't have to be completed for you to make your commission).

Be on the lookout for commission structures that reward you for good performance. These kinds of programs can add bonus percentages to the commissions you make and can be quite rewarding if you deliver substantial traffic.

In addition, some affiliate programs simply offer flat fees as incentives. For example, a web hosting affiliate program might pay affiliates $90 each time a visitor to the affiliate site signs up for a web hosting contract of a year or more.

$90 is, in fact, roughly the current going sales commission for an affiliate who sends a site visitor who signs up for a web hosting contract.

Also note that, depending upon the program, commission payout usually does not take place right away. Most affiliate programs build some time in for product returns (or buyer's remorse). Once it is clear that there will not be any returns, it can still be 30 to 90 days before you are paid.

Sales and commission tracking

Sales and commission tracking is a serious issue. It's very important to most affiliate site publishers. If you don't know that transactions originating from your site are being consistently tracked, then you have no way to be assured that you will be paid the commissions you are owed.

This implies that you should be careful to work only with third-party affiliate aggregators (see "Affiliate Aggregators," later in this chapter) or enroll in programs managed by an extremely reliable vendor, such as Amazon.com (see "The Amazon.com Associate Program," later in this chapter).

 You should test that each affiliate link on your site works by buying something and making sure that your sales commission shows up when you check the tracking software. You'd be amazed the number of times a problem with the linkage or the accounting is revealed by doing this!

Merchant support of affiliate programs

Will the merchant support your efforts with good promotions, incentives, and creatives? Ideally, an affiliate relationship is a long-term partnership. You'd like to know that the merchant supporting the affiliate program is in it for the long haul. Merchant support of affiliate programs makes a big difference in the following areas:

- To make an affiliate program work well, you'll want to be able to provide value to your site visitors in terms of special promotions.

- If you put great effort into an affiliate program and perform well, you should be rewarded with incentives.

- To keep your site visitors coming back to an affiliated merchant, you need a steady stream of quality, fresh creatives.

Matching affiliates with content

Perhaps the single biggest factor in successful affiliate marketing is the alignment of the content of your site with the affiliate merchant's offerings. In other words, visitors to your site should be genuinely interested in the products the merchant has to sell.

You'll have a tough row to hoe if you try to sell cosmetics to visitors to a digital photography site, but should find it easier to sell these visitors digital photo equipment and processing services. Visitors to a site that provides technical services of use to webmasters are likely candidates for web hosting affiliate programs, but unlikely to buy lingerie or refrigerators.

In the brick-and-mortar world, there used to be talk about a salesperson who could "sell ice to the Inuit." No web site can sell as well as this proverbial salesperson, so you need to use common sense and devise an intelligent strategy to provide affiliate links to products·and services that are relevant to your site visitors. Relevant links get clicked, goods get purchased, and publishers get their commissions. More than any other form of web site advertising monetization, affiliate marketing requires careful honing of site content with an intelligent choice of partners and creatives.

Working with an Affiliate Program

Generally, there are three affiliate marketing situations you may get involved with as a web content publisher:

- The affiliate program is managed by an affiliate aggregator (see "Affiliate Aggregators," next).
- An extremely well-known entity offers a broad and well-thought-out affiliate program (the Amazon.com associates program is the best example, as explained in "The Amazon.com Associate Program" section later in this chapter).
- A vendor with a limited line or products or service starts its own affiliate marketing program (see the "Ad Hoc Affiliation" box at the end of this chapter).

Affiliate Aggregators

Major affiliate aggregators provide the following benefits to web publishers:

- The publisher can use "one-stop shopping" to work with many different merchants.
- There's only one software interface to learn.
- Reporting and commission payments are consolidated.
- A third party (the aggregator) provides consistent tracking software and provides some recourse in case of disputes over sales.

Don't forget: affiliate aggregators are paid by merchants, not publishers. They exist to provide a service to merchants who want to effectively manage affiliate programs without having to roll their own. They primarily represent the interests of the merchants who are their clients, not the interests of the affiliates.

You'll need at least one content-based web site to enroll with an affiliate aggregator. Once you've signed up with an affiliate aggregator, the aggregator will provide a single web site that allows you to:

- Apply to individual merchant affiliate programs
- Get HTML for creatives
- Generate activity reports

It's pretty easy to add multiple web sites to your account with an affiliate aggregator once you have obtained an initial account. This is such an important point that it is worth rephrasing and repeating: as a publisher, you can use a single account with an affiliate aggregator to manage your relationship with multiple merchants and multiple content web sites.

Commission Junction, *http://www.cj.com*, and LinkShare, *http://www.linkshare.com*, are the two best-known affiliate aggregators.

The Affiliate Goddess

5-Star Affiliate Programs, *http://www.5staraffiliateprograms.com*, is an up-and-coming affiliate aggregator representing merchants, including the National Geographic Store and OneShare Stock Gifts. 5-Star is managed by PartnerCentric, a consulting company under the direction of Linda Woods, sometimes known as the "affiliate Goddess." 5-Star and PartnerCentric have an industry reputation of managing affiliate programs that are aggressively proactive in supporting affiliates.

Commission Junction

Commission Junction represents more than 1,000 merchants, ranging from Discover Card to Half.com, through dating sites, software publishers, and companies selling clothes—just about any kind of merchant you can imagine. If any legitimate product or service can be bought over the Internet, you can probably figure out a way to make a sales commission from selling it via Commission Junction. The Commission Junction home page is shown in Figure 4-4.

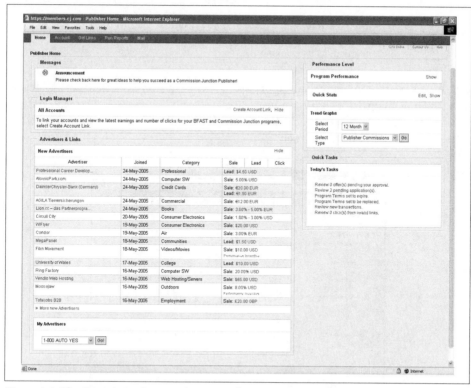

Figure 4-4. The Commission Junction home page lets you access much of the program's functionality from a single window

By choosing Account → Web site Settings, you can add a new web site for deployment with the Commission Junction affiliate programs (Figure 4-5).

Figure 4-5. It's easy to add web sites to your Commission Junction account or edit current site information

If you look carefully at Figure 4-5, you'll notice that a PID has been assigned as a site setting. The PID is the number that Commission Junction uses as its tracking ID.

The Run Reports tab, shown in Figure 4-6, provides a very complete set of metrics covering how many times ads have been displayed on your pages (called *page impressions*), how many times your ads have been clicked (called *click throughs*), and the sales commissions you have earned.

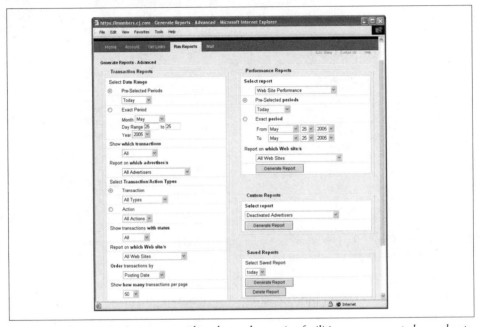

Figure 4-6. Commission Junction provides advanced reporting facilities you can use to learn about your page views, transactions, and sales

The heart of the Commission Junction interface is the Get Links tab, shown in Figure 4-7.

 A key metric at Commission Junction is EPC, or *earnings per click*. If you look at Figure 4-7, you'll note that the box on the lower right, listing Advertisers with special promotions, is sorted by EPC from highest to lowest. As a publisher, a high EPC is a great reason to sign up with a merchant.

Using the Get Links tab, you can find merchants—called *advertisers* in Commission Junction nomenclature—by category, by searching using various filters, or by listing

Figure 4-7. Using the Get Links tab you can search for participating merchants by category

the merchants with whom you have an existing relationship. You can also browse the entire list of Commission Junction merchants by clicking Advertiser List.

Once you've found a merchant you are interested in, you can apply to join the merchant's affiliate program by checking the program application box and clicking Apply to Program, as shown in Figure 4-8.

Figure 4-8. Check the box and click Apply to Program to join a merchant's affiliate program

You can view the links a merchant provides, and statistics such as EPC, before you join a program.

Your application to join a merchant program will either be approved automatically (if the merchant has decided to approve all would-be affiliates) or manually. During the manual approval process, which may take up to several days, your status with the merchant is set to "Pending Approval." With manual approval, you will be notified by email whether you've been accepted or rejected.

Once a merchant has approved your application to join its affiliate program, you can go grab the HTML required to make links. To do this, use one of the mechanisms provided by the Get Links tab to find the merchant that you have the relationship with.

A good approach to finding the merchants who have approved your affiliate application is to open the Get Links-By Relationship page shown in Figure 4-9.

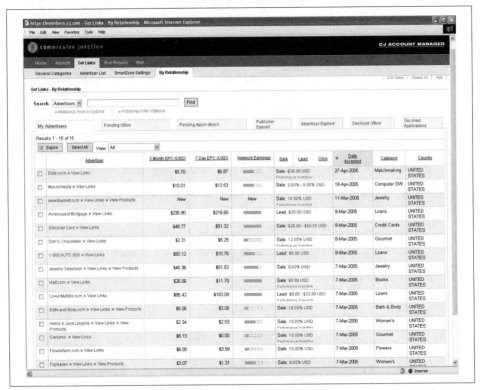

Figure 4-9. You can use the Get Links-By Relationship page to display all the merchants who have approved your affiliate account

Locate the merchant you want to add to your site. Click View Links. You can now scan all the creatives offered by the merchant. For example, Figure 4-10 shows some of the creatives offered by Half.com to participating affiliates.

Figure 4-10. You can view all the creatives supplied by a merchant to decide which ones will work best for your site

To grab the HTML for a specific creative, either click the creative or check the box next to it and click the Get HTML button at the top of the page. In either case, a Get HTML window, like the one shown in Figure 4-11, will open.

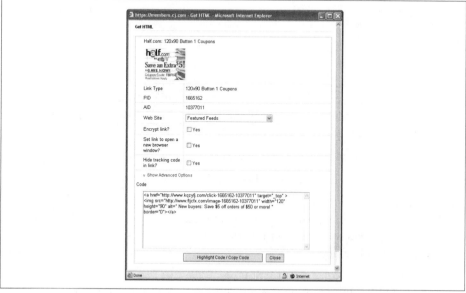

Figure 4-11. The Get HTML window lets you copy the HTML for a specific creative

If you are managing multiple web sites, make sure to select the right one on the web site drop-down list before copying HTML. You can also use the Get HTML window to set a variety of options, notably setting the affiliate to link to open a new browser window (an important choice because it helps to keep visitors on your site longer).

The HTML for the new affiliate link is pretty simple and includes the web publisher's PID (tracking identification) as part of the link:

```
<a href="http://www.kqzyfj.com/click-1665162-10377011" target="_top" >
<img src="http://www.ftjcfx.com/image-1665162-10377011" width="120" height="90"
alt=" New buyers: Save $5 off orders of $50 or more! " border="0"></a>
```

If you paste this HTML into the code for your web page, the new creative will now appear on your site (Figure 4-12).

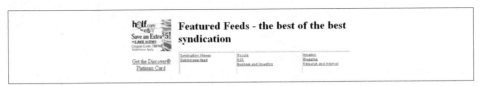

Figure 4-12. When you copy the HTML provided by Commission Junction into your page, the merchant's creative appears on your site with your tracking number embedded in the related link

 To maximize affiliate revenue, it's important to constantly tweak ads, for example, to respond to seasonal conditions such as holidays. To facilitate ad changes across a range of pages, it's vital to use an include architecture, as I explain in Chapter 1.

LinkShare

LinkShare, *http://www.linkshare.com*, is the oldest major affiliate aggregator, currently representing several hundred merchants ranging from David's Cookies to Overstock.com to Vermont Teddy Bear and beyond. LinkShare provides roughly the same functionality as Commission Junction.

The LinkShare home page is shown in Figure 4-13.

Within LinkShare, you'll find four tabbed windows in addition to the home page:

Join program
> Used to apply for approval to merchant's affiliate program (as with the merchant members of Commission Junction, some approvals will be automatic, and some will be manual)

Create links
> Used to builds and select merchant creatives (requires prior acceptance in a merchant's affiliate program)

Figure 4-13. From the LinkShare home page you can browse merchants, join programs, generate links, and more

Run reports
Used to generate detailed reports about site and program metrics

Your account
Used to change account information (for example, add a domain)

To obtain a creative, click the Create Link tab. A list of the affiliate programs for which you have been approved appears (Figure 4-14).

Figure 4-14. You can create links only if you have been approved for a merchant's affiliate program

If you have registered multiple web sites with LinkShare, be sure the one you want to use the creative with is selected from the drop-down list that will appear at the top of the page.

Click the name of the merchant you'd like to link with, for example, Sierra Trading Post, a discount retailer of sporting goods and clothes. A page that will let you generate creatives specifically for Sierra Trading Post will open. Choose the kind of creative you'd like to create from the Available Link Types box, shown in Figure 4-15.

Figure 4-15. Link types range from straight text to search boxes, banners, and more

 The Dynamic Rich Media category tends to produce creatives that are "blue plate specials," such as rotating deals of the day.

For example, suppose you want to add a box to your web site that searches the Sierra Trading Post product database. To do this, you'd click the Search Box link. A page showing a number of possible search boxes, such as the one shown in Figure 4-16, will open.

Figure 4-16. If you add this search box to your site, visitors can search the Sierra Trading Post product database

To add the search box to your site, copy the code and paste it into your page. Here's the code that generates the Sierra Trading Post search box:

```
<table width="150" height="150" border="0" cellspacing="0"
cellpadding="0" style="padding: 0px; background-image:
url
(http://www.sierratradingpost.com/assets/images/ppam/ad_images/LSsearchbox.jpg);">
<form action="http://click.linksynergy.com/fs-bin/statform" name="form1" id="form1"
method="get"><input type=hidden name=id value=RQUescWsfWI><input type=hidden
name=offerid value=42083><input type=hidden name=bnid value=740><input type=hidden
name="subid" value="">
```

```
                    <input type="hidden" name="Ntk" value="All">
                    <input type="hidden" name="Nty" value="1">
                    <input type="hidden" name="Ntx" value="mode+matchallany">
                    <input type="hidden" name="track" value="true">
<input type="hidden" name="DCMP" value="LS05">

<input type="hidden" name="KC" value="LS05">
        <tr>
                <td width="150" height="65"></td>
        </tr>
        <tr>
                <td width="150" align="center" height="25">
                        <input type="text" name="Ntt"
value="enter keyword or item #" maxlength="50" style="font-family:
arial,helvetica,sans-serif; font-size: 11px; width: 140px; padding-left: 2px;">
                </td>
        </tr>
        <tr>
                <td width="150" align="center" height="25">
                        <select name="N" style="font-family:
arial,helvetica,sans-serif; color: #000000; vertical-align:
top; font-size: 11px; width: 105px; height: 18px; width: 140px;">
                                <option value="0">All Departments</option>
                                <option value="9000310">Outdoor Gear</option>
                                <option value="9000154">Men's Clothing</option>
                                <option value="9000230">Women's Clothing</option>
                                <option value="9000342">Shoes & Boots</option>
                                <option value="9000335">Kids' Corner</option>
                                <option value="9000331">Home Decor</option>
                                </select>
                </td>
        </tr>
        <tr>
                <td width="150" align="center" height="35">
                        <input class="submit" type="submit"
value="Search Sierra Trading Post" style="font: 11px arial;
color: #ffffff; width: 140px; height: 30px; border:
outset 1px; background-color: #447744;">
                </td>
                </form>
        </tr>
</table><IMG width=1 height=1 border=0 src="http://ad.linksynergy.com/fs-
bin/show?id=RQUescWsfWI&bids=42083&type=5">
```

 The Sierra Trading Post search box code consists of an HTML form
formatted using table tags. The value of the affiliate tracking ID is
passed using a hidden form variable named id.

With this code pasted into your web page, the Sierra Trading Post search box will
appear on your site as shown in Figure 4-17.

Figure 4-17. Placing a search box on your site is a way to add value for your site visitors

If a visitor to your site enters a specific item, for example Men's socks, in the search box and clicks Search Sierra Trading Post, the results page for the item will open (Figure 4-18). This helps to increase the rate of conversion of clicks to sales, because visitors are looking only at items they have some interest in, and therefore increases the likelihood that you will make a commission.

Figure 4-18. Providing a way to search a merchant's catalog helps convert click throughs to sales because customers see items they are interested in

The Amazon.com Associate Program

If you belong to just one merchant's affiliate program, Amazon.com is probably the one to join.

In Amazon.com's terminology, affiliates are called *associates*, just as the sales help at a brick-and-mortar Wal-Mart (and other fine stores) are also associates. Becoming an Amazon.com associate sounds like the better of the two options to me!

Amazon.com makes a great partner for an affiliate (particularly if the affiliate is only going to be associated with one merchant program) for a number of reasons, including:

- Amazon.com is one of the oldest businesses on the Web.

- Amazon.com has a great reputation with customers for reliability and fair dealing.

- Amazon.com—at times in combination with partner merchants—can supply almost any conceivable product to your customers.

- Amazon.com provides creatives with great variety and flexibility; it's easy to use them to link to any product or Amazon.com search result, and the creatives fit well with most site designs.

Quick-and-Dirty Amazon.com Text Links

For an example of an Amazon.com text link, see "Creatives" earlier in this chapter. As many webmasters know, it's perfectly possible to build your own Amazon.com text links without visiting the Amazon.com site simply by inserting your own Amazon.com identifier in the link example, along with the ISBN or ASIN of the book or product you want to link to.

It's quick and dirty, but this hyperlink *http://www.amazon.com/exec/obidos/ISBN= 076457809X/xxxxxxxx/* points to one of my books by ISBN with an Amazon. com affiliate ID (represented in the link by *xxxxxxxx*.) If sales result from this link, Amazon. com will know to credit me.

If you create a link like this, you'll want to substitute your own account identification and change the ISBN to point to a book you are interested in. (Of course, I don't object if you just want to link to my book!)

To link to a product rather than a book, use the form ASIN=*asin number* in the URL.

The application process for becoming an Amazon.com associate can be accessed at *https://associates.amazon.com/gp/flex/associates/apply-login.html*. Essentially, Amazon. com approves all applicants who provide a valid email address and the required social security number (or EIN).

Amazon.com pays between 4% and 10% sales commissions, with the bulk of the commissions in the 4% to 7% range. In some cases, performance bonuses are given to affiliates who are extraordinary producers.

The home page for the Amazon.com Associate program, called Amazon.com Associates Central, is located at *http://associates.amazon.com*. Once you've joined the program, you can log in to update your account information, generate reports, and obtain creatives.

Click Build Links to specify creatives and obtain the corresponding code. There are five varieties of Amazon.com creatives:

Product links
> Link to a specific product that you select and display a product image.

Recommended links
> Link to Amazon.com recommendations by product category or keywords.

Banners
> Wide variety of banners, both rotating special promotions and by shopping category.

Text links
> Text link to any Amazon.com page, such as a product page, or a page that results from an Amazon.com search.

Search boxes
> You can put an Amazon.com search box on your site.

Figure 4-19 shows the launch panel for building this wide selection of creatives at Amazon.

For example, suppose you want to add a box on your digital photography site that will display a digital camera that Amazon.com recommends (and let Amazon.com take care of the specifics of which camera is highlighted).

To start, click Build Links with Recommended Product Links selected. The Choose Content panel, shown in Figure 4-20, will open.

In the Choose Content panel, select a product line and enter keywords or choose a subcategory. For example: if "Camera & Photo" is the primary category, "Digital Cameras" might be a good subcategory (but you could also limit the recommendations to a specific brand by entering "Nikon," "digital," and "camera" as keywords rather than selecting a subcategory.

With a content type selected, click Continue. You'll next be asked to select a size for the creative. With a size selected, you can now move to final adjustments (for example, to the colors used in the text and background of the creative) and copy the HTML, using the window shown in Figure 4-21.

Figure 4-19. The launch panel for building creatives at Amazon.com shows examples of what the finished link will look like

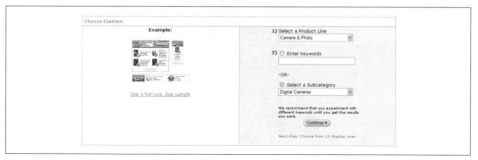

Figure 4-20. Use the Choose Content panel to specify what kinds of products Amazon.com will recommend

Here's the HTML produced for this creative:

```
<iframe src="http://rcm.amazon.com/e/cm?t=XXXXXXXXX&o=1&p=8&l=bn1&
mode=photo&browse=281052&fc1=&=1&lc1=&lt1=&f=ifr&bg1=&f=ifr"
marginwidth="0" marginheight="0" width="120" height="240"
border="0" frameborder="0" style="border:none;" scrolling="no">
</iframe>
```

Figure 4-21. By clicking the links shown, you can customize the creative or just copy the HTML for use on your site

In the example, the Amazon.com associate ID has been replaced with *XXXXXXXXX*.

When you copy this HTML into an include used by your digital photography site, the creative appears, as you can see in Figure 4-22.

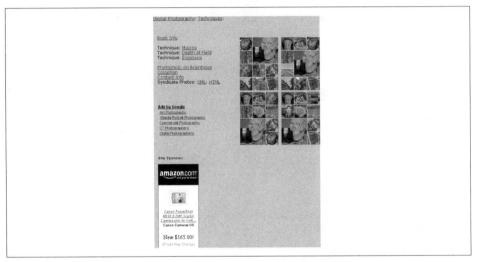

Figure 4-22. Once the HTML has been copied to your web site, the Amazon.com creative appears on your pages

With a recommended product creative that refers to a category of products, Amazon.com automatically rotates the actual products that are displayed in its creative.

Action Items

Here are some action items for you to consider to make money from your web content using affiliate programs:

- Identify merchants with affiliate programs that mesh well with your content.
- Explore, and sign up with, affiliate aggregators and individual merchants' affiliate programs.
- Integrate creatives as HTML links, banners, and search boxes on your web site.
- Monitor affiliate statements for traffic, click, conversion, and sales commission statistics.
- Experiment with your choice of merchants and their creatives to optimize your returns.

CHAPTER 5

CPC Advertising

CPC—cost per click—advertising is the most common way to make money by accepting ads on your site. With CPC, an advertiser pays a fee when someone clicks its link on your site, and you get a portion of that fee. CPC ads are mostly (although they don't have to be) text-only.

The idea of making ads *contextual*—that is, relevant to the content of the web page near the ad—is closely bound up with CPC advertising. CPC ads that are contextual are much more effective, and generate more revenue for a site owner, than ads that are not contextual. But, it is worth bearing in mind that you can have CPC ads that are not contextual, and, conversely, contextual ads that pay on some other basis than CPC.

 Affiliate advertising—where a visitor to your site clicks on a merchant's link, and you get paid when the visitor actually buys something from the merchant—is explained in Chapter 4.

CPC Terminology

When you first start working with a CPC program as a web site publisher, you will encounter some terms that may not be familiar to you. These concepts are actually pretty straightforward, so it makes sense to start a discussion of CPC by looking at the definitions of the most important terms you may not know or may mean something that is slightly different than in normal usage:

Ad unit
> A group of ads displayed by a single call to the server's script, usually from one to six text-only contextual ads.

Click
> Occurs when a site visitor to your web page clicks on a link in an ad unit. Not all clicks generate revenue (for example, fraudulent clicks that are detected and clicks on public service ads don't pay you anything).

Click fraud

> A click made without actual interest in the product or services offered. For example, clicks by a site publisher on the ads on a site or on the ads of a competitor (to jack up advertising costs for the competitor).

Click through rate (CTR)

> The number of clicks an ad unit receives divided by the number of times it is shown.

Effective cost per thousand impressions (eCPM)

> eCPM is a way to compare revenue from different kinds of advertising. eCPM is calculated by dividing the total earnings from an ad by its impressions in thousands. You can use this calculation to compare CPC revenue with its eCPM equivalent and decide which represents a better revenue opportunity.

 For more on CPM, see the "CPM Advertising" box in this chapter.

Impression

> Short for *ad impression*; the number of times an ad is displayed.

Page CTR

> The CTR for an individual web page.

Page eCPM

> The eCPM for an individual web page.

Page impressions

> The number of times an ad unit is displayed.

Public service ad (PSA)

> Public service ads are often served before relevant content has been specifically targeted.

Understanding Contextual Relevance

The basis of CPC advertising is having visitors to your web site click the links presented to them by ads. People are likely to notice ads, and click on ad links, only if the content of the ad is relevant to their current interests. This leads to the notion of contextually relevant advertising (usually referred to simply as *contextual advertising*) often being confused with CPC advertising, even though the two are not the same.

As I've already made clear, CPC ads don't have to be contextually relevant. But totally unrelated ads look odd on a web page and are unlikely to be clicked. How often would you interrupt your train of thought to click on an ad for "contact lens cleaner" when you are reading a site about C# programming? So as a web site publisher you are best off sticking with CPC programs, such as Google's AdSense, that do, in fact, provide reasonably good contextual placement.

How good, in fact, are these placements? It all depends; see the box "Contextual Ads—Not!" later in this chapter.

Serving Ads

How are ads placed on contextually relevant pages? As you can imagine, it isn't done by a roomful of gnomes scanning web pages and deciding what ads should go on them. There are simply too many web sites and web pages, and their content changes too quickly, for this to work (even if you had a few gnomes).

 Even with print media, such as newspapers and magazines, it makes sense to position advertising near contextually relevant editorial material (although it is not always possible). The manual mechanism that I mock (albeit using humans instead of gnomes) has always been used to try to come up with the best placement of ads, called ad *imposition*, in traditional print media.

Obviously, software, not gnomes, is used to automatically analyze the content of a web page to determine its content and which contextually relevant ads should be placed on it. This is fortunate for Google (and other search engine companies) because determining the content of a site for contextual ad relevancy is essentially the same task as determining the content of a site to match with the keywords used in a search.

 To make it easier for Google's AdSense and other contextual ad programs to accurately determine the content of your web pages, it's important that you follow the guidelines for web site and page optimization explained in Chapter 3.

Here's generally how the process of placing a contextually relevant CPC ad on your site works:

- A block of code on your web page calls a script on the server provided by the contextual ad program. This code also contains your tracking ID (discussed in Chapter 8) so the ad program knows who to pay when the ads are clicked.

- This code is activated when users load your web page in their web browser.

- The activated code invokes the script on the server. When the script is invoked on the server, the content of your page is analyzed. This process usually involves some time delay the first time; generic ads may appear until the server has had time to look at your web page. Once your page has been analyzed, the server doesn't have to parse it again (unless the page content changes, in which case there may be a time lag before the contextual ads have caught up with the new content).
- The software decides which ads to serve based on its analysis of your web page content.
- The designated ads are generated as HTML and served on your page.

These logistics behind serving contextual ads are shown in Figure 5-1.

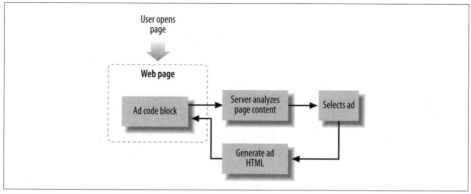

Figure 5-1. The program that generates the contextual ads figures out which ads are relevant and generates the HTML to display them on your web page

Dollars and Cents

The amount of money generated by an individual click on a contextual ad is a highly variable and murky business. In the case of Google and other contextual programs, the amount that is paid for an ad depends on an automated bidding process where advertisers bid for keywords. So the amount paid for a contextual ad varies day-by-day and even hour-by-hour.

> Google's terms of service (TOS) forbids the disclosure of any financial information about how much is made off the AdSense contextual ad program except an accurate account of the total paid to a publisher.

Essentially, a contextual ad program such as Google is acting as an agent or a broker: ads are sold by keyword to advertisers and publishers are paid on the basis of click throughs (see Chapter 7 for the details of Google's role as a broker). But Google doesn't say what percentage commission it takes, or what share of the pie it leaves for you, the web publisher. If you sign up for Google's AdSense, the leading contextual ad program, you just have to take what Google gives you, and trust Google.

 As companies go, Google is probably pretty trustworthy. Based on other CPC programs, the commission on contextual ads is between 25% and 75% of the total paid by the advertiser. (I know; that's a pretty big range!)

An individual click on a contextual ad is not going to make you rich. The net value to a web publisher of a click ranges from one or two pennies to a few dollars at the very high end. The average click is probably worth about $0.20. Combine this statistic with the fact that the click-through rates (the clicks an ad gets divided by the number of times it is served) are in the low single-digit percentages—2% is a quite respectable CTR—and you come up with the fact that to make good money from CPC, you need a lot of traffic. A six-figure income from CPC contextual advertising is not unheard of, but it takes monthly page views in the millions. Doing the math, this page-view volume implies either a broad site or some highly trafficked pages (or both).

Supposing you have a great deal of content—say 10,000 pages—it's possible to reach the target volume of more than 100,000 page views per month with an average of 10 page views per page per month—ambitious, in terms of the amount of content, but not impossible, and quite modest in terms of the traffic per page.

These 100,000 page views per month might theoretically give you an income of around $400 a month calculated by multiplying 100,000 times the 2% CTR, times the $0.20 average fee per click.

Of course, most sites are created to fulfill multiple needs and use a variety of mechanisms to generate income. But if your only consideration is creating revenue using a contextual CPC model, you should consider whether it makes more sense to get to 100,000 page views and beyond by creating a relatively few heavily visited pages—the *shallow-site approach*—or a great many, less trafficked pages—the *broad-site approach*.

If you take the broad-site approach, then you'll need to figure out a low-cost way to generate the content. The calculation that shows a $400 monthly revenue for a 10,000-page site—a broad site that is not heavily trafficked—implies a revenue stream of about $0.50 a page per year. For this to make sense as a business proposition, it can't cost you very much to generate this content (perhaps because you create it yourself).

Business modeling is only as good as its assumptions. If the hypothetical 10,000-page site averages 100 views per page rather than 10 views per page—not at all unreasonable for a worthwhile site—then the economics shift radically in favor of the site publisher. The site is now probably generating $50,000 or so annually in CPC contextual revenue (each page contributes an average of $5.00).

The point here is to understand the implications of site and advertising metrics on the economics of your site so you can take the steps required to meet your financial goals.

Site metrics, CPC advertising, and profitability are discussed further in Chapter 9.

CPC Program Vendors

Google's AdSense program, *http://www.google.com/adsense/*, is, of course, the largest of the contextual CPC ad programs, with features aimed at both large and small web publishers.

 See Part II for a lot more information about AdSense.

If you are large web publisher, you should also investigate Google's major competitor in contextual advertising: the Content Match service of Yahoo! Publisher Network (formerly Overture) at *http://searchmarketing.yahoo.com*.

AdSense is a truly great program and works extremely well for many web content publishers. But perhaps you'd rather not work with Google's AdSense and are not big enough to work with Yahoo!'s Content Match.

Here are some possible reasons to work with an alternative program:

- You'd like more control over the ads that appear on your site.
- Your site features content that is not acceptable to Google, such as adult content.
- You'd like to understand exactly what advertisers are paying for the ads and exactly how much commission is being deducted.

Some smaller CPC ad program vendors are shown in Table 5-1.

Table 5-1. CPC ad programs other than Google and Yahoo!

Program	URL	Comments
AdBrite	*http://www.adbrite.com*	The publisher interface is a little rough around the edges and provides CPC ads that are not very contextually relevant; however, this innovative program allows web site publishers a great deal of control over the specifics of advertising that will appear on their site.
AdPoint	*http://www.targetpoint.com*	Unlike AdSense, all kinds of content is acceptable.
BrightAds	*http://www.kanoodle.com*	Up-and-comer founded by executives who used to run a contextual marketing concern that was bought by Google.
DynamiContext	*http://www.kontera.com*	Requires a minimum of 150,000 page views a month for publisher participation.
Fastclick	*http://www.fastclick.com*	Offers both CPC and CPM (see the box on "CPM Advertising" programs later in this chapter).

CPM Advertising

With CPM (cost per thousand impressions) advertising you get paid a fee, based on thousands of impressions, when an ad is displayed on your site. This is the kind of web advertising that is the most like traditional media advertising: an advertiser pays for displaying its ad in a magazine, on television, or on a web site, end of story.

CPM ads can either be text-only or provide graphics. The bulk of banner ads that you see on the Web have been placed on a CPM basis. In fact, one of the pitfalls of accepting CPM advertising is getting stuck with garish imagery, Flash-based animations, as well as assorted pop ups and pop unders, which can irritate and distract visitors to your web site.

CPM advertising cannot be expected to generate a very high click-through rate and does not pay very much per impression. Typical CPM ad rates are in the $4 to $6 range per impression, although significantly higher fees can be achieved in special situations (for example, when a CPM sponsor underwrites an entire site).

Obviously, with these economics, making money from CPM is a volume affair. For the most part, to even participate in CPM programs you need a minimum of 500,000 monthly page views. If you do have this kind of volume, you can find a great deal of information about CPM advertising from the trade association that works with the Internet CPM industry, the Internet Advertising Bureau (*http://iab.net*). Depending on your organization, it's reasonable to negotiate directly with CPM advertisers or to sign up with an agency such as MaxOnline (*http://www.maxonline.com*).

While it remains true than you need high volume to make any real money from CPM ads, there are beginning to be some CPM options for lower-volume sites. You can join Fastclick's CPM program (*http://www.fastclick.com*) with as few as 3,000 site impressions per month. AdBrite (*http://www.adbrite.com*) has no minimum volume requirements and lets you set your own asking price for text ads running on your site (this is not technically CPM advertising because you are not paid per impression, but it can amount to pretty much the same thing depending upon the pricing structure you set).

As you may know, Google's AdWords program now accepts site-targeted CPM advertising. This means that if your site is enrolled in Google's AdSense program, you can automatically receive some CPM revenue (provided you choose certain settings in the AdSense program). For more details, see Chapter 8.

Placing CPC Ads on Your Site

You'll need to take the following fairly simple steps to place CPC ads on your site:

- Sign up with a program.
- Select the ad format that works best with your site.
- Add the code generated by the program to your pages.

Signing Up

Most CPC ad programs provide a mechanism for you to sign up online using a straightforward mechanism such as the one used by the AdBrite program, shown in Figure 5-2.

Figure 5-2. Simple contact information plus a tax ID number is all you need to enroll in a CPC program

You'll also need to provide contact information, who you want checks made out to, and a tax identification number (either a social security number or an employer identification number).

 Many programs also require that you complete and submit a W-9 tax form.

In addition, major programs such as Google will want at least one web site URL. They will manually vet the site for compliance with program content policies before accepting you into the program.

Selecting Ad Formats

Once you've been accepted, you can go ahead and choose ad formats—meaning size of the ad unit and number of ads—and colors for your site.

Some programs allow you to control adult content by specifying at the beginning whether it is unacceptable (and even what level of explicitness is permissible on your site). This is not an issue with Google's AdSense, since the AdSense program does not display adult ads at all or accept adult content sites into the program. In addition, some programs allow you to designate initial content areas, which is used until the contextual engine completes its job.

Most programs provide many sizes of ad units to choose from and a wide variety of preselected color schemes. Figure 5-3 shows the AdPoint program ad generator.

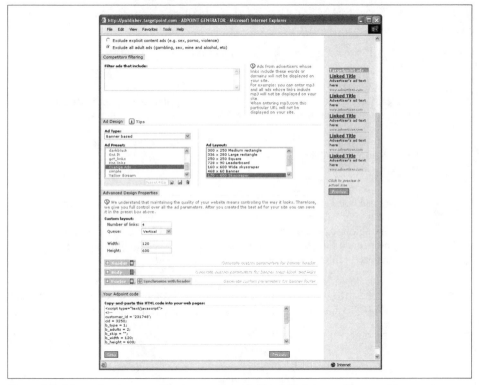

Figure 5-3. Most ad generators, like the ones provided by AdPoint, provide you with a great many ad format and color choices

The design choices you make in relationship to ad format and color are quite important. See Chapter 1 for some discussion of ad placement. In addition, you should consider two possible, but incompatible, strategies: making ads seem like they are part of a site's content, and making ads different, so they really stick out.

Adding Code to Your Pages

Once you've selected your ad format and colors, simply copy the code provided into your web pages where you'd like the ad units to appear.

 It's important to place ad code in include files, as I explain in Chapter 1, so that your ad settings can easily be modified sitewide.

Ad unit code consists of settings, which depend on your choice of format and color, and a JavaScript call to the program on the ad server that actually displays the ad on your site (see "Serving Ads," earlier in this chapter, for an explanation of this mechanism).

For example, an AdBrite ad unit looks like this in code:

```
<!-- Begin: AdBrite -->
<style type="text/css">
.adHeadline {font: bold 10pt Arial; text-decoration: underline; color: blue;}
.adText {font: normal 10pt Arial; text-decoration: none; color: black;}
</style>
<script type="text/javascript" src="http://3.adbrite.com/mb/text_group.
php?sid=XXXXX&amp;newwin=1&br=1"></script>
<!-- End: AdBrite -->
```

 You can tweak the settings in the ad code easily enough to change the format and, in some cases, the colors of the ads displayed. Although working directly with the generated code is prohibited by some programs (including AdSense), no one will mind if you are just adjusting things to fit in with your site's look and feel.

With the code copied into your web pages, and the web pages placed on your server, the CPC ad units are displayed, like the AdBrite unit shown in Figure 5-4.

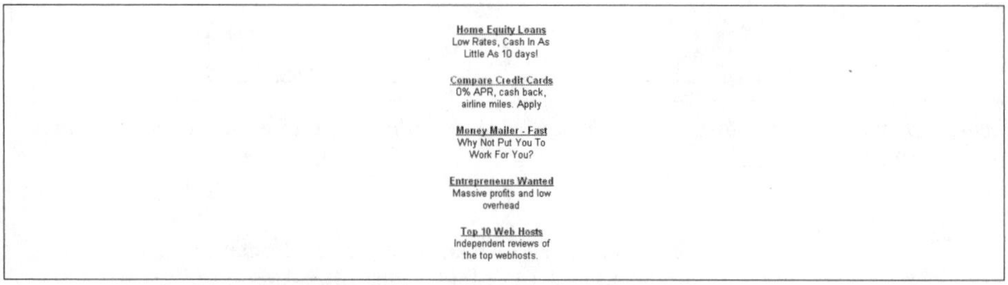

Home Equity Loans
Low Rates, Cash In As
Little As 10 days!

Compare Credit Cards
0% APR, cash back,
airline miles. Apply

Money Mailer - Fast
Why Not Put You To
Work For You?

Entrepreneurs Wanted
Massive profits and low
overhead

Top 10 Web Hosts
Independent reviews of
the top webhosts.

Figure 5-4. If this ad group in AdBrite's default style doesn't go with the look of your site, you can edit the styles to change its appearance

Action Items

Here are some action items you may wish to take to make (more) money from CPC ads:

- Understand the logic behind CPC and contextual ad programs.
- Create a realistic plan based on the revenue you can expect from CPC advertising.
- Enroll your site in a CPC ad program.
- Use a server-side include so that the CPC ad code is replicated across your site.
- Choose ad format and colors to match or complement your site design.
- If your site has enough volume to make it feasible, investigate CPM advertising programs.

CHAPTER 6
Profiting from Adult Sites

The standard adult web site disclaimer goes something like this: "This site contains adult material. If you are under 21 years of age, or if it is illegal to view adult material in your community, or if adult material offends you, please do not enter this site!" In a similar spirit, if you are uninterested in making money from advertising on adult sites, or if this subject offends you, please simply skip this chapter.

However, adult content is an interesting business because it is undoubtedly the Web's most lucrative fee-based content area. The exact figures are controversial and murky, but there's no doubt that subscription and per-item fees for adult content are in the billions of dollars in the aggregate. This compares favorably, from a business perspective, with other kinds of content on the Web, where the attitude is often that "information wants to be free," and it is hard to get consumers to pay for content from even the most prestigious institutions.

 You probably don't need a formal definition of what I mean by *adult content*. But just in case you aren't clear about this term, "adult" means that content (or a web site) features, discusses, depicts, or portrays explicitly sexual activities.

The popularity of adult content on the Web means that:

- Adult advertising for content represents one of the largest segments of the advertising business on the Web
- Advertising for adult content, and on adult sites, can be more profitable to independent site operators than advertising on any other kind of site

In other words, it's possible for small, or solo, entrepreneurs to make money advertising adult content provided they can draw traffic interested in adult content to their site.

The adult-content industry on the Web in many ways works the same way as the rest of the world on the Web. Just as with nonadult web sites, to make money from advertising on your adult site you need to:

- Create a site (or sites) that draws traffic with an interest in what you are advertising
- Understand the advertising options to make money from your site
- Publicize your site to drive traffic to it

Many, but not all, aspects of constructing, making money from, and driving traffic to a site that involves adult content are the same as when adult content is not involved. After all, HTML is HTML is HTML.

 You can review many of these general content techniques by having a look at Chapters 1 through 5 to review the basics of constructing a web business based on advertising.

However, there are some considerable differences in how each of the steps towards making money from advertising is achieved when adult content is involved. Some mechanisms are simply not available for sites in the adult-entertainment orbit. For example, Google's AdSense program will not accept adult sites, and mainstream press release services will not accept press releases that include references to adult content. The good news for operators of sites related to adult content is the willingness of users to pay for content; this creates opportunities not available elsewhere.

In effect, the adult-content industry on the Web is a vast parallel universe: to some extent it is part of the Web in general, but in some significant ways it operates according to its own rules. To a large degree the adult Web is omitted from conventional search engines and uses its own portals. Much of the adult Web has a home-spun feel to it, although it is also true that new web technologies are often deployed by the adult industry before these technologies migrate to conventional content areas.

 From within the adult web industries, the portions of the Web that exclude adult content, explicit sexual content, and porn are sometimes called the *vanilla Web*, terminology I'll use as shorthand in this chapter.

This chapter explains how the adult industry operates on the Web, what the options for monetizing content via advertising are, and how to get traffic to a site that features adult advertisements.

Creating Adult Sites

Putting together an adult web site is very much like creating a vanilla web site from a site construction viewpoint. It's very important, just as with a vanilla site, to use includes in your site architecture (see Chapter 1 for information about using includes) so that you can easily tweak advertising across an entire site.

One key difference with an adult site is that you need to take steps to prevent people who don't want to see your content from viewing it. It's wrong—for ethical, moral, and legal reasons—to have the index page for your domain open with content that may be offensive.

As a start, to protect unsuspecting visitors, it's a simple matter to make sure that all sites with adult content open with a bland, vanilla page containing appropriate warnings. This page should describe in inoffensive words the content of the site and make it easy to exit without proceeding.

 For more information about the law and adult sites, see "Legal Issues," next. Please also take a look at "Protecting the Children," later in this chapter.

As with vanilla sites, adult site content can be generated in a number of different ways. You can:

Create content yourself
> Feasible if you are a talented pornographer (for X-rated stories), videographer, or photographer—and have attractive models.

Purchase content
> There's a great deal of available adult content you can license. You can also contract to have custom content made for you. You can find a good list of providers with content to license or purchase in the Content Providers section of the XBiz Directory at *http://xbiz.com/directory.php*.

Find a way to obtain free site content
> Among the many strategies for putting together a site with free content are using submissions from visitors and creating specialized directory and review sites. In addition, in the adult-content industries, quite a few affiliate programs will provide their affiliates with sample content, with the hope that this will send traffic to the program site.

 See "Making Money with Advertising," later in this chapter, for more information about adult affiliate programs.

Legal Issues

Publishing a web site that draws adult traffic raises some special legal issues. First, in some communities sites with adult content might be considered obscene and therefore illegal and subject to criminal penalties.

Adult web traffic and obscenity

The First Amendment to the United States Constitution protects you from criminal prosecution for what you write or publish, including adult content—for the most part. However, the First Amendment does not protect obscene content.

There's no hard-and-fast standard for what is obscene. As Justice Harlan Stewart once famously observed, he couldn't define obscenity but he knew it when he saw it. Essentially, obscene speech, which is not protected by the First Amendment, has come to be defined as violating community standards, or as speech that is utterly without redeeming social value.

The problem with this from the adult webmaster's viewpoint is that it is not a hard-and-fast definition, and it is subject to different interpretations by different jurisdictions. And unlike most other media, web sites can be opened in almost any jurisdiction. Your takeaway should be that there is always some possibility, however remote, that some prosecutor in a benighted jurisdiction might decide to go after a particular adult web site, with consequences that are hard to know in advance. This happens very rarely, if it all. If you can't live with this level of uncertainty, don't start a business that draws adult traffic. And by all means consult a lawyer with knowledge of First Amendment law if you are in doubt about any specific content. A good source for general information about legal issues and adult content is the Legal Articles section of XBiz, located at *http://xbiz.com/article_bycat.php?cat=40*.

 Adult webmasters are also, of course, potentially subject to jurisdictions in countries other than the United States (meaning the rest of the world). This is primarily of concern to webmasters who live in the jurisdictions in question. If you live in a country with strong sanctions for involvement with adult content, obviously the risk profile for engaging in this activity increases.

Common sense, and common courtesy, strongly suggests that you place a waiver on the opening page of your site. This practice will help to avoid offending unsuspecting people and would afford some legal defense if a site is ever accused of obscenity, along the lines of "they were warned, and they decided to have a look anyhow." The wording of this waiver can be complex, and it can require users to check a box or click a button to signify agreement.

However, it is probably just as legally efficacious to put simple text along the lines that I've already suggested:

> This site contains adult material. If you are under 21 years of age, or if it is illegal to view adult material in your community, or if adult material offends you, please do not click the link to enter this site, and leave this site immediately.

Children in pornography

Obscenity is not the only legal concern of those involved with adult content. Title 18 U.S.C. Section 2256 and 18 U.S.C. 2257 forbid a variety of sexual conduct involving minors. If there is any possibility that photographs or video on your site might depict a minor in any situation, then you must comply with the record-keeping provisions of this law to make sure that minors are not involved. You are also required to post an 18 U.S.C. 2257 notice on the opening page of your site affirming that no minors were involved, and stating where the required records can be reviewed.

 Not only should you comply with the provisions of this law, you should also make sure that any site sponsors do as well.

Celebrities

Provocative images of celebrities are immensely interesting to many people and are therefore desirable content for any site that hopes to draw adult traffic. There are a great many provocative, erotic, or nude photographs of celebrities in circulation. Some were taken before the celebrity became famous, others are of look-alikes, some were released by the photographer without permission, and still others were intentionally released by the celebrity for publicity purposes. If you are thinking of publishing photos of celebrities on your site, you should get competent legal advice and take the following steps:

Make sure all copyrights are in order
> It's important to have a signed model release with an authenticated signature as well as a license from the owner of the copyright to an image.

Consider celebrity rights of publicity and to privacy
> Depending on the jurisdiction, a celebrity may have rights to publicity over imagery that depicts them and rights of privacy relating to their imagery that can provide a cause of action when photos are published.

Run the celebrity photo in an editorial context
> Adding editorial content to a photo of a scantily clad celebrity lends the image the protection of the First Amendment, which is usually gained at a low threshold of some redeeming content. In other words, if you write something (indeed, almost anything that isn't derogatory) about the celebrity you are less likely to run into trouble.

Avoid any negative characterization of the celebrity
You don't want to give the celebrity a possible cause of action for defamation.

Protecting the Children

Protecting children should be a top priority. As a parent, you can make sure that children do not surf the Internet without supervision. As an adult webmaster, you can take a series of successively stronger steps to protect your content from access by minors.

Reporting Child Pornography

If you see child pornography—defined as lewd images of children under 18—on the Web, you can report the site to ASACP, the Association of Sites Advocating Child Protection, at *http://www.asacp.org/index.php*. The mission of ASACP is to help self-police the adult industry via a code of ethics, a logo indicating compliance with the code, and a program for reporting child porn sites to the appropriate government agencies.

You'll need to know the exact URL of the page containing the child pornography. You can't use ASACP to report P2P child porn, emails, etc., only web pages. Please be sure to read the ASACP FAQ, at *http://www.asacp.org/faq.php*, for all the details before reporting a site.

An opening page that provides a description of the content and makes the visitor affirmatively click through to the adult content is an easy step that won't dissuade any traffic, but it probably won't stop any children either.

 Many sites provide an exit link for users unhappy with the content described on an adult site. These exit links are a profit opportunity for webmasters: they can open G-rated properties run by the webmaster.

A step up from a simple warning and disclaimer forbidding minors is the requirement that visitors certify or affirm that they are adults using a mechanism such as the BirthDateVerifier Age Verification System, *http://birthdateverifier.com*. Like a site warning label, this probably won't turn any traffic away, including minor traffic, although it may help mitigate any liability you might have for that traffic.

Yet another step you can take is to place content and graphics on your home page urging visitors to install "parental control" software such as Net Nanny or CyberSitter on their computers. The downside to these programs is that it's easy to find out online how to defeat them. In addition, many of the adult sites with links to this software are making money off referral fees and conversion.

Adult verification systems such as Adult Check and CyberAge do effectively monitor age by requiring a credit card. But they charge a small fee, which once again, depending on the situation, can result in income to the adult site that sends traffic to sign up for the adult verification. Additionally, many users resent credit card verification, which can result in lowered traffic.

 Since teenagers are now often issued credit cards, credit card age verification may not be entirely effective in any case.

Expect changing technology and legislation to impact this aspect of adult-content access. Biometric measuring hardware and software may become a standard way to verify identity (and age) at some point. And, if the pending Child Internet Protection Act becomes law, many sites will have to require a credit card before allowing entry to the site (a measure the credit card industry is fighting bitterly).

Adult Web Hosting

The terms of service (TOS) of most vanilla web hosts forbid adult content on their servers. You should not try to ignore the TOS and host a site oriented towards adult traffic on a vanilla host. It might take a little while before your adult site is noticed, but it certainly will be noticed if it draws traffic—putting your entire business in jeopardy and exposing you to legal risk for violating the TOS.

Fortunately, there is an entire industry of adult web hosts ready to serve you. One of the best of these is MidPhase, *http://www.midphase.com*. You can also find many web hosts specifically geared towards the adult industry in XBiz's Service Providers directory at *http://xbiz.com/directory_showcases.php?id=4*. Adult.TopHosts.Com, *http://adult.tophosts.com*, also provides an extensive directory of adult web hosts (as well as resources for adult webmasters).

You can expect essentially the same technologies and services from an adult web host as from a vanilla web host. However, adult web hosts tend to be slightly more expensive for comparable specifications—and slightly rougher around the edges when it comes to customer service.

Adult web hosts will protect your privacy to a greater extent than vanilla web hosts. For example, you can expect an adult web host to provide its own contact information to the domain registrar for your domain, so you don't end up connected with your adult traffic in a whois registry.

 Some adult sponsors will give you free web hosting provided you refer a specified amount of traffic that converts to the sponsor.

Converting Traffic

To *convert* a sales prospect means to get the prospect to actually plunk down money for something. Generally, for you to make money with adult advertising, the traffic you send to adult sites will have to convert (and spend money), as is the case with affiliate advertising in general (see Chapter 4).

 In some cases, you can make money on an adult site on a CPC (cost per click) basis, although it is a less viable approach than with the vanilla Web. For more information, see "Making Money with Advertising," later in this chapter.

The three "secrets" of converting adult-oriented traffic are:

- Instant gratification
- Product credibility
- Targeting content to your traffic

Instant gratification

Adult traffic wants what it wants when it wants it—which is now! If you are counting on making money based on site visitors' making a purchase, assume that they won't buy anything, such as a mail-order product, that won't lead to instant gratification.

The purchase of products online that can be enjoyed online either on a subscription or per-item basis is the name of this game, because these products can be consumed and enjoyed in real time without ever leaving the computer. Examples include X-rated personals, downloadable videos, and content sites aimed at a specific interest (see "Adult Site Segmentation," later in the chapter).

Product credibility

The for-fee adult products available on the Web can be junky and cross the line into outright rip-off. It's good to start from the assumption that your site visitors are smart enough to know this and don't want to be ripped off.

This means that product credibility is paramount. Brand names help with credibility (as, of course, they also do on the vanilla Web). For example, Jenna Jameson and Vivid are powerful brands in the adult-content world.

Product endorsements that seem authentic also help to establish credibility for links to site sponsors. Good adult webmasters have learned to research the content their site sponsors provide and place enthusiastic reviews of the content on their own sites along with the link to the sponsor's content.

Targeting content to traffic

Visitors to sites with an adult orientation tend to have very specific—and different—interests. For example, straight men are probably uninterested (and even turned off) by gay male adult content. The implication is that you cannot sell straight male traffic sponsored gay content (and vice versa).

 See "The Taxonomy of Desire" next for more information about adult site segmentation.

When you create your site, you need to be very clear about what specific sexual interests your content appeals to and what kind of traffic you are drawing. You need to target your content to the interests of your traffic.

What's more, traffic may not be segmented when it comes into your site, and your site may present material geared to a number of different interests. You should take care to differentiate the topic areas of your site and use mechanisms to present material that is as relevant as possible.

An easy way to segment content is to provide a separate page for each content area. However, this runs counter to the site architecture principle of using a single include for ads in one position across a site. You can solve this problem by checking, within an include, for which page you are on and displaying a different ad based on the content of the page.

For example, suppose a site has content aimed at people interested in bondage and submission (commonly known as *BDSM*) and in lesbian sex (to pick two interests at random). Supposing a site was written using PHP, the include file used to display an ad in a given page location (such as the upper right) could test to see which page was being displayed, and then display relevant content, like this:

```php
<?php
if ($_SERVER['PHP_SELF'] == "/bdsm.php") {
    echo '<!-- Display BDSM HTML ad content here -->';
}
if ($_SERVER['PHP_SELF'] == "/lesbian.php") {
    echo '<!-- Display lesbian HTML ad content here -->';
}
?>
```

The Taxonomy of Desire

Specific groups of people are interested in specific kinds of content and they have very little interest in other kinds of content. There are at least a dozen major adult subject-matter categories and quite a few specialty niches on top of that. So people

---

interested in spanking are probably only going to purchase from sponsors providing spanking content. This content may only appeal if it is primarily addressed to giving spankings (as opposed to receiving spankings). The gender of both the giver and receiver is probably important. The implements used in the content—a hairbrush on a naked bottom, for example, as opposed to a bare hand—may matter.

There are innumerable variations of human sexual proclivities. These proclivities are of vital obsessive interest to particular groups and bizarre and unattractive to others. For instance, some people like to give or receive enemas, and others get a sexual charge out of being dressed up like a baby (both of which are hard for me personally to appreciate). However, if you want to make money from your site you should appreciate the specific interests of your visitors and target advertising to their interests and needs.

 It's obviously beyond the scope of this chapter to provide a catalog of the vast variety of human sexual preferences. If you are interested in this topic, you might take a look at the resources and information provided by the Kinsey Institute at *http://www.indiana.edu/~kinsey/*.

Although cataloging these sexual tastes is a scientific (and possibly anthropologic) task, adult webmasters do need to consider the taxonomy of the different market segments.

Perhaps the best way to look at this is to see the categories used by the adult industry itself. Figure 6-1 shows the table of contents for Persian Kitty, *http://www. persiankitty.com*, a leading directory of adult sites.

![Persian Kitty Jumpstation table of contents]

JUMPSTATION
Free Sites

| Free Sites | Fetch Sites | Amateur Sites | Fresh Sites |
| Updated Jun 10th | Updated May 10th | Updated May 3rd | Updated May 3rd |

PK's Thumbnail Gallery Post Updated Jun 10th

Hourly And Daily QuickPics - "1,950" Fresh Pics Daily

Other Sites by Category - **Updated Jun 10th**

*NEW!*Solo Amateur Girls*NEW!*

Pix of Men	Gay	Erotic Stories	Sex/Relationships Advice & Info
Interesting Sites	Other Lists	CDRom/Video	Toys/Clothing
Other Products	BBS	Phone/Video Sex	Personals/Dating Services
Other Services	AVS Sites	Chatrooms	Membership Sites
WebCams		Models/Pornstars	

PK Exclusive Free Pix & Vids

Purrfect Pose of the Week - Every Tuesday	This Week	Last Week
Purrfect Panoramic Background of the Week - Every Saturday	This Week	Last Week
Purrfect Video of the Day	Hardcore	Softcore	Busty

*NEW!*PK Live*NEW!* - Chat FREE with PK's Live Cam Babes!

PK's Hot Movies - First 10 Minutes FREE!

Persian Kitty's Videos On Demand - Free Daily Clip!

*NEW!*Persian Kitty's Live Cams*NEW!*

Persian Kitty's Chat

| Submit/Update a link | TGP Submissions | Download a PK Banner | Webmasters |
| Email PK | Advertising Info | Making Persian Kitty Your Start Page | |

Figure 6-1. Persian Kitty is a leading directory for adult sites; its table of contents can be used to glean taxonomic information about adult interests

The Persian Kitty table of contents is a little misleading because it combines categorical information with method of delivery information (and also whether sites are free or for-pay). Still, the following major categories can be gleaned from Persian Kitty:

- Amateur girls
- Erotic stories
- Fetish sites
- Gay men
- Models and porn stars

Most of the categories could be labeled differently, and each of these major categories has subcategories, but you probably get the point: visitors will expect a certain kind of content on your site and expect to find this content using specific topic keywords. You should deliver this targeted content and advertising that relates to it, not random content of a sexual nature, and make it easy for visitors to your site to find the content that interests them.

 Take away "sex" as the subject matter, and the concept of making it easy for site visitors to find content they care about applies to web sites in general.

Another way to look at this issue is to consider the content that site sponsors, who also have targeting content to your traffic in mind, make available. The content offered by your sponsors will to some degree limit the traffic you can hope to service—and convert.

Figure 6-2 shows the broad taxonomic categories offered by one major adult sponsor. Within each broad category (called niches by this sponsor) there are usually multiple individual sites catering more specifically to tastes and proclivities.

Figure 6-2. You can select individual sites from these broad categories for site advertising

To learn more about adult content niches, you might also want to take a look at Cozy Academy, which bills itself as a free school for adult webmasters. Cozy Academy presents an entire course on *nichology*—the study of sexual niches, or preferences—at *http://www.cozyacademy.com/classrooms/nichology/index.asp*. The course provides information about 37 separate adult content niches!

Making Money with Advertising

In principle, making money with advertising related to adult content isn't all that different from making money with vanilla content. The good news for operators of sites related to adult content is that the willingness of users to pay for content creates opportunities. Site visitors are happy to be able to purchase adult content privately, and instantly, without a (potentially embarrassing) trip to a video or adult store.

As with other kinds of affiliate programs, adult sponsors work by providing you with an identification code that you embed in the links you place on your site (see Chapter 4 for more information about the general process of affiliate linking). The steps involved in adding a sponsor link to your site—the same as with a vanilla affiliate program—are:

Registering with a sponsor
> This may require manual approval, and you'll need to provide a name and social security number to receive checks.

Selecting banners or other content for your site
> Most sponsors provide a huge array of ads for you to choose from, with the HTML, including your identification code, generated for you.

Copying and pasting the code to your site
> You should use include files for all ad code, as explained in Chapter 1, so they are easy to modify.

Testing the link
> You should make sure the sponsor site opens when the link is clicked.

Types of Programs

For the most part, adult advertising is for sponsors—the kind of relationship known as an affiliate program in the vanilla world (see Chapter 4 for information about non-adult affiliate programs) in which the sponsor is called a *merchant*. Within the adult-content world, "types of programs" means the offering of the sponsor.

The major categories, or types, of programs which in almost all cases are segmented by niche (see "The Taxonomy of Desire," earlier in this chapter, for more information about adult niches), include:

- Online erotic content such as text, pictures, and video feeds (see Figure 6-3)
- Sites specializing in streaming video feeds
- Interactive sites providing services such as interactive phone sex, directed webcams, etc.
- Adult personal sites

In addition, some sponsors provide a classic merchant offering: online stores provide merchandise for shipment such as sex toys and adult DVDs.

Figure 6-3. This well-known sponsor offers for-pay access to sites built around individual porn stars

Payment Plans

Adult sponsors pay commissions to sponsored sites carrying their ads in a number of different ways, including:

Pay per sale
> A flat fee, often as much as $30 to $40, each time a visitor subscribes or signs up (this kind of payment plan is also called *Pay Per Sign-up*, or *PPS*).

Pay per click (CPC)
> Works just the same way as vanilla CPC (see Chapter 5); usually worth a few pennies per click.

Revenue sharing
> The promise is that you'll receive a share of whatever your traffic pays into the indefinite future; see "Webmaster Programs," next, for an interesting extension of this arrangement.

It's hard to know in advance which arrangement will work best for you. Obviously, if you knew that your visitors would click and not buy, you'd go for CPC; if you knew that they'd subscribe and not renew, you'd go for "pay per sale"; and if your average site viewer subscribed forever, you'd want to revenue share.

If you believe in the sponsor's offering, and think that it works for your traffic, you are probably best off going along with a revenue-sharing arrangement. The best approach is trial and error. For example, suppose you work with two sponsors. You could try one on a pay-for-sale basis, and the other on a revenue-sharing basis, and see which does best. Eventually, you could switch the lower-yielding program over.

 Most adult-site sponsors allow you to switch program payment plans easily, although this will often involve pasting new code into the ad code on your site.

Webmaster Programs

Webmaster programs allow you to refer other webmasters to your adult-site sponsor. Not only do you get a payout when the other webmaster enrolls in the sponsor's affiliate program, you also get an override commission on anything the other

CPC Contextual Ads on Adult Sites

Don't confuse CPC as a form of payment basis from an adult-site sponsor with CPC contextual advertising. Sites with adult traffic can host contextual ads (contextual and CPC ads are explained in Chapter 5). So it's perfectly possible to expect to use contextual ads as an additional source of revenue on an adult site.

However, Google will not knowingly accept adult sites into the Google AdWords program; you need to work with an alternative contextual ad vendor (some are mentioned in Chapter 5). Another alternative, also described in Chapter 5, is to use a service such as AdBrite, which allows bidders to place ads on your site subject to your approval.

Oddly enough, although Google will not place ads via AdWords on an adult-oriented site, it will accept ads (with some limitations) through the AdSense program intended to drive traffic to adult content. See "Advertising Your Site," later in this chapter, for more information.

webmaster brings in. In a sense, a webmaster program is a great deal like a multilevel marketing (MLM) scheme: it is possible to make a great deal of money at the early phases of a webmaster program (or MLM), but the good times, even in theory, cannot go on forever; there are only so many webmasters to enroll.

> Some adult sponsors require different identification codes in links intended for webmaster traffic (as opposed to normal site visitors). To work with a site sponsor with this requirement, you need to be sure to use the right identification code with the appropriate ads to get properly credited for your traffic.

Ads intended for webmaster traffic tend to have a different look and feel than ads for site visitors: more about metrics and profitability, and less about sex (Figure 6-4).

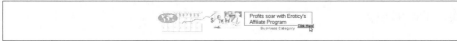

Figure 6-4. Ads targeted at webmasters, like this one from a leading adult classified site Eroticy, tend to emphasize dollars and cents at the expense of sex

Finding Sponsors

Experience is the best teacher, and the best way to know the right sponsors for a given niche in the adult market is to have an in-depth understanding of the category. You may have a good gut-level idea of the kind of content your site visitors will pay for.

If you are unfamiliar with adult sites, you can find listings of sponsor programs on these web sites:

Adult Chamber

Adult Chamber is an adult webmaster resource center; ad sponsors can be found at *http://adultchamber.com/adprograms.htm*.

Cozy Academy

Site sponsors organized by topic niche are at *http://www.cozyacademy.com/classrooms/nichology/index.asp*; a complete directory of sponsors can be found in the Cozy Academy "library": *http://www.cozyacademy.com/library/index.asp*.

XBiz

XBiz publishes newsletters and syndication feeds and maintains bulletin boards aimed at informing the adult community; see the XBiz directory at *http://xbiz.com/directory.php* for listings of potential site sponsors.

 Keep in mind that links to sponsor offerings in directories such as Adult Chamber, Cozy Academy, and XBiz are themselves likely to be sponsored. In other words, by clicking through a banner or link on one of these sites and signing up with a sponsorship program, you are likely generating revenue for the directory either on a PPS or revenue sharing basis. It's entirely possible that placement within a directory is determined on an economic basis rather than on the basis of desirability of the content.

Publicizing Your Site

As with a vanilla site, if you build an adult site and no one comes, you won't be able to make any money off advertising on the site. Traffic is a basic requirement for monetization. Some of the mechanisms you can use to publicize a vanilla site work with adult sites, and in some cases you need to modify your approach.

Adult Directories

It's a good idea to list adult sites in Google and other search engines (as explained in Chapter 2). You should also list your site in the appropriate category of the ODP–Adult, located at *http://dmoz.org/Adult/*, or one of the specialized subcategories of the Adult category. Listing with the ODP will help your site gain status with Google and the other search engines of this world.

 For more about working with the ODP, see Chapter 2.

Most adult traffic does not come through Google, but rather through specialized directory and review sites that categorize and evaluate adult content. Persian Kitty, *http://www.persiankitty.com*, is a leading adult directory categorized alphabetically and by content niche. The Persian Kitty site submission form can be found at *http://www.persiankitty.com/links.html*. JanesGuide, *http://www.janesguide.com*, is a categorized directory and review site with a great reputation for honest reviews in the adult industry.

You can find a great listing of alternative search engines and directories aimed at the adult industry that accept unpaid listings in the resource section at Adult Chamber, *http://www.adultchamber.com/freelistings.php?maincat=8*.

 Read the FAQs carefully before submitting a site to an adult directory. Adult directory and review sites expect a reciprocal link. Often, the link must be placed before the site is submitted to the directory. The details for reciprocal link graphics and placement are spelled out precisely in webmaster FAQs.

Advertising Your Site

Advertising your site may be the easiest way to draw traffic, although, of course, it does cost something.

 Link exchanges within the adult industry are way to exchange traffic— by providing reciprocal site links—without money changing hands.

For adult-industry advertising resources, link exchanges, and related programs to drive traffic, visit:

- The Traffic Programs category at Adult Chamber, *http://www.adultchamber.com/freelistings.php?maincat=7*
- The lesson links within the Traffic Lounge at *http://www.cozyacademy.com/classrooms/traffic/index.asp*
- The Traffic and Marketing section of XBiz, *http://xbiz.com/directory_showcases.php?id=6*

A better bet than advertising within the adult world may be advertising for adult traffic using the mainstream search engines such as Google. Although Google will not accept adult-content sites into its AdSense content network, it will accept ads into the AdWords program that direct traffic to adult sites.

The AdWords program is explained in Part III.

The catch is that a certain amount of adult-content ads submitted to Google are rejected. For example, the ad shown in Figure 6-5 was rejected for supposedly promoting prostitution, but the ad shown in Figure 6-6 for the identical site was acceptable.

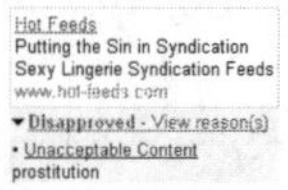

Figure 6-5. Ads submitted to Google can be rejected arbitrarily (like this one which was disapproved for supposedly promoting prostitution)

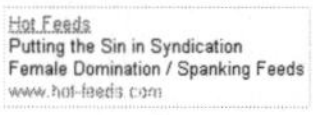

Figure 6-6. Some ads aimed at adult traffic are fine with Google

The moral: if you advertise for adult traffic through Google, be prepared to have some ads rejected. You should expect to replace rejected ads with alternatives—there's no real appeal from a Google decision of this sort.

Syndication

In Chapter 2 I explained how to use syndication to create syndication feeds using your web site content. Once you've created your feed, you can use it to drive traffic to your site. Syndication works especially well as a promotional tool for adult web sites because, generally, there's no mechanism within syndication readers to discriminate against adult content. Web users interested in adult content like syndication feeds because they see it as a way to uncover adult content on the Web without paying for it.

Two syndication aggregators that specialize in adult feeds are:

Hot Feeds
> This specialty site, focused on syndication feeds created by sex blogs but also including niche adult-content categories, is located at *http://www.hot-feeds.com*; you can submit your feed at *http://www.hot-feeds.com/submit.php*.

Web Nymph

The adult section of Web Nymph, located at *http://www.webnymph.com/?page=adult*, provides links to hundreds of adult syndication feeds that your mainstream RSS aggregator may have "missed." You must register to submit a feed. After a time delay, you can use your Options page to submit your own feed.

Adult Press Releases

Unfortunately, you can't submit a press release covering adult topics to the mainstream press release services.

 You'll find information in Chapter 2 about crafting an effective press release and submitting it to mainstream press services.

There's no completely acceptable alternative for the widespread coverage these mainstream wire services provide. But you can (and should) submit an initial press release describing your content to adult-industry press release services.

This process should be repeated every time you have something newsworthy to report, for example, a brand-spanking-new content area. Adult industry sites that accept press releases include:

- Adult Buzz (*http://www.adultbuzz.com*)
- XBiz (*http://www.xbiz.com*)
- YNOT.COM (*http://www.ynot.com*)

Action Items

If you are considering creating an adult web site, or are already an adult webmaster, you should:

- Understand legal issues surrounding adult web content
- Work with a web hosting company specifically geared to adult sites
- Understand the taxonomy of adult content niches
- Create, commission, or license content, or obtain it from site sponsors
- Provide content that caters to specific niches and interests
- Forge relationships with a few good adult sponsors
- Display ads from these sponsors that are relevant to your traffic

- Get listings in adult directories
- Consider advertising via the Google AdWords program to drive traffic
- Syndicate one or more feeds based on your site content
- Submit your syndication feeds to specialty adult feed aggregators
- Create an initial (and subsequent) press release
- Submit your press releases to adult-industry press release services

PART II

Getting the Most from AdSense

Chapters 7–9 explain how to work with Google's AdSense, the premier contextual advertising program for content sites. Participating in the AdSense program is probably one of the best ways to monetize your site.

CHAPTER 7

Understanding Google, AdSense, and AdWords

Google is a colossus that sits astride access to information on the World Wide Web. Ubiquitous, useful, and often imitated—but seldom equaled—Google has lent its name to a verb: to *google* something (or someone) is to search for the thing or person on the Web. Google is also a forward-looking corporation filled with brilliant thinkers and one of the largest companies in the world in terms of market capitalization.

The primary focus of this book is making money with the Google advertising applications: the AdSense and AdWords programs. These programs are closely related to Google's searching technology. AdSense ads are placed on your web site depending on the context of your site (in other words, Google's analysis of how your site is likely to be found). And AdWords ads are targeted using keywords and phrases—the same keywords and phrases used when searching for something with Google.

The close relationship between Google web searching technology and the advertising programs means that it is important to understand a little about the syntax of Google searches when working with the AdSense program or crafting AdWord campaigns. It's not that I propose to teach you how to use Google to search in this book. Rather, you need a sense of how *others* may be using Google to search when they come across your sites or ads.

To get the most out of working with Google, you also need to understand the parts of Google. It's not easy to get a grasp on what Google is and what Google does, besides web searching. For a phenomenon of its magnitude, the parts of Google are surprisingly unintegrated. This chapter starts with an overview explaining the parts of Google and what they do so that you'll get a sense of what Google resources may be available to you and how all these moving parts work together (or don't work together).

After explaining Google's search syntax and exploring what Google has to offer generally, this chapter drills down on Google's role as an automated advertising broker with these programs and explains, in general terms, how these programs relate and how you work with them.

The Syntax of a Google Query

The primary Google search interface, the Google home page, is famously simple and uncluttered (as shown in Figure 7-1).

Figure 7-1. In its simplest form, Google search returns results for keywords entered in the search box

You enter a word or words, also called *keywords,* in the Google search form. (Several keywords make up a *search term*, also called a *query*.)

As you probably know, when you click the I'm Feeling Lucky button, Google opens the page that is the top-ranked search result for your query.

 Experienced researchers don't usually bother with the I'm Feeling Lucky button because it is unlikely that you will find what you need this way, and it wastes time—even if it is fun!

Clicking the Google Search button opens the first page of Google's search results for your query. Google's search result pages also display AdWords ads that are contextually relevant to the query that generated the page.

Google Syntax and Operators

Google searches support a number of operators, including:

AND

The AND operator tells Google to explicitly join two keywords in a query. It must be uppercase (cannot be written and).

OR

The OR operator, which can also be written using the pipe character (|), matches any of the terms joined with this operator in a query. It must be uppercase (cannot be written or).

+

The "plus" operator, called the *inclusion operator*, forces Google to include words, such as stop words (defined below), in a search.

The "minus" operator, called the *exclusion operator*, looks for results that do not have the specified keyword in them. For example, a search for virus-computer finds results that have to do with viruses, but not computers (particularly useful if you are looking for biologic viruses).

> To avoid confusion, all search terms are printed in this book in literal font (as in Google AdWords). If quotes are shown in the search term—as in "Computer Programming"—then those quotes are part of the search term and would be typed in by the user.

You should also know that Google searches omit many common words, called *stop words*. Stop words that are omitted include "and," "for," "the," and most punctuation. If you want to include a stop word in your search, you need to include it within double quotes.

Double quoting also serves the purpose of searching for an entire quoted string. For example, to search for the film Star Wars III, you could use the query "Star Wars III". Without the quotes, the III would be omitted as a stop word.

The Rules of Simple Search

Searching with Google can be really simple, but it helps to keep some basic rules of Google search syntax in mind:

Implicit AND *connection*
> Google assumes that two or more words in a query are connected by an AND operator, even when the AND is omitted. A search for Landscape Photography is the same as a search for Landscape AND Photography.

All-word search
> Google searches for all words in a query, unless they are stop words.

Results can be anywhere
> A successful search finds results anywhere in a document (such as in HTML and meta information) not just in its text.

Word order matters
> The words in a search are ordered in terms of importance from left to right.

Proximity counts
> Words in a query that are close together in a search result are returned ahead of results where the words are farther apart.

Google is not case sensitive
> Unless your query is double-quoted, Google does not care about capitalization. For example, new york matches New York in a Google search (but "new york" would not, because of the quotes).

Effective Searching

Google searches tend to be more effective—producing better search results—if the following concepts are kept in mind:

Google looks for words, not meaning

Google's algorithms look for the occurrences of words and phrases, not the meaning of words. This implies that it helps to think about how words are likely to be used in context and in web pages when formulating a search.

Specificity and distinctiveness in keyword choice helps

If you search using generic words—words that are used in a great many documents on the Web—you won't get as useful a result set as if you can pinpoint more unusual words that are relevant to your search.

Use singular, plural, and alternate word forms

Since Google is looking for words, not meaning, you may need to use alternative forms of words in your searches to get the widest results. A search for photograph, photographs, and photography may each yield different results.

> You can use the OR operator to search for several forms of the same word: photograph | photographs | photography.

These concepts related to effective searching have big implications for participants in the AdWords program (see Part III for more about AdWords). An important part of AdWords is selecting the right keywords to target your ads against. It's hard to cost-effectively target generic words that generate massive search results; it makes much more sense to target narrow quirky words (and phrases).

The Google Results Page

A typical Google results page is shown in Figure 7-2. It's a good idea to learn a little more about what to expect on a results page and what ads to expect, because Google search results pages are where more than half of all AdWords ads turn up.

> Ads placed with the Google network using AdWords show up on web content (via AdSense), in third-party pages with whom Google has contracted, and on Google's search results. The Google search results are the most important of these from a dollars-and-cents viewpoint and also have the best click-through rates (CTR).

Results are returned in the order of their PageRank—the complex formula Google uses to determine the importance of a web page—in Google's index. Each search

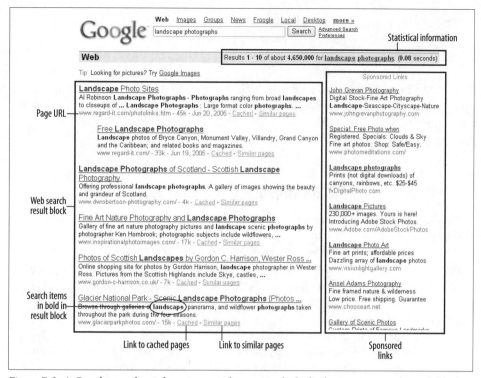

Figure 7-2. A Google search results page provides a great deal of information in each result block as well as "sponsored links" (AdWords ads)

results page provides statistics in the upper-right corner (above the actual search results) that show you an estimate of how many results were found and how long a search took.

Each of the results on the page is represented by a snippet of text from the web page the result points to, called a *search results block*. A link to the web page is part of the search results block, with the title of the page as the text for the link if it is available (the page's URL is used if the title isn't available).

Each result block also provides a Cached link and a Similar Pages link. If you click the Cached link, a copy of the page saved by Google's servers will open. This is useful in case the page has changed since it was indexed by Google. It's also handy for finding where on a page the search terms are located: they are highlighted in the cached version.

The Similar Pages link opens pages that Google determines bear a close relationship to the page found in the search results.

Using the Google related operator in a search is equivalent to clicking the Similar Pages link following a search result.

Following Similar Pages links for a search is a great technique for participants in AdWords to ferret out keyword alternatives. The sites that are in part of the similar results may be what the traffic you are interested in selling to is interested in visiting; you can get ideas from these sites about what keywords to bid on.

Learning More About Google Search

This section provides enough about the mechanics of working with Google search so that you can skillfully use the Google AdSense and AdWords programs. But, obviously, it is not a complete guide to becoming an experienced researcher with Google.

For more information about researching with Google, begin with the Google Help documentation. A good starting place on the Web is *http://www.google.com/help/basics.html*.

Google: The Missing Manual (O'Reilly) is a great introduction to Google search tools and techniques. *Google Hacks* (O'Reilly) provides more in-depth technical information. My own *Building Research Tools with Google for Dummies* (Wiley) explains how to use Google as a professional research tool, what information you can expect to find in Google (and what isn't there), and how to evaluate the credibility of information you do find on the Web.

Google's Parts

Google's parts can, roughly speaking, be divided into the following categories:

Services
> These let people do something (for example, search the Web or create a blog).

Tools
> Software to make chores easier (for example, the Google Toolbar or the Picasa image software).

Developer tools
> Programs aimed at software developers, such as the AdWords API.

Advertising solutions
> Programs such as AdSense and AdWords.

Business solutions
> Products intended to be used as part of an enterprise infrastructure, such as the Google Enterprise search appliance.

Obviously, many of these aspects of Google are beyond the scope of this book, which focuses on making money with Google advertising and the AdSense and AdWords programs. This section explains the parts of Google you should know about with this selective focus.

More Google Parts

Parts of Google not discussed in this section (because of limited relevance to Google and advertising) include:

- Alerts (automatic notifications of news and search results by email)
- Answers (humans answer research questions using Google)
- Desktop Search (searches the files on your desktop computer using an interface that looks like Google's web search)
- Groups (bulletin board posts on every conceivable subject)
- Images (lets you search for pictures on the Web)
- Language Tools (automatic translation of text and web pages)
- Maps (maps, satellite pictures, driving directions, and access to local search)
- MySearch History (tracks the history of your searches)
- News (lets you search news items)
- Picasa (image management and lightweight image editing)
- RideFinder (find taxi, limousine, or shuttle services, with real-time location of vehicles)
- SiteMaps (service for webmasters; lets you submit a site map to Google in XML format showing areas of your site that have changed and need reindexing)

These Google parts may not be the primary focus of this book, but even a quick glance should help give you respect for the breadth and depth of Google's offerings.

Google is a moving target; it's constantly innovating, releasing software, and acquiring software companies. No static list of Google parts is ever likely to be up-to-date or final.

 Google has the custom of releasing software and services as *beta* (meaning still in a test period) and calling the software beta for a long period of time, even though most other companies would consider it up to normal release standards.

You'll find software that Google is still playing with at Google Labs, *http://labs. google.com*. If you go to Google Labs, you can try out this software. Many of the "graduates" of Google Labs are now real, live Google parts.

Some of the parts of Google can be opened directly from the Google home page, *http://www.google.com*. If you don't see the link you are interested in on the Google home page, open the Google Services and Google Tools page by clicking the More link on the Google home page.

 You can reach this page directly by opening the address *http://www.google.com/options/* in your browser.

You'll find links to almost all the parts of Google from the Google Services and Google Tools page; I'll also provide a direct address to each Google part I discuss in the body of that section.

Advanced Search

Google Advanced Search, shown in Figure 7-3, can be opened using the URL *http://www.google.com/advanced_search*. Google Advanced Search implements the operators explained in "Google Syntax and Operators" earlier in this chapter (and a number of additional operators which I didn't explain) using a visual interface, so you don't need to enter the operators as part of a search query.

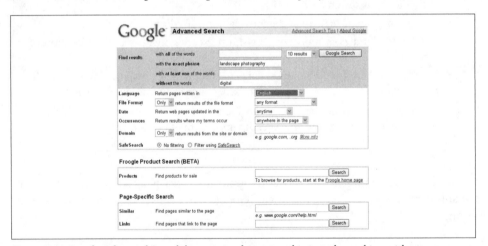

Figure 7-3. Google Advanced Search lets you implement sophisticated searching without understanding Google's query language

Blogger

Blogger, *http://www.blogger.com*, is one of the largest hosted blogging services on the Web. Blogger hosts hundreds of thousands of blogs, and it is free and easy to use. From an advertiser's viewpoint Blogger (and other hosted blogging services) are interesting, because they provide Google with a venue for AdWords contextual ads, categorized by the specific interest of the blog author.

Catalogs

Google Catalogs, *http://catalogs.google.com*, is a library of scanned mail-order catalogs that users can search. There's no charge for getting a catalog included in this list, and Google does not currently place advertising on the catalog search results pages. But you may want to know that the listings from Google Catalogs can show up in regular Google search results and accept that these listings are possible competition for merchandise items of your own.

Code

Google Code, *http://code.google.com*, is a centralized repository of all the APIs, documentation for developers, Google open source projects, and everything else related to programming Google (see Part IV for information about programming the Google AdWords API).

Directory

Google Directory uses the categorization scheme and sites selected by the Open Directory Project (ODP) to find information that has been vetted by volunteer editors familiar with a particular subject. The URL for Google Directory is *http://directory.google.com*. As I explain in Chapter 2, the ODP is important to you if you want to drive traffic to your site. You can use Google Directory to explore Google's use of the ODP taxonomy.

Froogle

Froogle, *http://froogle.google.com*, is a comparative, searchable shopping service. It's currently free for merchants to list their offerings with Froogle, and as far as can be told, Google makes no money from Froogle. It should be in the sites of businesses working with the Google advertising programs, however, because Google will eventually do something to monetize this service and Froogle may end up competing with merchants who advertise on other parts of the Google network.

Local

Google Local, *http://local.google.com*, is used to pinpoint information related to a particular place. This is achieved by searching billions of web pages for information about local businesses, then cross-checking those results with Yellow Pages data.

There are several implications for advertisers: Google Local results pages are excellent advertising venues for local businesses who have signed up with AdWords. Google Local has excellent mapping features and is very convenient to use. The trend that is underway of advertising moving from newspapers and Yellow Pages to the Web will only accelerate as people become more accustomed to using Google Local, meaning that it will become even more important for advertisers to learn to work with AdWords.

 Businesses whose traffic is local should take steps to design campaigns that interact properly with Google Local (see Chapter 11 for more information).

Personalize Your Home Page

Personalize Your Home Page, *http://www.google.com/ig*, presents a variety of news feeds and other information on the Google Home Page. Figure 7-4 shows a generic version of this customized home page.

Figure 7-4. Google's personalized home page feature lets you add news feeds, weather, stock quotes, and more

At this time, it's hard to know for sure where Google is going to go with the home page personalization feature, but it's worth watching for advertisers because opening up the Google start pages to different kinds of information suggests that Google may extend the kinds of advertising it accepts.

Print

Google Print, *http://print.google.com*, lets users search through books submitted to the program by publishers and other copyright holders. Google takes care of scanning the books and hosting the resulting pages on Google servers. These pages are then used by Google to display contextual ads. A portion of the revenue from the ads is paid by Google to the owner of the materials.

Scholar

Google Scholar lets you search for academic, peer-reviewed articles and citations. You can open Google Scholar at *http://scholar.google.com*. Although Scholar has had some rather mixed reviews, it is certainly one of the largest free repositories online of scholarly materal, and Google Scholar search results are another place Google displays contextual advertising.

Automated Ad Brokering: AdSense and AdWords

Google places ads on its own properties—most significantly on search results pages—and on web sites that have signed up for the AdSense program.

 Google also places ads in third-party content networks to extend the range of its ads even further.

Advertisers—businesses and people with something to sell or promote—sign up with Google via the AdWords program. Working with AdWords, which involves bidding a maximum amount for particular keywords, is explained in detail in Chapter 10.

Google's software sits like an automated advertising broker between the two halves of this equation, as shown in Figure 7-5. It's a really important point. If a content ad is hosted by Google and appears on your site, you could theoretically cut out the company in the middle (Google), if advertiser and publisher knew who each was, and could negotiate a price both felt was fair. For example, if I publish a site with information about digital photography, and I notice that online camera stores often provide the Google AdSense ads that appear on my site, I could theoretically approach one of these camera stores and negotiate a deal to carry ads for the store on my site that did not pay Google a commission. However, that assumes that I know who to contact and want to take on the added responsibility of a direct interface with the stores. Since many people don't want this extra responsibility, using Google as an intermediary turns out to be a good solution.

Like all successful intermediaries, Google's job is introducing parties and establishing a market pricing mechanism that both sides feel is fair (or, at least, that they can live with).

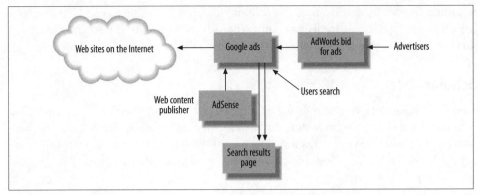

Figure 7-5. Google is the intermediary between AdSense accounts and AdWords advertisers

In the case of advertisements that are placed on web sites participating in the AdSense content network, the business model is really simple. Google takes in money from the advertisers and pays out money to the owners of the web content. Your goal if you are web site content owner should be to maximize your share of this revenue stream, and Google's game is to make the most of the difference between what it has to pay for ad space (AdSense) and what it can take in placing ad inventory (AdWords).

The Google inventory of pages that can host ads is bifurcated, however, and Google's model with its own search results pages is different, and more complex. Google's search result pages make Google a content owner of an incredibly valuable web property—one that is, however, difficult and expensive to maintain. Google's profit in this portion of its business comes from taking in more in ad revenue than it pays out to maintain and improve its search application (and, to some degree, the other parts of Google). The goal of a participant in the AdWords program who is looking to place ads on the Google search network is to maximize the effectiveness of its expenditures on the AdWords program.

Action Items

To become an effective and productive user of the Google AdSense and AdWords programs, you should:

- Learn the basics of Google's search syntax
- Think about the queries users are likely to use to find your products or services (or products and services similar to yours)
- Spend some time getting a grasp on what the main parts of Google contain
- Understand Google's brokering function between the AdSense and AdWords program

What About Click Fraud?

Click fraud means clicking on contextual ads with no interest in purchasing the goods or services advertised, usually with the intention of defrauding the advertiser or enriching the contextual publisher. Most often, click fraud occurs as part of an effort to raise expenses for a competitor—by making them pay for the bogus clicks—or as an attempt at self-enrichment by a publisher (by clicking on ads on its own pages).

Click fraud is a major problem, at least in terms of perceptions, on the Internet for contextual advertising vendors like Google and Yahoo.

Google has major efforts underway to detect click fraud, which are in the aggregate fairly successful, but the details of these programs are (for obvious reasons) secret. The bottom line:

- On a very small scale, it is possible to commit click fraud and get away with it. However, as a publisher, you should take care to be totally aboveboard. If Google suspects you of click fraud, it will most likely close your account, and possibly ban your sites from the Google search index.

- Detecting click fraud is a statistical matter. Once the fraud becomes statistically significant, it will probably be detected.

- Contextual advertising does work and delivers targeted prospects much more effectively than any other method. A small amount of click fraud is a fact of life—most advertisers regard it as a cost of doing business that does not diminish the relative effectiveness of CPC advertising. (Despite the publicity that click fraud gets, a recent study shows that less than 6% of all advertisers regard it as a problem.)

CHAPTER 8

Working with AdSense

As Karl Marx said, "Being determines consciousness," meaning, in part, that the way you make your living influences how you think about things. Google makes its living from advertising, and the Google AdSense program in particular earns its keep by placing ads in web content. It's therefore not surprising to see AdSense promoting itself as the way to reap "the reward of great content"; of course, you should remember what else determines great content from Chapter 1.

 It's worth having a quick look at the web content scenarios that Google presents as AdSense successes. You can view these case studies at *https://www.google.com/adsense/success*.

This chapter explains the details of how to work with the Google AdSense program. Once you know how to work with AdSense, you can start making money from your web sites by placing Google's ad code in your web pages.

Premium Service for AdSense

High-volume sites deserve more service. According to Google, if your site receives more than 5 million search queries, or 20 million content page views per month, you are eligible for AdSense *premium service*. To apply, fill out and submit the form you will find at *http://services.google.com/ads_inquiry/*.

The benefits of the AdSense premium service include:

- Access to technical and sales support
- A greater variety of customizable ad formats than standard AdSense offers
- Assistance with ad optimization
- Sophisticated filtering options
- More ways to make money from ads than standard AdSense offers

---

Applying for an AdSense Account

To apply for a Google AdSense account, visit the Google AdSense home page, *http://www.google.com/adsense/*, and click the Click Here to Apply button. The form shown in Figure 8-1 will open.

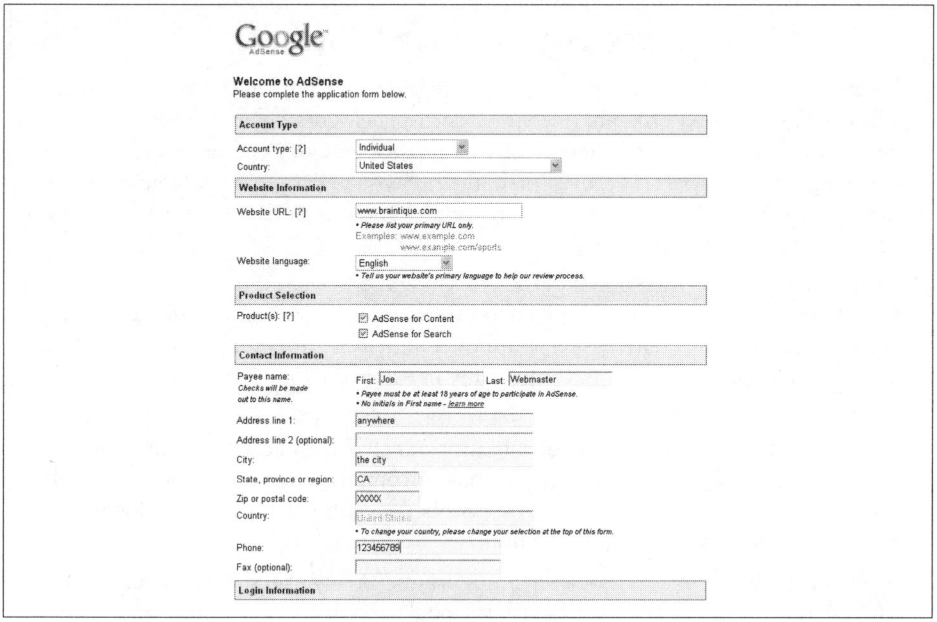

Figure 8-1. You apply to open an account with the Google AdSense program using this simple form

There are only a few issues you'll need to bear in mind as you complete this form:

Type of business entity
> You need to tell Google whether your web site is published by an individual or a corporation.

Web site address
> You need to provide Google with the URL for your primary web site (see "Providing a Web Site Address" in the nearby sidebar).

Product selection
> You can sign up for AdSense for Content or AdSense for Search or both (see "AdSense Content and AdSense Search" later in this chapter for information about the distinction between the two programs). There's really no reason not to sign up for both.

Contact information
> You need to tell Google what name to put on the checks and where to mail those checks.

Login information

You need to set up an email address and password for logging into your AdSense account. If you have a Google AdWords or Google Print account, you can use the same login; otherwise, you should provide this information.

Providing a Web Site Address

Google will review the web site address you provide for compliance with the content policies of the AdSense program (see *https://www.google.com/adsense/policies* for more information about AdSense policies). It is not unusual for Google to reject web sites for noncompliance with content provisions of the AdSense policies; the prohibitions range from excessive advertising content through adult content, content about hacking, and content using excessive profanity.

It is permissible (and often done) to use one Google AdSense account across multiple web addresses. If you are maintaining half a dozen sites, it is easier to work with a single AdSense account than to keep up with statistics on multiple accounts (see Chapter 9 for information about what you need to do to monitor your AdSense performance).

This leads to the possible scenario of submitting one URL for acceptance into the program and eventually placing AdSense ads on noncompliant sites. You could probably get away with doing this for a while, but it is a bad idea. If you are caught, Google will most likely terminate your entire account.

The best approach is to apply for a separate account for any web site with questionable content. That way, you are aboveboard. If Google accepts the account application, it can have no beef with you because of the content. If Google rejects the application, then you'll need to work with one of the less squeamish vendors mentioned in Chapter 5.

It's pretty simple, really, to fill out the AdSense form; as these things go, it is not a lot of red tape. The next step is to wait for Google to review your application, which usually takes one or two days.

Setting Account Options

You will be notified by email that your AdSense application has been accepted. Once you've been accepted into the AdSense program, you can modify your initial account options using the Account Settings page. To open that page, just click the My Account tab once you have logged into AdSense.

Ad Type Preference

Besides the account options you set in your application, the Account Settings page is used to set global preferences for whether you want to display text ads only or both text and images. This Ad Type Preference option sets your global default; you can override your choice when you specify options for a block of Google ad code that will be placed on a particular page.

Text ads are the delivery format of most of Google's contextual advertising. Some content owners may want to avoid image ads because they can clutter sites and may work to the detriment of content. However, Google's (relatively new) CPM advertising program uses image ads; so if you'd like the possibility of displaying Google CPM ads (which pay when they are displayed and not when they are clicked), you'll need to allow image ads on your site. See Chapter 5 for more information about the distinction between CPC and CPM advertising.

Filing Tax Information

Filing appropriate tax information forms with Google is really part of the account application process, and your account won't be activated until you file these forms.

If you are operating as a sole proprietorship under your own social security number, you will need to file an IRS form W-9 with Google.

For instructions and forms, with the Account Settings page open, click the Tax Information link. Once your form has been filed with Google, when you click the Tax Information link you'll see a message saying that "our records indicate that you have already submitted the appropriate information."

Reviewing Payment History

The Payment History link on the Account Settings page opens a display of your earnings and payment history. Although it's reasonable to want to know how much money one is owed, the information in this display is quite sketchy and not very useful for tracking your account activity. See Chapter 9 for information about how to monitor the activity in your AdSense account.

AdSense Content and AdSense Search

Google AdSense provides two programs you can use to make money from your web content:

- AdSense for Content
- AdSense for Search

These are different programs and work in different ways. AdSense Content places ads on your web pages, similar to the ad unit shown in Figure 8-2, and you make money when a site visitor clicks on the ad.

Figure 8-2. A typical AdSense Content unit provides text ads with links; you get paid when someone clicks one of the links

With AdSense Search, you put a Google search box, like the one shown in Figure 8-3, on your site.

Figure 8-3. In the AdSense Search program, a search box goes on your site

The AdSense search box displays Google search results when a user enters a query. These search results show relevant ads. You receive a portion of the revenue generated when a visitor uses your search box and then clicks on an ad from the search results returned by Google.

 Adding to the power of the AdSense search program, you can use the SiteSearch option to search your site rather than the Web (see "AdSense Search Settings" later in this chapter for details). You can also configure the AdSense search results page (whether searching your site or the Web) to match the look of your web site (see "Working with Search Styles" later in this chapter for more information).

To summarize, AdSense Content and AdSense Search are two very different ways to make money from your content, but both are lumped (a little confusingly) under the AdSense program umbrella; it's important to be clear about the distinction.

AdSense Content or AdSense Search?

Is AdSense Content or AdSense Search right for your site? It's hard to say, and there's very little reason not to try both to see which works best.

From a general viewpoint, AdSense Content works best on *destination sites*. If visitors to your site tend to linger a while, and regard your site as conferring some authority on the ads you present, then AdSense Content will probably work well.

On the other hand, if your site is a way station leading toward further information (usually on other sites), then it is probable that visitors will frequently use AdSense search if it is available on your site, and this program may make you quite a bit of money.

AdSense Ad Settings

Once your AdSense account has been approved, you probably want to get started by adding the code that will place Google's ads on your site. To get started with AdSense for Content, log into Google AdSense, and click the Ad Settings tab. The Ad layout code page will open.

Getting Ad Layout Code

The Ad layout code page is used to generate code for content ads that you will place in your web pages. There are a number of sections of the Ad layout page used for choosing options, including:

- Ad Type
- Ad Layout
- Color palettes
- Channel choice (see "Using Channels" later in this chapter for more information)

Ad type

Ads are supplied by Google in *units*. An *ad unit* contains from one to six ads. A *link unit*, shown in Figure 8-4, contains four or five links to pages listing ads.

Your first choice is to decide which kind of unit—ad or link—you want to display (Figure 8-5).

Figure 8-4. A link unit displays links to Google ad pages

Figure 8-5. You can choose between ad units and link units

If you select an ad unit, the drop-down list to the right of the ad unit radio button (shown in Figure 8-5) is used to determine whether only text ads will be displayed in the unit, only image ads will be displayed in the unit, or both.

> You can also just leave the text ad/image ad setting for the unit at the default you selected when you signed up for the AdSense program or that you chose in your account options.

When you choose to generate code for a link unit, the drop-down list to the right of the link unit radio button is used to decide whether the link unit will provide four or five links.

Ad units display ads directly on your pages, where they are probably more likely to be clicked than link units. Link units, a relatively new kind of Google unit, are in some ways one step removed; a link unit presents links to ads rather than the ads themselves. But the advantage of the link unit is that it takes up almost no space. This effective use of real estate makes sense if your site visitors are affirmatively looking for additional resources related to a topic rather than "impulse clicking." Once again, experimentation and trial and error is the best way to find what works on your site.

Ad layout

The Ad Layout section of the ad layout code page is used to specify a size for your ad or link unit. Figure 8-6 shows the drop-down list of choices for ad units, which are also shown in Table 8-1.

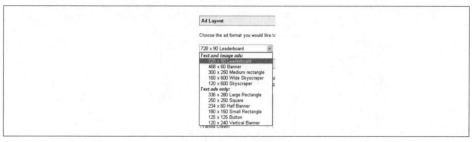

Figure 8-6. If you are specifying an ad unit, you select its size from this drop-down list

Table 8-1. Ad unit names and sizes

Unit name	Size (in pixels) (width first)	Contains
Leaderboard	728 × 90	Text and images
Banner	468 × 60	Text and images
Large Rectangle	336 × 280	Text ads only
Medium Rectangle	300 × 250	Text and images
Square	250 × 250	Text ads only
Half Banner	234 × 60	Text ads only
Small Rectangle	180 × 150	Text ads only
Wide Skyscraper	160 × 600	Text and images
Button	125 × 125	Text ads only
Skyscraper	120 × 600	Text and images
Vertical Banner	120 × 240	Text ads only

If you are specifying a link unit (in pixels, width first), your size choices, shown in below are different:

> 728 × 15
> 468 × 15
> 200 × 90
> 180 × 90
> 160 × 90
> 120 × 90

Color palettes

Color palettes are schemes for the text and graphs of ad units that Google provides so that your ad units will work well with your site. These color schemes, as you can see in Figure 8-7, have fanciful names, like Wicked Witch and Black Night.

Figure 8-7. *You can choose from a number of existing color schemes, called a color palette, for your ad unit*

The best way to see which (if any) of these color palettes is right for a given web page or site is to run through the list of possibilities in the drop-down list shown in Figure 8-7. When you select a color palette, an example showing the appearance of the ad elements using that scheme will display.

 You can select multiple palettes by holding down the Control key (Windows) or Command key (Mac). If you do this, the ad display will rotate using the palettes you've selected.

You can also create your own color palettes from scratch, if nothing that is available out of the box meets the needs of your site (see "Custom Ad Colors" later in this chapter for details).

What Color Choice Works Best?

There's a lot of discussion in webmaster circles about what AdSense color (or color palette) choice works best. Ultimately, nobody really knows; it is different for different sites, and experimenting and watching the results make sense.

That said, there are two circulating theories that have strong advocates (but happen to be contradictory):

- Use the color palette to match your site (if you do this, it is speculated, some users may click on the ads because they think they are part of your site, not ads).
- Make a color choice that starkly contrasts with your site (by doing this, the ads are made more noticeable, and thus it is more likely that they may be clicked).

Alternate URL or color

If Google doesn't have an ad to display on your web page—because it hasn't figured out what would be contextually relevant, or because there's nothing in the Google ad inventory that matches your content—Google will display a public service ad of its choice. There's nothing wrong, in my opinion, with public service ads, and personally I always elect to display them. However, some webmasters do not like to give away their "real estate" without getting something in return.

You can change the behavior of a Google ad unit when it doesn't have an ad to serve by choosing either an alternate URL or a color code (Figure 8-8). The obvious use for an alternate URL is to use it to link to a standby ad of your own, so that the real estate occupied on your site by the Google ad unit can be productive even when Google doesn't have any ads to serve. The Color code box is used to enter a color specification in hexadecimal RGB notation. To get the hexadecimal for a color, you can click the Choose a color link. Select the color you'd like from a palette and Google will supply the hexadecimal code. This color will be displayed in the Google unit when there is no ad to serve.

Figure 8-8. If you choose an alternate URL, or a color code, Google will not display public service ads

 The best use for the color alternative is to specify the background color of your site. That way, if Google doesn't have an ad to serve, the Google ad unit will not be visible—it will just look like part of your site background.

Selecting a channel

Channels are a mechanism for keeping track of which part of a site—or which site if you are managing multiple sites in one AdSense account—is generating clicks. *Custom channels* are channels that you define in advance of ad deployment. A Google unit can be assigned to a custom channel you've created, as shown in Figure 8-9.

Figure 8-9. Custom channels are user-defined and can help you keep track of pages and groups of pages and their click throughs

In addition to custom channels, *URL channels*, which tracks ad-unit clicks by URL, can help you keep track of how your Google ad and link units are doing. See "Using Channels" later in this chapter for more information about channels.

Putting the ad on a frame

HTML frames allow publishers to present documents in multiple views, which may be independent windows or subwindows. One view may be kept visible while other views are scrolled or replaced. An HTML page made up of frames (views), called a frameset, is defined using the <frameset> tag. The location of each view is specified in a <frame> tag.

If you intend to put your Google ad unit on a page that is part of an HTML frameset, it is important that you ensure the ad will be placed on a framed page box.

Frames are pretty unpopular these days among people who construct web sites because users can find them irritating and they sometimes don't work well with web browsers.

Grabbing the Code

With your Google unit selections made, it's time to grab the code for your unit and place it in your web page.

Ad unit example

Suppose you decided to create a Leaderboard (728×90) ad unit using the Steely Gaze palette (otherwise accepting the default options from Google). The next step is to click the code box shown in Figure 8-10 to select and then copy the code for the unit you have specified.

> **Your AdSense code**
>
> Click anywhere in this box to select all code.
>
> You may copy-and-paste the code into any web page that complies with our program policies.
>
> ```
> <script type="text/javascript"><!--
> google_ad_client = "pub-xxxxxxxxxxxxxxx";
> google_ad_width = 728;
> google_ad_height = 90;
> google_ad_format = "728x90_as";
> google_ad_type = "text_image";
> google_ad_channel ="2144598502";
> google_color_border = "CCCCCC";
> google_color_bg = "FFFFFF";
> google_color_link = "000000";
> google_color_url = "666666";
> google_color_text = "333333";
> ```

Figure 8-10. The next step is to copy and paste the code from the box into your web page

Here's the complete code for the ad unit:

```
<script type="text/javascript"><!--
google_ad_client = "pub-XXXXXXXXXXXX";
google_ad_width = 728;
google_ad_height = 90;
google_ad_format = "728x90_as";
google_ad_type = "text_image";
google_ad_channel ="2144598502";
google_color_border = "CCCCCC";
google_color_bg = "FFFFFF";
```

```
google_color_link = "000000";
google_color_url = "666666";
google_color_text = "333333";
//--></script>
<script type="text/javascript"
  src="http://pagead2.googlesyndication.com/pagead/show_ads.js">
</script>
```

 The actual Google publisher ID has been replaced with Xs in this example.

If you look at the code that makes up this Google ad unit, it is really a very simple affair, built using JavaScript. First, a variety of variables are set, such as the ad size, colors, and publisher ID. Next, a remote script on Google's server, *show_ads.js*, is called. This script generates the HTML for the ads that are displayed on your page.

 It's best to place AdSense code within includes so you can modify one file and have the changes displayed simultaneously on many pages. See Chapter 1 for more information on using includes for your advertising.

Figure 8-11 shows the Leaderboard ad unit displayed with ads on a web page.

Figure 8-11. The Leaderboard ad unit is displayed on this web page

Link unit example

Suppose you decided to display a link unit with five links, 200 × 90, in the Black and Blue palette (otherwise accepting the default options). Here's the code AdSense would generate for you to copy and paste:

```
<script type="text/javascript"><!--
google_ad_client = "pub-XXXXXXXXXXXXXXXX";
google_ad_width = 200;
google_ad_height = 90;
google_ad_format = "200x90_0ads_al_s";
google_ad_channel ="2144598502";
google_color_border = "000000";
```

```
google_color_bg = "F0F0F0";
google_color_link = "0000FF";
google_color_url = "008000";
google_color_text = "000000";
//--></script>
<script type="text/javascript"
  src="http://pagead2.googlesyndication.com/pagead/show_ads.js">
</script>
```

Paste the link unit code into an include file, copy the include file to your server, and modify your content pages so they include the link unit file. The link unit will then appear on your site, hardly taking up any space at all, and just look like more links, as shown in Figure 8-12. If you click on one of the links in the link unit, a Google page consisting of contextual ads will open (Figure 8-13).

Custom Ad Colors

The Ad Colors page can be opened by clicking the Ad Colors link on the Ad Settings tab or from the Manage color palettes link on the Ad code layout page.

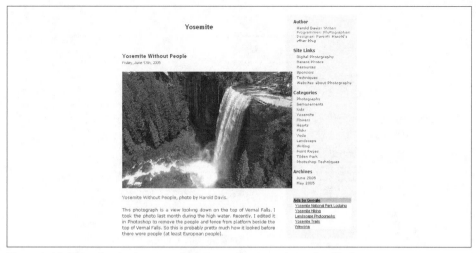

Figure 8-12. This ad unit, shown on the lower right, consists simply of links

Figure 8-13. The links in each link unit open a page of contextual ads

Using the AdColors page, you start with one of the built-in Google palettes. Next, you can modify each of the colored elements of the palette, either by specifying an RGB hexadecimal color value or by choosing colors from a color picker (see Figure 8-14).

Once you have the color scheme you want, you can save your custom palette (using any name you'd like). Your custom palette will be added to the list on the Ad layout page (Figure 8-15), which opens if you click Save and get code.

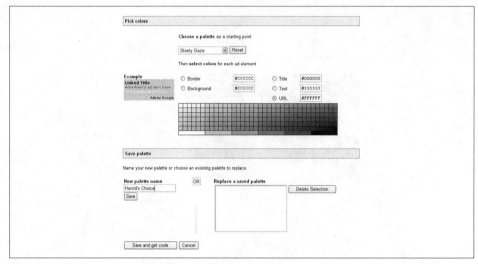

Figure 8-14. Creating your own custom palettes makes it easy to match the design of your site

Figure 8-15. Custom palettes are available on the Ad layout code page

Using Channels

The Channels page, opened by clicking the Channels link on the Ad Settings tab, lets you define URL and custom channels.

URL channels are tracked by web address, and you can add these at any point. You can use URL channels to track a single page, a directory in a domain, or an entire domain. For example, the URL channel `www.digitalfieldguide.com` will track ads served and clicked on this URL and ads on any page below that address (for example, ads on pages in *www.digitalfieldguide.com/blog/*). In contrast, the URL channel `www.digitalfieldguide.com/index.php` tracks activity only on the page *index.php*. Figure 8-16 shows the interface for creating and managing URL channels.

> For information about using URL channel information to understand your Google AdSense activity, see Chapter 9.

Custom channels are not limited by the domain and directory structure of your web server and track activity from an ad unit—wherever it is located—that is linked to the custom channel. The catch is that for this to work, you need to have created the

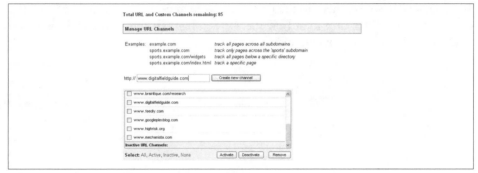

Figure 8-16. URL channels track activity by web address, so you can use them to monitor impressions and clicks on specific pages, directories, and domains

custom channel and associated the ad unit with that channel *before* deploying the ad unit. In contrast, you can always add a URL channel (but URL channels are not flexible in terms of the information they report).

 The need to specify a custom URL channel before you deploy your ad code is a serious drawback. Things do change often and quickly on the Web. Adding, or changing, custom channels means changing the actual ad unit code in your pages.

Figure 8-17 shows the interface used to create custom channels.

Figure 8-17. Custom channels must be defined before they can be deployed but can be used for granular ad unit tracking

Applying Competitive Filters

Some times it's a good idea to filter ads so that they *don't* appear on your site. The most common reason for doing this is to make sure that competitors' ads don't appear on your site, but you might also simply want to make sure that ads from organizations you find offensive don't appear beside your web content.

To block ads, based on their destination URL, from appearing on your site, click the Competitive Ad Filter link found on the Ad Settings tab. Enter the addresses you want to ban in the box shown in Figure 8-18.

Figure 8-18. You can easily filter out ads from your competitors or that you find offensive

---

Finding That Offensive URL

Suppose an AdSense ad appears on your site that you really don't like and want to ban. How do you determine what URL to use in the Competitive Ad Filters dialog to exclude the ad?

Following these steps will let you find the URL you need to ban:

1. Right-click the ad title (the portion of the ad that is a hyperlink).
2. If you are using Internet Explorer, select Copy Shortcut. On Mozilla or FireFox, the command will be something like Copy Link Location.
3. Paste the selection into a text editor like Notepad.
4. The destination URL for the ad will appear following the `adurl=` portion of the URL, and continue up to the ampersand (&).

For example, if the pasted selection is something like this (portions of the ad string have been omitted):

```
http://pagead2.googlesyndication.com/pagead/adclick?sa=l&...&adurl=http://www.
competitiontermite.com&client=...
```

then the destination URL is *http://www.competitiontermite.com*.

AdSense Search Settings

To get the code for placing a search box on your web pages, click the Search Settings tab followed by the Search Code link. On the Search Code page, enter your site language from a drop-down list and select your country.

Web Search Boxes

To add a web search box, make sure Google Search is selected, as in Figure 8-19. There are a few simple choices you can make about the layout of your search box, and you can also decide to exclude adult content from searches by enabling SafeSearch. When you are satisfied with your search box selections, click Update Code.

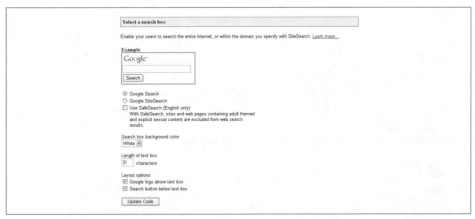

Figure 8-19. Google web search boxes give you some layout choices, along with the possibility of filtering adult content from your searches

Site Search Boxes

The site search box is a nifty alternative to Google's web search box. You can set this box up in a number of different ways, depending upon the options you choose:

- Users can search the Web using Google.
- Users can search the Web *and* additionally search within one to three domains that you designate.

Google can only return results from pages it has indexed, so the site search box results of your domains will only be as good as Google's job of indexing your site.

To implement a search box, choose the Google SiteSearch radio button (rather than the Google Search button), as shown in Figure 8-20.

Next, enter the domains you would like the ability to search (from one to three, separated by semicolons). Make your selections of graphic elements, and click Update Code.

Figure 8-20. You can include up to three domains as sites to search

 With both search and site search boxes, as with ad units, you can use channels—in this case called *search channels*—to track the performance of your search boxes. You can also apply competitive search filters to block ads from specific URLs from appearing on the pages generated by your search results.

Getting Simple Search Code

Scroll down to the bottom of the Search Code page, and select and copy the Google search box code. For example, for a site search box, the code would look more or less like this:

```
<!-- SiteSearch Google -->
<form method="get" action="http://www.google.com/custom" target="google_window">
<table border="0" bgcolor="#ffffff">
<tr><td nowrap="nowrap" valign="top" align="left" height="32">
<a href="http://www.google.com/">
<img src="http://www.google.com/logos/Logo_25wht.gif"
border="0" alt="Google"></img></a>
</td>
<td nowrap="nowrap">
<input type="hidden" name="domains" value="www.braintique.com ;
www.digitalfieldguide.com ; www.googleplexblog.com"></input>
<input type="text" name="q" size="31" maxlength="255" value=""></input>
<input type="submit" name="sa" value="Search"></input>
</td></tr>
<tr>
<td> </td>
<td nowrap="nowrap">
<table>
<tr>
```

```
<td>
<input type="radio" name="sitesearch" value="" checked="checked"></input>
<font size="-1" color="#000000">Web</font>
</td>
<td>
<input type="radio" name="sitesearch" value="YOUR DOMAIN NAME"></input>
<font size="-1" color="#000000">YOUR DOMAIN NAME</font>
</td>
</tr>
</table>
<input type="hidden" name="client" value="pub-XXXXXXXXXXXX"></input>
<input type="hidden" name="forid" value="1"></input>
<input type="hidden" name="ie" value="ISO-8859-1"></input>
<input type="hidden" name="oe" value="ISO-8859-1"></input>
<input type="hidden" name="cof"
value="GALT:#008000;GL:1;DIV:#336699;VLC:663399;AH:center;BGC:FFFFFF;LBGC:336699;
ALC:0000FF;LC:0000FF;T:000000;GFNT:0000FF;GIMP:0000FF;FORID:1;"></input>
<input type="hidden" name="hl" value="en"></input>

</td></tr></table>
</form>
<!-- SiteSearch Google -->
```

As you can see, internally the site search box is implemented as an HTML form and table. If you copy this code into your web site, you'll see a search box that allows you to search the Web (or specific domains) like the one shown in Figure 8-21.

Figure 8-21. With a site search box, users can search the Web, or the specific domains you chose

If your site visitors use this box to search the Web or your domains, the page that Google returns will carry ads that are contextually relevant to the search. If the visitor clicks on one of them, you'll make some money.

Working with Search Styles

Google has made some effort to help you customize the search page that visitors see when they search using the Web or site search boxes. After all, in some sense the search results page—particularly if you are using site search to search through your own domain—is an extension of your content, even if Google is serving it.

To customize the search results page that visitors will see when they use your Google search or site search boxes, click the Styles link on the Search Settings tab to open the Search Styles page.

On the Search Styles page, choose a built-in palette as the starting place, and select a color for each element of the page (Figure 8-22).

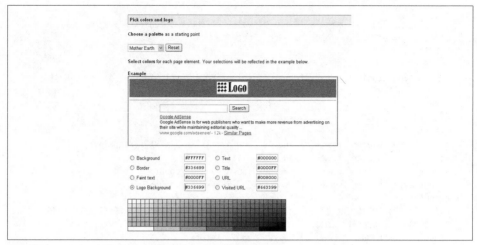

Figure 8-22. You can pick the color scheme for your search results page

Next, you can specify a logo (by location) to appear on the search results page (see Figure 8-23). This logo can be used to click back through to your site, so it's a good thing to provide, because it helps you keep control of your traffic.

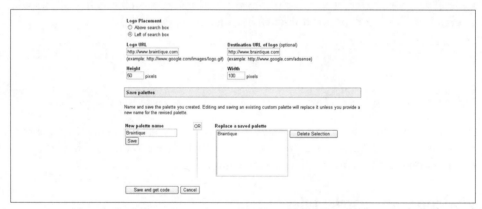

Figure 8-23. The search results page template is saved as a "palette"

Finally, name and save the scheme for the search results page (Figure 8-24).

> If you click the Save and get code button, the Search Code page will open with your custom palette selected.

Your custom palette will now appear on the list of palettes in the Search Code page (Figure 8-24). Select it, and click the Update Code button to get the new code for your search box. Copy and paste the code into the code in your web pages.

Figure 8-24. The custom palette appears in the Search Code page list of palettes

Now, when visitors use the Google web or site search box, the results page that they see will be customized with your choice of colors and, if you specified one, your logo (see Figure 8-25).

Figure 8-25. With the custom palette selected, your color scheme and logo are used to create the search results page

Action Items

To start making money with AdSense:

- Apply, and get accepted by Google's AdSense program.
- File an IRS form W-9 (or other appropriate tax form) with Google.
- Generate AdSense for Content ad and link unit code for your site.
- Place the code in your pages, preferably within includes.
- Add AdSense web and site search boxes to your site.
- Create a custom search results page that echoes the look and feel of your site.

CHAPTER 9

Making Sense of AdSense

Putting AdSense code on your web pages is only the beginning to making money with Google AdSense advertising. Once you've added AdSense Content and AdSense Search to your pages, you need to know how well your AdSense revenue is doing in relationship to how well it could be doing. Monitoring your performance so you can make changes to make more money is a very important part of successfully working with AdSense.

This chapter explains the reporting and performance tracking tools available in the AdSense program and what you should be looking for in terms of performance.

Ad Performance

When you log into AdSense from the AdSense home page at *https://www.google.com/ adsense/* (after your account is up and running and you have ads on your site), the first thing you'll see is the Reports Overview window, with the current day's earnings displayed, as shown in Figure 9-1.

 Clicking one of the AdSense for content or AdSense for search links shown at the bottom of Figure 9-1 opens the Advanced Report tab for content or search preloaded with the specified report.

Click the top channels link shown in Figure 9-1 to see the statistics for your top-performing channels (Figure 9-2).

When you click the Advanced Reports–Ad Performance link (Figure 9-1) or the view all AdSense for content channels link (Figure 9-2), the Advanced Reports window opens, as shown in Figure 9-3. This is used to monitor your performance in the AdSense Content program.

Figure 9-1. When you open AdSense, you'll see your page impressions, clicks, and earnings for the current day

Figure 9-2. The top channels display lets you see at a glance which of your channels are performing

To monitor your AdSense search results, click the Search Performance link on the Reports tab.

It's quite appropriate that the Ad Performance statistics should be the first thing you see in the AdSense application, because as an AdSense publisher, you need to keep a close watch on these statistics. This chapter goes into the details of slicing and dicing the information you can get from the Report screen, but let's start with the mile-high view first.

The most important statistic for you to pay attention to is the *Page CTR* (or *Page click-through rate*). This statistic measures what percentage of ads are clicked. Page CTR should be in the 0.5% to 2% range (meaning from 1 to 4 of every 200 ads are clicked). As you'll see when you learn about the AdWords program in Chapter 10, a 2% CTR is a home run; it's more normal to expect something slightly below 1%.

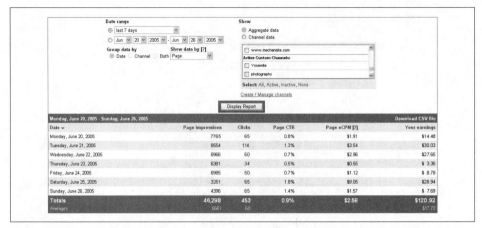

Figure 9-3. You can see at a glance how many times your pages have been displayed (page impressions) and how many people have clicked on the Google ads on your pages

Click-through rates are higher for ads displayed on Google search results pages than they are on web content pages, perhaps because it is easier to serve really relevant ads when people are searching for something specific rather than simply surfing web pages.

If your CTR is consistently below 0.5% for more than a day or two, meaning that fewer than 1 in 200 ads are clicked, then you need to take remedial action—fast! Your traffic is going to waste.

Most likely, the problem is that Google is not able to accurately serve relevant ads on your pages, because you haven't written the pages to make clear the most important content they contain (see Chapter 3 for information about how to fix this). Try tweaking your pages to emphasize their significant content areas. In addition, try changing the position on your page of the AdSense ad units, the kind of ad units, and the graphic schemes used in these ad units (see Chapter 8 for information about changing ad units and their palettes). Carefully monitor the Reports tab to see which of these measures improves your CTR.

You should also be monitoring your comparative performance. Over time—using fairly broad time slices such as weeks or months—is the absolute number of impressions going up (or down)? And what about CTR? If either the number of impressions or your CTR is declining, you should be concerned and consider revisiting your ad layouts and site content and positioning.

Running Reports

The Ad Performance interface is designed to generate reports. To generate a report, pick your date range, select page or unit impressions, choose aggregate versus channel data (and select your channels), and click Display Report.

 The initial AdSense settings are to display an aggregate, page unit report for the current day. When you log into AdSense subsequently, it displays the settings for the most recent report you ran. The best idea probably is to generate daily reports to get a sense of how your AdSense account is doing in real time. You may also want to generate weekly and monthly reports to get a more long-term perspective.

Choosing a date range

You can choose any data range you'd like, by date, from the inception of your AdSense account to the current point in time, all using the interface shown in Figure 9-4; or you can choose one of the preset time spans that Google always has available.

Figure 9-4. You can choose a preset time span or a date range

The preset time spans are:

- Today
- Yesterday
- 2 days ago
- Last 7 days
- This month
- Last month
- This week (Monday–Sunday)
- Last week (Monday–Sunday)
- Last business week (Monday–Friday)
- All time

 The "all time" preset time period means from the beginning of your AdSense account through the current day; it does not include the age of the dinosaurs or the birth of the Roman Empire.

Page or unit impressions

Google lets you put up to three AdSense ad units, plus one link unit, on a single page; accordingly, you can display impressions (the number of times something is displayed) by either page or unit, using the drop-down list shown in Figure 9-5.

Figure 9-5. Individual ad unit impressions are likely to be a higher number than page impressions, because you can have more than one ad unit per page

 If you put a single ad unit on each of your pages, then displaying data by page or unit will show the same thing.

It's easy to be tempted to throw four AdSense units (three ad units and one link unit) up on each of your pages, but try to resist this temptation. Experienced webmasters generally find that CTR goes down as pages become too loaded with ads, even AdSense ads.

Aggregate versus channel data

You can choose to display AdSense data for your entire account by selecting the Aggregate data radio button shown in Figure 9-6.

Figure 9-6. If you display data by channel, you can choose from URL channels or from Custom channels

Alternatively, you can select Channel data to show as many or as few channels as you'd like.

 As explained in Chapter 8, URL channels display information from the specified web address. In contrast, Custom channels can be applied to whichever ad units you'd like to group together—for example, they can span multiple domains and not include all units in those domains—but must be specified before the ad units are created and included in the ad unit code.

When you are showing data by Channel, you can use the Group data by radio buttons to display statistics organized by date, channel, or grouped using both.

Statistics

A famous aphorism says, "There are three kinds of lies: lies, damn lies, and statistics," meaning you can support any statement, and sound authoritative, so long as you quote statistics. Fortunately, the statistics shown in an AdSense Ad Performance report are simple enough that they are hard to misinterpret, but you should be clear about the terminology used.

Each report will show you daily statistics (each of these is a column in the AdSense report, as shown in Figure 9-7):

Impressions
> An *ad impression* is recorded each time an AdSense ad unit is displayed. A *page impression* is recorded each time a web page containing an AdSense ad unit is displayed. A single display of a web page containing three ad units would produce one page impression and three ad impressions.

Clicks
> A visitor's click on an ad on a publisher's page. Public service ad clicks are not included in this statistic.

> Google reserves the right to audit clicks and retroactively remove clicks that it deems invalid, for example, if Google finds you have been clicking ads on your own pages. These clicks will show up in the report that is displayed, even though you won't make any money from them.

CTR
> CTR (click-through rate) the number of clicks an ad unit receives divided by the number of times the ad unit is displayed (ad unit impressions).

eCPM
> eCPM—effective CPM (cost per thousand impressions)—is calculated by dividing the total earnings by the number of impressions in thousands. For example, if a publisher earned $100 from 20,000 impressions, the eCPM would equal $100/20, or $5.00. The point of this metric is to provide a way to compare AdSense's CPC revenue with the money you might make from other forms of advertising, namely CPM (see Chapter 5 for more information about CPM advertising).

Your earnings
> This column shows your earnings, either in aggregate or for selected channels. These are not final numbers, and may be subject to adjustments. (See "Your Earnings" later in this chapter for information about final earnings numbers.)

The Point of eCPM

eCPM is related to CTR—the higher the CTR, the better the eCPM comparison. Google includes this metric as a way to compare apples to apples—AdSense CPC with conventional CPM advertising—and stacks the deck slightly in its own favor while doing so. (I would, too, if I had a program that delivers as well as AdSense.)

The normal cost of CPM advertising is in the $3 to $4 ballpark. If you have a reasonable CTR (anything better than about 1.5%), your eCPM will demonstrate that you are doing significantly better than you would have with conventional CPM advertising.

Monday, June 20, 2005 - Sunday, June 26, 2005					Download CSV file
Date ▾	Page impressions	Clicks	Page CTR	Page eCPM [?]	Your earnings
Monday, June 20, 2005	776	6	0.8%	$1.91	$1.48
Tuesday, June 21, 2005	855	11	1.3%	$3.54	$3.03
Wednesday, June 22, 2005	896	6	0.7%	$2.96	$2.65
Thursday, June 23, 2005	638	3	0.5%	$0.55	$0.35
Friday, June 24, 2005	698	5	0.7%	$1.12	$0.78
Saturday, June 25, 2005	325	6	1.8%	$9.05	$2.94
Sunday, June 26, 2005	439	6	1.4%	$1.57	$0.69
Totals	4,627	43	0.9%	$2.58	$11.92
Averages	661	6			$1.70

Figure 9-7. You should monitor your earnings for trends and inconsistencies (such as the relatively poor result shown on Thursday of the week in this figure)

 You can sort the report by one of these columns by clicking the column header (Figure 9-5). For example, if you have a month's worth of data displayed and want to see it with the day with most clicks displayed first, clicking on Clicks will accomplish this sort.

Downloading a CSV File

You can download the data in your AdSense report by clicking the Download CSV file link (shown in the upper right of Figure 9-7). The file is a plain text file formatted with comma-separated values, and it can be opened in a spreadsheet program such as Microsoft Excel (shown in Figure 9-8) for further analysis.

Search Performance

You can display an AdSense Search report in almost exactly the same way as an AdSense Content report. To generate a Search report, on the Reports tab, click the Search Performance link. You can then display a report, as shown in Figure 9-9.

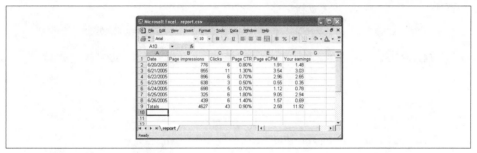

Figure 9-8. Downloading AdSense report data into Excel allows you to use the full power of Excel to manipulate and display the information

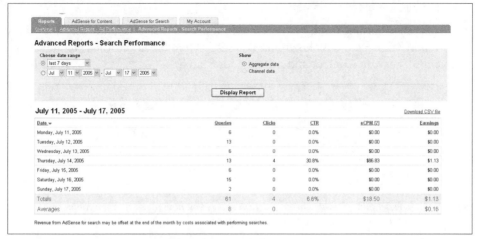

Figure 9-9. You can display reports for AdSense Search pretty much in the same way as for AdSense content

The only difference between an AdSense Search report and an AdSense Content report is that AdSense Search can't display information by unit impressions, only by page impressions (because ads are displayed on Google's search results pages, not your pages).

Your total earnings, of course, are the sum of AdSense Content and AdSsense Search earnings.

Your Earnings

To monitor your actual earnings (as opposed to your ad performance), choose the My Account tab and click the Payment History link. As you can see in Figure 9-10, you will be shown your month-by-month earnings for any time period you select.

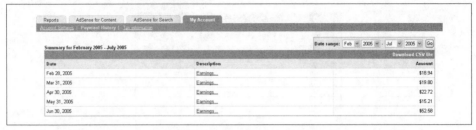

Figure 9-10. Your actual earnings are displayed on the My Account tab

Your earnings can be downloaded as a comma-separated value file (by clicking the Download CSV file link shown in the upper right of Figure 9-8). This file can be imported into Excel for further analysis.

If you click an Earnings link in the Description column for a particular month, a detail report (an example is shown in Figure 9-11) will break out the revenue source between AdSense for Content and AdSense for Search.

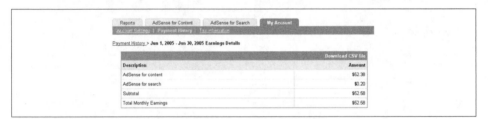

Figure 9-11. The detailed monthly earnings screen shows you how much revenue came from AdSense for Content, and how much from AdSense for Search

 Detailed monthly information can also be downloaded as a CSV file.

Tools Beyond AdSense for Tracking

"Trust, but verify" is an excellent motto in life. It's nice to have independent verification of Google's numbers and also better analysis tools of visitor behavior than the AdSense reports provide.

To get third-party information about your traffic, a good starting place is to visit Alexa, *http://www.alexa.com*. On Alexa, click the Traffic Rankings tab. Enter your site domain in the box, and click Get Traffic Details. The Related Info page for your site will open. Next, in the Explore this Site box, click the Traffic Details link.

A number of different measures of your site traffic, including the daily page views graph shown in Figure 9-12, will be displayed.

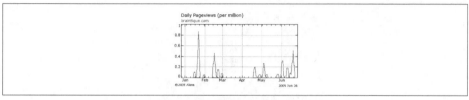

Figure 9-12. Alexa can help give you an idea of how many daily page views your site receives

You can use the Alexa metrics as a reality check in terms of whether it agrees with Google that your page views are going up (or down) over time, but you cannot use Alexa as an absolute measure of anything because of how the Alexa statistics are compiled. Alexa's page-view metrics are based on information uploaded from a small toolbar, mostly installed by business users. This information is notoriously flawed for consumer sites, particularly ones without high traffic.

The next place to turn is your web server's logs.

Listening to Web Logs

Depending on your web host, you should have access to a number of tools used to generate usable information from your web logs files.

 Raw web log files provide copious and dense information, but it is hard to extract anything usable from them.

Webalizer, shown providing monthly statistics in Figure 9-13, is available for almost all sites that are hosted on a Linux-based web server. If your web host doesn't make Webalizer available to you, it almost surely will provide comparable software.

Web Log Analysis Programs

There are many good web log analysis programs available with much the same functionality as Webalizer, the one shown in this section. Popular offerings include Access Watch, Microsoft Web Trend Analytics, ModLogAn, NetTracker, and WebTrends.

Many of these programs are free; others, such as WebTrends, which offers additional facilities for tracking visitors through your site as explained in "Web Analytic Software" later in this chapter, are fee-based.

Which web log analysis program you have access to depends upon the operating system of your web server and (assuming you are working with a web hosting company to serve your web pages) the software made available by your web host.

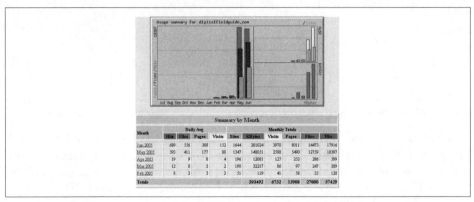

Figure 9-13. Webalizer uses your web logs to display accurate statistics about your site

You can use the Webalizer summary shown in Figure 9-11 to verify Google's accounting of your page views. Next, click a specific month to get more detailed information about a whole range of topics, including:

- Daily usage (Figure 9-14)
- Hourly usage
- Top URLs on your site (your pages that have the most visitors)
- Top entry pages on your site (the pages most often used as the entry point to your domain)
- Top exit pages on your site (the pages most often used as the exit point for leaving your domain, Figure 9-15)
- Top referrer pages (the pages, by address, that have referred the most traffic to your site, Figure 9-16)
- Top search strings used (in search engines) to find your site (Figure 9-17)

A great deal of the information that is provided is quite valuable. You should certainly keep an eye on daily usage statistics (Figure 9-14).

You probably already have a good idea of your entry pages, the pages that visitors first open when they access your site (but it's still a good idea to verify this information with your web log analysis tool). These pages are also often called *landing* pages. But you may not know about your top exit pages—the last page a visitor opens in your site—shown in Webalizer in Figure 9-15.

Exit pages are significant because you may wish to make an attempt to keep traffic on your site on the top exit pages, for example, with an "Are you sure you want to leave" message. More importantly, studies have shown that exit pages are a particularly good place to site AdSense ads. The logic is your visitors are ready to leave your site anyhow, so they are likely to be more willing to click on a link in an ad. Therefore, it makes sense to pay special attention to your top exit pages when you tweak your AdSense content ads.

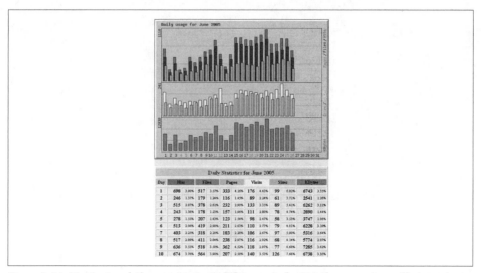

Figure 9-14. Monitoring daily usage statistics helps you make sure that your site traffic is staying steady or gaining

	Top 10 of 153 Total Exit Pages		
#	Hits	Visits	URL
1	1703	9.51%	925	23.57%	/blog/
2	1148	6.41%	888	22.62%	/blog/feed/
3	966	5.39%	581	14.80%	/
4	463	2.58%	318	8.10%	/blog/feed/atom/
5	104	0.50%	57	1.45%	/blog/entries/yosemite/
6	89	0.50%	44	1.12%	/blog/26
7	42	0.23%	26	0.66%	/blog/50
8	33	0.18%	22	0.56%	/blog/14
9	50	0.28%	21	0.54%	/blog/date/2005/06/
10	46	0.26%	20	0.51%	/blog/entries/yoda/

Figure 9-15. Exit pages are the final page viewed in your domain before leaving your site

Referrers are sites that refer traffic to you. It's good to know where your traffic is coming from. Figure 9-16 shows some top referrers for the site *www.digitalfieldguide. com.*

The first entry shown in Figure 9-16, Direct Request, represents visitors who simply entered the URL for the site in their browser and didn't come via a link from another site.

Using information about your top referrers, you can work to strengthen your relationship with these referrers and also consider if there are other sites like a particular referrer that you might be able to approach for traffic (see Chapter 2 for advice about how to approach a site).

Figure 9-17 shows a table of the top search strings used in search engines to find your site.

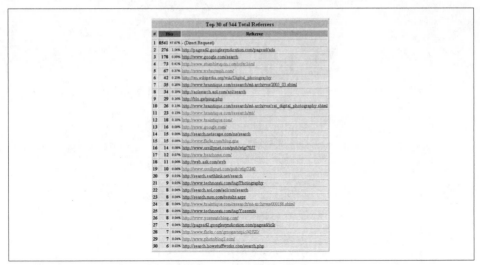

Figure 9-16. The top referrer table helps you to know where your traffic is coming from

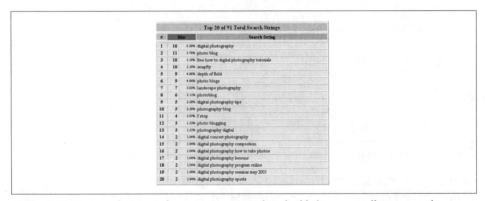

Figure 9-17. Top search string information is extremely valuable because it allows you to hone your site content

Knowing the top search strings used to find your site is extraordinarily valuable to an AdSense publisher. Honing your site to provide information relevant to these searches sets you up to benefit from a virtuous circle: more targeted information draws better search engine rankings for these queries, which in turn draw more traffic and at the same time generate better click-through rates because it's easier for Google's contextual engine to figure out what your site is about.

As you can see, there's a great deal of information to be had from your web log data, and it is important to keep on top of it to get the most revenue out of the AdSense program. Pay particular attention to the overall direction of traffic volume, the flow of traffic through your site via entrance and exit pages, and top referrers and search strings.

Web Analytic Software

When your web log software is not enough, because you really need to understand visitor behavior in detail through your site, it's time to turn to web analytic software such as Urchin (now owned by Google), *http://www.urchin.com*, and WebTrends, *http://www.webtrends.com* (which also does web log analysis). These are relatively expensive software packages. WebTrends is available as a standalone product (you install it on your web server) or as a hosted solution. Urchin is only available as a hosted solution.

 In a hosted solution, you add a small bit of code to your pages—much in the way Google AdSense works—and the software company takes care of the rest.

This sophisticated category of software can be used to track almost everything about every visitor to your site. For example, Urchin will also tell you how many people bounced off your landing page, meaning they didn't go beyond the first page of your site. If you have a high bounce-off rate, you need to know it so you can redesign your site to pull visitors in.

 If you are using AdWords to advertise and are selling a product, as I explain in Part III, a key feature in Urchin allows you to track how many visitors are converted into customers and what they buy, and even which link they clicked to make the purchase.

Action Items

If you are enrolled in the AdSense program, you should track your progress by:

- Regularly displaying reports—perhaps as often as daily—to monitor your AdSense Content and Search performance
- Using Custom or URL channels to display results to get a better handle on performance on different parts of your site
- Learning to use the web log analysis programs available to you to get a better understanding of how your site is performing in relation to the AdSense program

PART III

Working with AdWords

Chapters 10–12 explain the nuts and bolts, and metrics, of the Google AdWords program, a highly successful mechanism that anybody with a valid credit card can use to place advertisements that reach over 80% of users of the Internet.

CHAPTER 10

Using AdWords

Google's AdWords program is a marvelous way for big and small advertisers to reach precisely the people they would like to reach. Ads placed via AdWords are almost always relevant to people viewing the ads; the ads are targeted using keywords selected by the advertiser and placed on Google search results pages where users have searched for these keywords (AdWords *search network*) or on web pages that publish content including the targeted keywords (AdWords *content network*). In addition, it's estimated that ads placed using AdWords reach more than 80% of all Internet users.

Unlike old-fashioned advertising, the AdWords delivery mechanism is completely managed from the Web and can be used by anyone who has a credit card. There's not even a minimum budget. You can design effective AdWords campaigns that drive traffic to your site for just pennies a day; of course, it always helps to have a bigger budget!

This chapter explains how to open an AdWords account and how to create ad campaigns, ad groups, and keyword-targeted ads. Although the mechanics of the AdWords program can appear a little daunting at first, after reading this chapter you'll be armed with the information you need to create sophisticated and cost-effective targeted web ads.

Signing up for an Account

To create an AdWords account, start by opening the Google AdWords home page at *https://adwords.google.com/select/*. Open an account using the Click to Begin button under the Sign Up Now headline (Figure 10-1).

Targeting Customers

The first window that opens involves targeting customers (Figure 10-2).

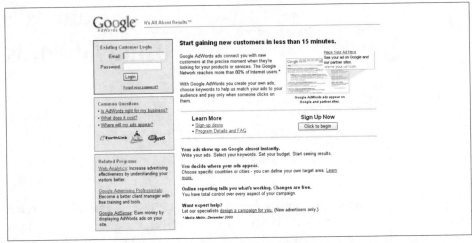

Figure 10-1. Google makes it very easy to sign up for AdWords

Opening an AdWords Account by Working Backwards

As you'll see, while Google makes it pretty easy to sign up for an AdWords account, the whole process can seem a little backwards: you go through the steps to create an initial ad and then finally—at the end of the process—provide contact information and establish your account. Once your account has been established, but before your ad is run, you provide your credit card information.

If you are like me, it would probably feel more natural to do this in reverse order: first establish an account with your credit card so you can get to understand the various account options and then set up your first ad. Alas, that's not an option, so backwards it is for now.

This window is used to provide a name for the Ad Group you are creating (see the nearby sidebar "Ad Campaigns and Ad Groups" for more on Google's AdWords terminology).

Next, choose a language for your ad from the long list of available languages in the Target customers by language drop-down list.

You can target multiple languages by holding the Control key (Windows) or the Command key (Mac) when choosing languages from the drop-down list.

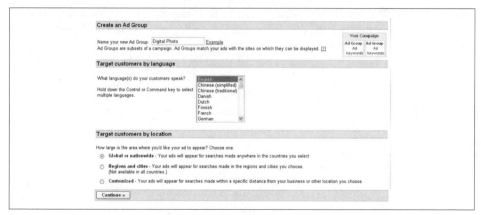

Figure 10-2. You can target customers by language and location

---

Ad Campaigns and Ad Groups

In AdWords terminology, an *Ad Campaign* is a way to group all the related ads used for a similar purpose. Using your AdWords account, you can have as many Ad Campaigns as you'd like. The concept of the "Ad Campaign" is borrowed from traditional advertising. For example, a car company might use an advertising agency to plan an ad campaign that could include television ads, print ads, Internet advertising, and product placements.

Within each AdWords campaign, you have one or more *Ad Groups*. (The relationship between Ad Campaigns and Ad Groups is shown graphically at the upper right of Figure 10-2, as well as in Figure 10-17.) Each Ad Group contains a specific ad and the keywords related to that ad. Without an Ad Group, there are no ads in a Campaign.

Finally, target a geographic area. The choices are:

- Globally, or by country
- By specific region or city
- Within a designated distance from an address or geospatial coordinate (*custom geographic targeting*)

Click Continue. The window that will open depends upon your choice of geographic targeting.

Global and national targeting

If you choose to target global or nationwide customers (the most common and simplest choice), you'll see a window with two list boxes like that shown in Figure 10-3.

The list box on the left shows the available countries you can choose from, and the list box on the right shows the countries you have selected. Use the Add and Remove buttons until you are satisfied with your selection of countries.

 The top choice in the Available Countries list box (not shown in Figure 10-3) is All Countries. If you add All Countries to the Selected Countries list box, then you are done and there are no further choices to be made.

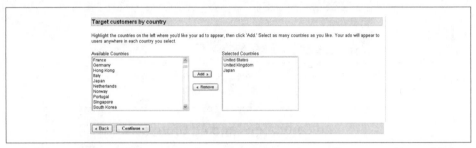

Figure 10-3. When you target customers by country, you can choose All Countries (the world) or a specific country (or countries)

Regional and city targeting

Regional and city targeting is a useful choice if you suspect that the bulk of your customers may come from a specific region or city within a country. For example, a service that supplies inflatable jumpers and slides for children's birthday parties located in the San Francisco area is unlikely to get customers from outside the Bay Area. It is likely this business will want to target only the San Francisco–Oakland–San Jose metropolitan area within California. Alternatively, some advertisers may target cities and regions as a way to reach specific demographics. For example, if you are selling agricultural products online, you may wish to target very carefully areas that do not include major cities.

Although you pay for ads only when they are clicked, targeting ads to customers for whom they are relevant still is in your best interests, because targeted ads will produce higher click throughs, and Google will give ads with a demonstrable track record of high CTRs better placement.

 Regional and city targeting is not available for all countries; for example, if you are targeting Romania, you can only target all of Romania, not regions or cities within the country. The countries currently with regional and city targeting are shown in the countries drop-down list in Figure 10-4.

Use the Add button to move regions and/or cities from the Available areas list box to the Selected areas list box shown in Figure 10-4. When you are satisfied with your selection or selections, click Continue.

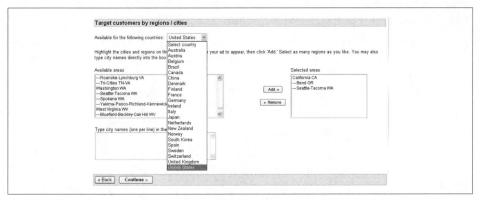

Figure 10-4. Regional targeting is available for many countries, including the United States

Custom geographic targeting

Custom geographic targeting is primarily intended to benefit businesses with a very local focus. For example, if you deliver pizza, it makes sense to limit your advertising to potential customers within your delivery area.

Targeting customers by location involves two steps (both shown in Figure 10-5):

1. Define a location (probably your business location) either by address or by latitude and longitude coordinates.

2. Specify the distance, as the radius of a circle, from the defined location for those who are to be shown the ad.

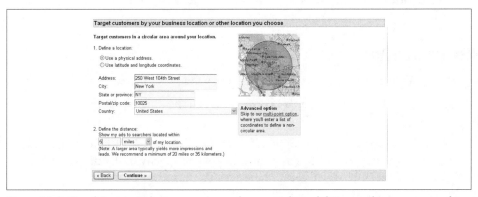

Figure 10-5. Google's extraordinary mapping and geospatial capabilities are the resources used to provide you with a number of different ways to target locations

If you are delivering pizzas, your service area may not be exactly a circle and may in fact be a highly irregular area, for example, an area comprising the communities of North Berkeley, Kensington, and Albany (all in California). To target an area based on any kind of shape, click the multipoint option link shown in Figure 10-5. The Multi-Point Option window, shown in Figure 10-6 will open.

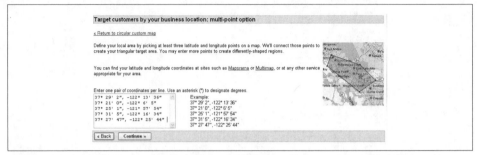

Figure 10-6. In the real world, neighborhoods containing potential customers are contained in irregular areas, and Google lets you specify these with the multipoint location option

Each of the pairs of latitude and longitude coordinates you enter in the text box shown in Figure 10-6 becomes a point in the two-dimensional shape that Google draws to target an irregular, custom area.

 A number of free online services, including Maporama, *http://www.maporama.com*, and Multimap, *http://www.multimap.com*, will tell you the latitude and longitude corresponding to any address you enter.

Whether you choose a circular custom geographic area by radius, or define a custom area using latitude/longitude points, click Continue when you are ready to move on to the next step.

Creating an Ad

The next step is to create an actual ad using the window shown in Figure 10-7.

As you can see in Figure 10-7, an ad consists of the following elements:

The Headline
> A Headline appears at the top your ad and is a hyperlink. When the user clicks the link, the user is redirected to the address you specify in the destination URL. The Headline is what will capture the eye of a prospect.

Two Description lines
> Each Description line is limited to 35 characters. The Descriptions are the heart of your ad. Once an ad's Headline has captured the attention of a prospect, it is up to the Descriptions to provide enough specific information to motivate the

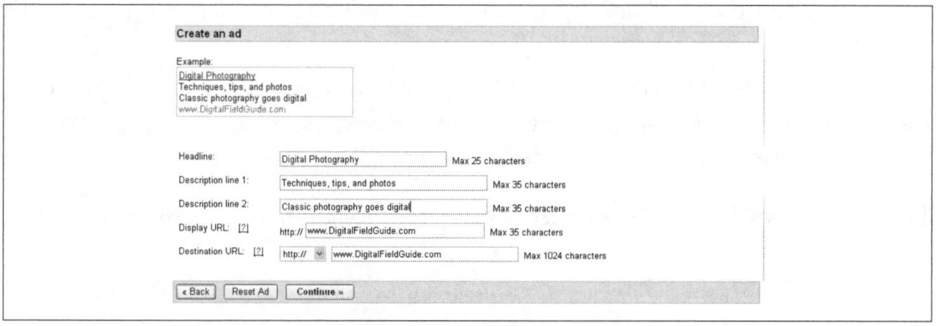

Figure 10-7. *An ad shows a headline, two descriptions lines, and a display URL*

prospect to click the hyperlink provided by the ad. It's therefore important to think through how best to achieve this goal using the 70 characters available (which is not much) in the two Description lines.

The Display URL

The Display URL is the address that shows in the displayed ad, not necessarily the one the ad links to.

The Destination URL

This is the actual address that the hyperlink associated with the Headline element of the ad sends traffic to.

When a user clicks the hyperlinked Headline on your ad, an address on one of the Google ad servers is opened. The Google ad server then automatically redirects the user to the address you specified in the Destination URL field when you created the ad. This allows Google to meter the click throughs on your ad, so that Google can assign you, the advertiser, a CPC-based charge and pay an AdSense CPC-based fee to the web site on which your ad that was clicked appeared as applicable.

Providing the ability for you to use distinct display and actual (destination) URLs also gives you some flexibility when you create your ads. For example, you can use this capability to display a single, simple URL for your site while directing click throughs on different versions of your ad to different internal portions of your site. You can also embed information in the destination URL to programmatically track where clicks are coming from (see Part IV for more information).

> Bear in mind that as soon as your account is activated your ad will start running and you will be charged for it. So, although it seems somewhat bizarre to create an ad before your account is activated, take the time to craft your first ad with care; the ad you are creating is real, and not just a trial run.

Of course, the mechanics of creating an ad are not nearly as important as understanding how to craft an ad that will get people's attention and make them want to click your link and also not violate Google's editorial policies (for more on Google's policies, see the box "Complying with Google's Editorial Guidelines" later in this chapter).

Generally, you should realize that AdWords ads are very short. Specifically, when you create an AdWords ad, you have 130 characters, including spaces and the display URL. These characters are divided as shown in Table 10-1.

Table 10-1. You need to keep the character limitation of each line in mind when you create your ads

Line	Purpose	Maximum characters
1	Headline	25
2	Text of ad	35
3	Text of ad	35
4	Display URL	35

Crafting an Ad

If you stop to think about it, these four lines, with their rigid maximum number of characters, present a writing challenge a bit like that involved in writing a formal haiku (a Japanese poetic form with three lines and a specific, limited syllable count for each line):

Fancy headline leads

Describe, interest, compel

My hyperlink: yes!

 Since the fourth line is used for the display URL, you ad really has only the 25-character headline and the 70 characters of text. This compares with the Japanese haiku convention of 5-7-5 syllables in three lines!

You'll want to abbreviate and be as succinct as possible, while still being intelligible and inviting. The best AdWords ads don't bang surfers on the head, rather they appear to provide a solid and calm way to get information or services needed by the reader of the ad (who, after all, has already been prequalified by ad targeting). Good AdWords ads are pared down to the essentials.

The following guidelines are also basic to crafting good AdWords copy:

- Try to include the keywords you targeted with the text of the ad.
- Short, clear, nonrepetitive phrases work best.
- Make sure the words in your ad are all spelled correctly.
- Identify your unique selling proposition (what makes your site special?).
- Provide a call to action ("Join our photo club!").

For example, the ad:

> Wi-Fi Antennas
>
> Large selection, good prices
>
> Immediate shipping

will probably generate a respectable click-through rate if properly targeted. The ad is clear, simple, and informative and contains an implicit call to action.

In contrast, the following ad for the same merchandise is poorly written and contains too much jargon (although perfectly acceptable under Google's editorial guidelines). Most prospects will probably be unclear about what the ad is selling and what benefits clicking the link will provide:

> Wireless Boosters Blog
>
> IEEE 802 standard devices
>
> Rectify and amplify

Complying with Google's Editorial Guidelines

AdWords provides an extensive list of "thou shall" and "thou shalt nots" when composing your ad (you can review the complete list at *https://adwords.google.com/select/guidelines.html*.) Working with Google's Editorial Guidelines can sometimes feel like working with a particularly rigid and unimaginative high school English teacher—yes, spelling and punctuation do count. Google enforces its rules with an automated check of your ad before it is accepted. In fairness, Google's rules are generally intended to make everybody's web experience better on the (probably true) premise that respect for web visitors on the part of advertisers yields better ad results.

The good news is that in some cases—for example, if Google believes you have misspelled a word when in fact you are spelling the word differently as part of your branding—you can request a waiver as part of the approval process. This waiver is automatically granted pending Google's manual review of the matter.

Here are some of the highlights of Google's editorial strictures:

- Use proper spelling and grammar.
- Ad content and keywords must directly relate to the destination web page.
- Local services must indicate their location in their ads.
- No exclamation point in the ad headline, and only one in the ad text.
- No unnecessary capitalization or repetition.
- No use of superlatives such as "best price" without third-party verification on your site.
- No universal call-to-action phrases (such as "click here") that could apply to any site (but site-specific calls to action are generally encouraged).
- The third line of text cannot reference the display URL immediately below it.

When you are satisfied with your ad, click Continue to move to the next step. After you click Continue, Google will test your ad to make sure that the URLs you supplied are valid and to see if the ad complies with editorial policies (see previous box). Assuming all is in order, the Choose keywords window will open.

Choosing Keywords

The next step is to choose the keywords or phrases that you will be running your ad against, using the window shown in Figure 10-8. The keywords or phrases you select will determine which search results pages your ad appears on. Users will see the ad when they search for the keyword or phrase in Google. If you've elected to display your ad on the Google AdSense network as well, your keywords are used by Google to determine relevancy for placement purposes. (See "Ad Groups" later in this chapter for information about targeting Google search, content, or both with an ad.)

The keywords or phrases you choose will also determine the cost of your ad. Enter the keywords you would like to target in the text box shown on the left of Figure 10-8.

 See Chapter 11 for more information about estimating the costs of an ad based on the keyword selected.

Figure 10-8. "Digital photo" and "aperture" are examples of keywords; you can even use special characters within your keywords, as "f/stop" does

If you can't think of the best words to target, or even if you think you have a pretty good idea of which keywords and phrases make the most sense for targeting your ad, it's a good idea to use the *Keyword Tool*, shown in Figure 10-9, to get additional ideas for keywords and phrases to target.

To use the Keyword Tool, once you've opened the Choose keywords window, enter a keyword or phrase in the text box on the right side of the window and click Get More Keywords. The Keyword Tool will show two lists of keywords:

More specific keywords
> These are keywords or phrases that include the keyword or phrase that you entered in the tool but are based on popular Google search queries and are more specific then your original term.

Similar keywords

> These are keywords or phrases that were searched for by users who also searched for your original term. This methodology of coming up with result B because users who liked result A (your entry point) also liked B is sometimes called *collaborative filtering* and is the basis for many recommendation engines on the Web, including the one provided to users by Amazon.

Check the boxes next to the keywords in the Keyword Tool window you would like to add to your keyword list, and click Add Selected Keywords. Next, back in the Choose Keywords window, click Continue.

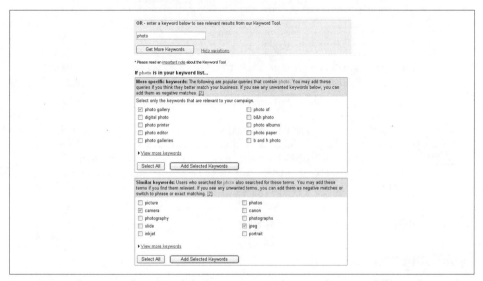

Figure 10-9. The Keyword Tool can help you come up with "more, better, or different" keywords

Setting Pricing

The next step is to set up the economics of your new ad. You'll need to:

- Choose a currency to pay for your new account
- Set a maximum cost per click for the ad (CPC)
- Set your daily budget for the ad

Google will by default set the maximum CPC, as well as a daily budget for you (you can see these settings in Figure 10-10), but most of the time you should take care to override Google's idea of the size of your wallet and set your own maximum CPC and daily budgets.

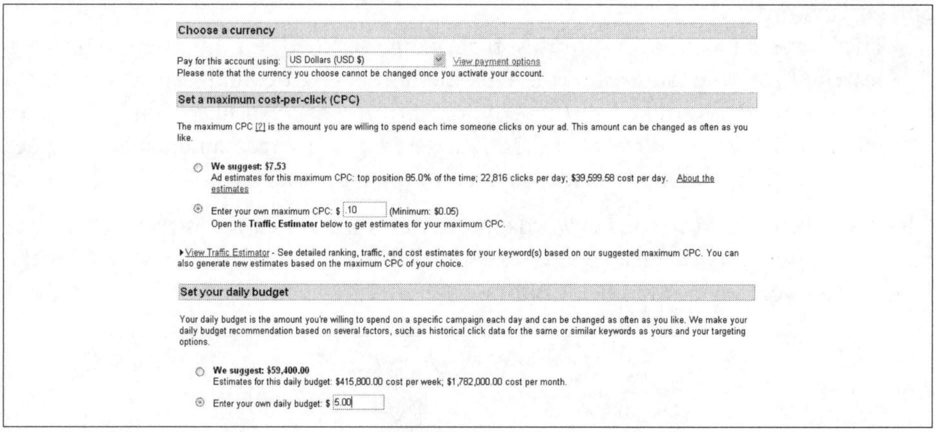

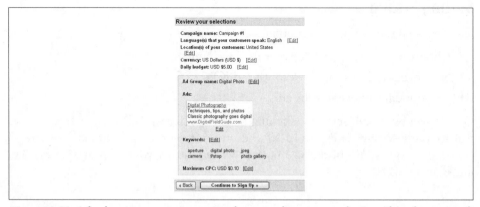

Figure 10-10. By setting a maximum cost per click (CPC) and a daily budget, you are establishing both how much you are willing to pay for a click and how much your credit card is likely to be charged

Google's suggestions are often wildly extravagant, like the suggested monthly budget of almost $1.8 million shown in Figure 10-10. Also, don't get too worried about the outsize suggestions you'll often see. Google is just trying in its crude way to be a pushy sales agent by getting you to spend more than you intend.

Click Continue to move on to the next step.

Reviewing Your Account

You now have the opportunity to review and edit your selections for your new ad group (Figure 10-11).

Figure 10-11. A final review screen gives you a chance to change your selections if you have second thoughts

When everything is the way you want it, click Continue to go on to the Sign up window.

Signing Up

In the Sign up window, shown in Figure 10-12, enter a valid email address and a password that is seven characters or longer.

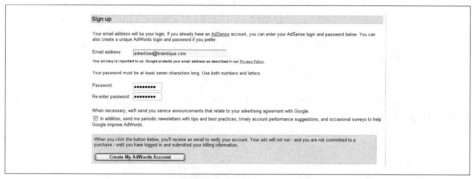

Figure 10-12. At this stage of the sign-up process, all you need to provide are a valid email address and a password

Click Create My AdWords Account. This phase of your account creation is now complete.

Providing Payment Information and Activating Your Account

Once you've created your AdWords account by completing the steps needed to create an Ad Group, and an ad, and providing a valid email address (along with a password), Google will send you an email containing a link. You must click this link to verify the email address you supplied.

After you've clicked the link to verify your email address, you can use the email you supplied and your password to log on to your AdWords account. The first time you log on, AdWords will note that your account hasn't been activated (signified by the text in the pink box at the top of Figure 10-13).

To activate your account, open the My Account tab and click the Billing Preferences link. The Account Setup window will open (Figure 10-14).

In the Account Setup window, select the country in which you (or your business) are located and click Continue.

Next, the Terms window will open. Review the AdWords terms and conditions and print a copy for your files if you like. Continue with the activation process by selecting the Yes radio button and clicking Continue. The Form of Payment window, shown in Figure 10-15, will open.

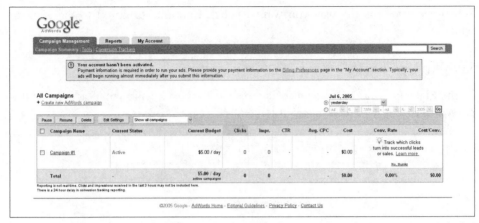

Figure 10-13. Once your email address has been validated, you can log on to your account (which hasn't yet been activated)

Figure 10-14. The first step in activating your account is to tell Google the country in which you are located

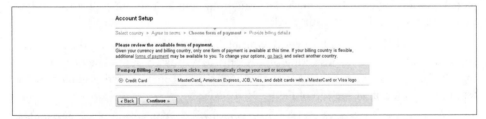

Figure 10-15. If you are located in the United States, your only payment option is to post-pay by credit or debit card

Click Continue to enter your credit card information, contact information, and business type, as shown in Figure 10-16.

To enter your card information, choose a card type from the Type of card drop-down list and provide the requested information. Next, provide your name, billing address, and telephone contact information. The penultimate step in the account creation

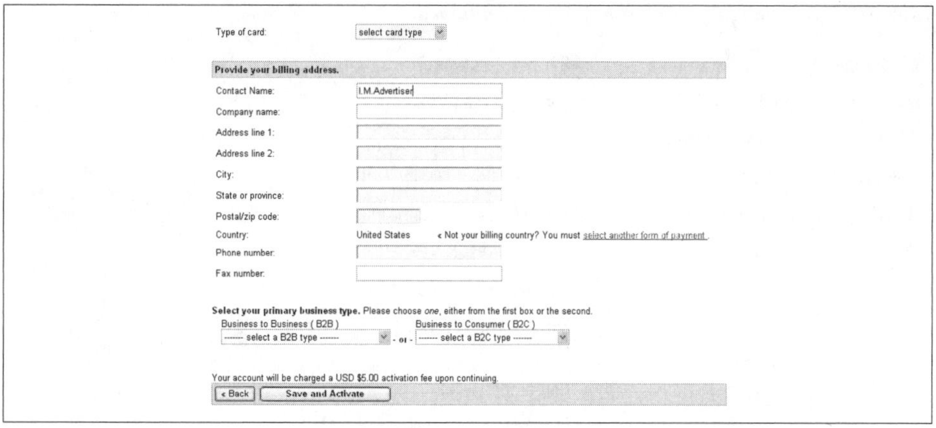

Figure 10-16. *Activating your account is as simple as entering your credit card information, address, and business type*

process is to tell Google whether your business is categorized as business to business (B2B) or business to consumer (B2C) and to select a specific category of B2B or B2C business. Google's B2B and B2C categories—which are somewhat idiosyncratic and do not correspond to government business categorization schemes or any recognized taxonomy of businesses—are shown in Table 10-2.

> Many businesses may find themselves choosing Other (in Business to Business or Business to Consumer) because nothing else matches very well.

Table 10-2. *Google's primary business types*

B2B business types	B2C business types
Advertising, Marketing, SEO	Adult & Gambling
Affiliate Marketing	Affiliate Marketing
Agriculture	Antiques and Collectibles
Automotive	Apparel
Business Services	Automotive
Construction & Real Estate	Beauty Products
Finance	Books & Magazines
Government & Regulated Industries	Careers & Classifieds
Healthcare	Consumer Electronics
Legal Services	Consumer Packaged Goods
Manufacturing	Dating & Personals
Printing & Office Supplies	Education, Religion
Technology: Commerce	Flowers, Gifts, Greetings

Table 10-2. Google's primary business types (continued)

B2B business types	B2C business types
Technology: Enterprise	Games (non gambling)
Telecom, Communications, Network	Healthcare
Transportation & Logistics	Home & Garden, Furniture, Art
Web Hosting and Domain Registration	Jewelry, Gems, Watches
Other Business to Business	Legal Services
	Mass Merchants & Auctions
	Music, Movies, TV, Tickets, Media
	Non-profit
	PC Hardware & Software
	Personal Finance & Insurance
	Real Estate
	Telecommunications & ISP
	Travel
	Other Business to Consumer

Finally, click Save and Activate. Congratulations! You now have an active AdWords account containing an Ad Campaign (named *Campaign #1*), the Ad Group you created, and a running ad within the Ad Group, targeted against the keywords you chose, using the budget you designated.

 Once your account has been established, you can change your personal information, billing information, and account options by opening the My Account tab and clicking the Billing Preferences and User Preferences links.

Creating and Editing Ad Campaigns

When you create and activate an AdWords account, as I've just explained, you must create an Ad Campaign and an Ad Group at the same time as you open your account. But once your account is in use, it is likely that it will contain multiple Ad Campaigns. Many of these Ad Campaigns will contain multiple Ad Groups.

For example, if you are a webmaster attempting to generate traffic to multiple sites, it makes sense to create an Ad Campaign for each of your sites. Within each Ad Campaign for a particular one of your web properties, create an Ad Group containing a specific ad, along with the keywords it targets.

Ad Campaigns allow you to organize your AdWords account along functional lines, by creating a separate Ad Campaign for each web site, for instance. Within each Ad

Campaign, multiple Ad Groups—one per ad—allow you to experiment with how ads are written and which keywords they target.

The relationship between an AdWords account and the AdWords Campaigns and Groups it contains is shown in Figure 10-17.

AdWords account
Ad campaign #1
Ad group 1
Ad group N
Ad campaign #2
Ad group 1
Ad group N
Ad campaign #N
Ad group 1
Ad group N

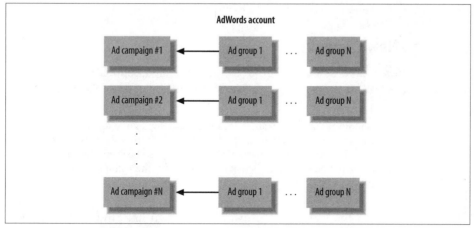

Figure 10-17. An AdWords account usually contains multiple AdWords Campaigns, each of which usually contains multiple AdWords Groups

For example, a webmaster might have campaigns defined for a photography site and a wireless networking site. Each campaign would probably contain several different ad groups, with each ad group containing a different ad and targeted at somewhat different keywords.

When you log on to AdWords, the first thing you will see is the Campaign Summary window, and you will probably have multiple Ad Campaigns defined in it, as shown in Figure 10-18, for example.

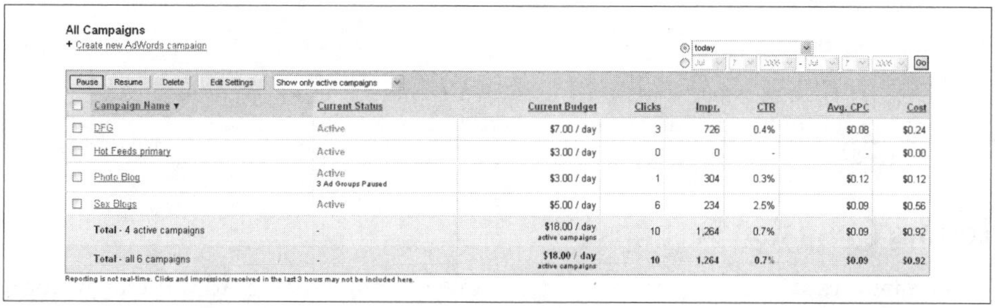

All Campaigns
+ Create new AdWords campaign
today
Go
Pause
Resume
Delete
Edit Settings
Show only active campaigns
Campaign Name ▾ | Current Status | Current Budget | Clicks | Impr. | CTR | Avg. CPC | Cost
DFG | Active | $7.00 / day | 3 | 726 | 0.4% | $0.08 | $0.24
Hot Feeds primary | Active | $3.00 / day | 0 | 0 | - | - | $0.00
Photo Blog | Active 3 Ad Groups Paused | $3.00 / day | 1 | 304 | 0.3% | $0.12 | $0.12
Sex Blogs | Active | $5.00 / day | 6 | 234 | 2.5% | $0.09 | $0.56
Total - 4 active campaigns | - | $18.00 / day active campaigns | 10 | 1,264 | 0.7% | $0.09 | $0.92
Total - all 6 campaigns | - | $18.00 / day active campaigns | 10 | 1,264 | 0.7% | $0.09 | $0.92
Reporting is not real-time. Clicks and impressions received in the last 3 hours may not be included here.

Figure 10-18. It's common to define multiple Ad Campaigns within your AdWords account

When you created your AdWords account, the Campaign you created as part of the account creation process was named *Campaign #1*. Once your AdWords account is activated, you'll want to change this name to something recognizable by checking the box next to the campaign name and clicking Edit Settings. Ad Campaign names should let you know at a glance what the campaign is about.

Creating a New Campaign

To create a new AdWords Campaign, from the Campaign Summary window, click the Create new AdWords campaign link (shown in the upper left of Figure 10-18).

You shouldn't have any trouble locating the Campaign Summary window, since it is what opens first when you log on to your AdWords account. The Campaign Summary window can also be found by clicking the Campaign Management tab followed by the Campaign Summary link.

Once you've clicked the Create new Adwords campaign link, things work almost identically to the campaign creation process you followed when you created your AdWords account (see "Signing up for an Account," earlier in this chapter), *except* that you can name your new Ad Campaign anything you like, as shown in Figure 10-19.

Figure 10-19. It's good to name new campaigns so that you can identify the purpose of the campaign at a glance

Just as when you signed up for an account, you must create an Ad Group as part of the process of creating an Ad Campaign.

Editing Campaign Settings

You'll often want to change the settings for one of your existing Ad Campaigns for a whole host of reasons, including:

- You want to temporarily pause, resume, or permanently delete an Ad Campaign.
- You'd like to change the budget for a campaign.
- You'd like to access certain settings that cannot be changed from the default when the Ad Campaign is created.

Pausing, resuming, and deleting an ad campaign

Proactive advertising managers find themselves often temporarily stopping (pausing) an Ad Campaign. This is a good way to see which of several campaigns works best—you can pause each of several campaigns in turn. After your comparison is complete, you can resume the Ad Campaign that works best. You may also want to delete an Ad Campaign if you no longer have any interest in it.

Another reason for pausing an Ad Campaign is that your budget may have temporarily run dry.

To pause, resume, or delete an Ad Campaign, check the box in the Campaign Summary window next to the campaign to select it (the campaign *DFG* is shown selected in Figure 10-20). Next, click Pause, Resume, or Delete, as desired.

Figure 10-20. Webmasters often find they are pausing and resuming campaigns to meet the needs of their budget, and this window makes it easy to perform the operation on multiple campaigns at once

You can select more than one campaign and perform an operation on all of the selected campaigns at once.

Clicking Edit Settings with one or more campaigns selected lets you change Ad Campaign settings.

The campaign summary

There's more to Ad Campaigns than whether they are running—in fact, much more! To start editing campaign settings, click the Ad Campaign link in the Campaign Summary window. A window like the one shown in Figure 10-21 will open, providing access to a campaign's Ad Groups.

The summary window for the specific Ad Campaign is used to drill down into the campaign's Ad Groups (see "Ad Groups," later in this chapter). You can also use it to change settings for the entire Ad Campaign.

Excluding sites. Excluding a web site means making sure that your ads do not appear on that site. You may wish to exclude specific web sites for an entire campaign, for example, because you don't want your ads to appear on a competitor's site. Or, you

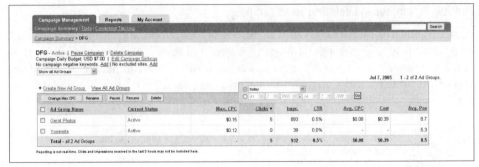

Figure 10-21. The Campaign Summary window lets you review information about all the Ad Groups within a campaign

may have seen a site that is contextually relevant but that you don't think provides a good environment for your ads.

Whatever your reasoning, it's easy to exclude specific domains by clicking the Add link that follows the words "no excluded sites," shown in Figure 10-21. The Site Exclusion window, shown in Figure 10-22, will open.

 If you have already excluded sites, instead of the Add link shown in Figure 10-21, the link for excluding sites will say Edit.

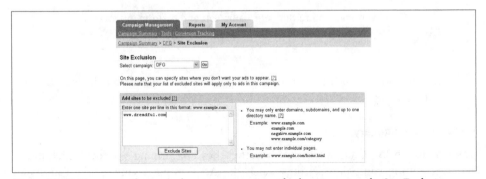

Figure 10-22. You can make your ads not appear on specific domains using the Site Exclusion window

To exclude a domain, subdomain, or directory within a domain, add it to the text box shown in Figure 10-22, and click Exclude Sites.

Adding negative keywords. *Negative keywords* are used to make sure your ad *doesn't* run on a content site with the specified negative keyword. For example, if you are trying to drive traffic to a digital photography site by targeting keywords such as "photo," you might want to add "film" as a negative keyword to make sure your ads don't run on sites that primarily cover older, film-based photography. Negatives keywords can be added at the Ad Group or Ad Campaign level.

To add a negative keyword to an Ad Campaign, from the summary screen for the campaign (Figure 10-21), click the Add link following the words "No campaign negative keywords". The Edit Campaign Negative Keywords window, shown in Figure 10-23, will open.

If you've already added negative keywords to the campaign, the Add link changes to Edit.

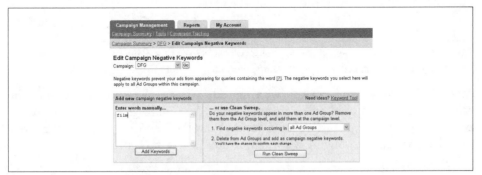

Figure 10-23. Using negative keywords is a good way to make sure that ads in a campaign don't end up targeted to inappropriate content by allowing you to paint with broad strokes and then eliminate inappropriate matching (for example, a match against "photography" that uses "film" as a negative keyword is likely to target digital photography)

In the Edit Campaign Negative Keywords window, add words you want to negatively target in the Enter words manually text box and click Add Keywords.

The Clean Sweep option, shown on the lower right of Figure 10-23, is a mechanism that lets you aggregate negative keywords applied to individual Ad Groups with an Ad Campaign up to the Ad Campaign level.

Changing campaign settings. To edit Ad Campaign settings themselves, click the Edit Campaign Settings link in the Campaign Summary window for the campaign (Figure 10-21). The Edit Campaign Settings window will open (Figure 10-24).

You can also open the Edit Campaign Settings window directly from the Campaign Summary window by checking the box next to a campaign to select the campaign and then clicking Edit Settings (see Figure 10-20).

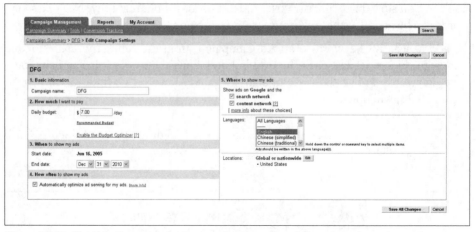

Figure 10-24. The Edit Campaign Settings window is used to change many campaign settings, including whether ads appear on search results, on content, or both

Most of the settings you can edit with the Edit Campaign Settings are exactly the same as the settings used when creating a new Ad Campaign. However, there are two important settings that you can access from the Edit Campaign Settings window that you cannot configure when setting up a new campaign:

- How often to show ads
- Where to show ads

Optimizing ad service. By default, the Automatically optimize ad serving box shown under How often to show my ads in Figure 10-24 is checked. This means that AdWords will give priority in ad placement to your keywords that are performing well (meaning a better click-through rate). The logic here is that since these keywords are performing better than your other keywords, they will probably continue to do so.

However, there are a couple of reasons you might want to experiment with turning this option off. You might want to give your underperforming keywords a chance by serving ads against them in equal proportion with the better-performing keywords (after all, if the underperforming keywords never get to serve ads, they have no way to better their performance).

 You might also intentionally choose to target ads to keywords that don't perform so well if you are primarily interested in getting your ad text noticed, and less concerned about actual click throughs.

By unchecking this option, all your keywords will be served equally, not just your high-performing keywords.

Where ads display. All AdWords ads are displayed on Google search results pages. By default, your ads will also be displayed on the AdSense search and content networks (see Chapter 8 for information about these programs).

In the Where to show my ads category shown in Figure 10-24, uncheck search network if you don't want your ads to appear on AdSense search results pages, and uncheck content network if you don't want your ads to appear in AdSense web content.

 Ads that appear in search results have a much higher click-through rate than ads appearing in web content, so much so that Google itself doesn't count ads placed in content towards official click-through rates (although, of course, clicks on these ads do cost you money).

Ad Groups

The most granular level within the AdWords programs is the Ad Group, which lets you create individual ads and target the ads against keywords.

Creating a New Ad Group

Each Ad Group must be created from within an Ad Campaign. To create an Ad Group, start from the Campaign Summary window that will contain it (such as the Campaign Summary window shown in Figure 10-21).

Next, click the Create New Ad Group link. The New Ad Group Set-up sequence of windows will open. These windows (the Create Ad window is shown in Figure 10-25) work the same way as entering your initial ad when you created your AdWords account to start with (see "Creating an Ad," earlier in this chapter).

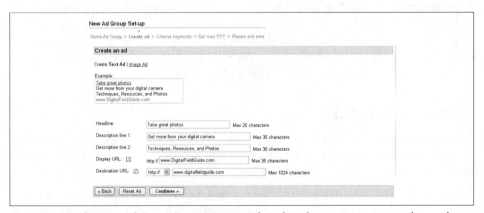

Figure 10-25. The New Ad Group Set-up sequence of windows lets you write a new ad, provide keywords for targeting, and set the maximum CPC for your ad

Editing an Ad Group

To edit an existing Ad Group, from a Campaign Summary window (such as the one shown in Figure 10-21) click on an Ad Group link. A detailed Ad Group window, such as the one shown in Figure 10-26, will open.

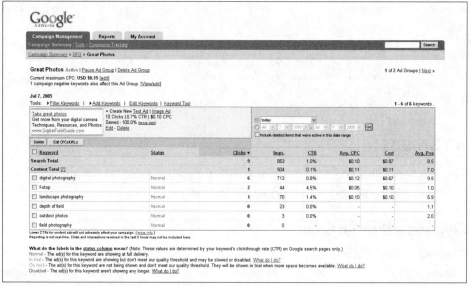

Figure 10-26. The Ad Group window provides an opportunity to review, and edit if you desire, the text of an ad and the keywords it targets

The detailed Ad Group window lets you modify the text on an existing ad, as well as to delete, edit, or add keywords.

See Chapter 11 for information about how to make effective use of the keyword and CPC metrics shown in the detailed Ad Group window. In addition to keyword, click-through, and CPC metric data, the detailed Ad Group window gives you access to some functionality not available when you first create an Ad Group; most importantly, you can create an ad with graphics, called an *image ad*.

Creating an Image Ad

To create an image ad, from the detailed Ad Group window, click the Create New Image Ad link (shown just to the right of the text ad in Figure 10-26). The Image Ad creation window, shown in Figure 10-27, will open.

To create an image ad, click the Browse button to upload a *.gif*, *.jpg*, or *.png* graphics file from your computer that is one of the sizes shown in Table 10-3 and is less than 50k in file size.

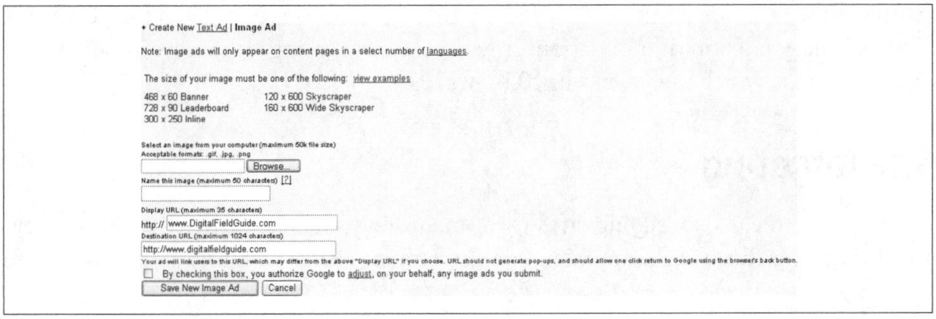

Figure 10-27. It's easy to create image ads in a handful of acceptable sizes that will run with AdWords

Table 10-3. Sizes for image ads

Size (in pixels)	Adjusted size (in pixels)	Size called
468 × 60	468 × 49	Banner
728 × 90	728 × 79	Leaderboard
300 × 250	300 × 239	Inline
120 × 600	120 × 578	Skyscraper
160 × 600	160 × 578	Wide skyscraper

Next, give the image a name, and verify the display and destination URLs. Click Save New Image Ad to create the image ad.

The adjusted size column shown in Table 10-3 represents the actual size of the graphics that Google will run in ads it serves. The "missing" 11 or 22 horizontal pixels are taken up with your display URL and a Google feedback link.

It is best practice to resize your graphics yourself to the adjusted size. However, you can alternatively check the box that authorizes Google to adjust your graphics from the nominal size to the adjusted size.

If you authorize Google to make this adjustment, be aware that the resizing will probably not be proportional; watch the results carefully.

Google AdWords editorial guidelines are nothing very extraordinary and about what you'd expect. Google takes its role in preventing users from being bombarded with offensive content, or ads that blink and gyrate, quite seriously. You can see the full text of the editorial guidelines for image ads at *https://adwords.google.com/select/ imageguidelines.html*.

Google AdWords is not known for primarily serving image ads, and the vast majority of AdWords ads served are text ads. For one thing, image ads do not appear on Google search results and in only some of the formats chosen by AdSense content participants. Still, it's an important facility to be able to serve targeted image ads via Google, and you should know about it for those advertising situations in which you feel a picture is worth many—well, 105—words.

Site Targeting

Site targeting means specifying sites by domain for your ads, rather than using keyword targeting. Each Ad Campaign can implement either keyword targeting or site targeting.

Implementing site targeting is a two-step process. You must:

* Enable site targeting in your AdWords account
* Choose site targeting for new Ad Campaigns

In other words, once you've turned on site targeting globally, you can then elect to use site targeting in a specific campaign (but not keyword targeting for the same campaign).

 Site targeting essentially means using Google as an agent for CPM, rather than CPC, advertising. Site-targeted ads appear on Google's content network only and not on Google search results pages.

By site-targeting your ads, you are saying that you don't really care about click throughs and that the primary purpose of your ad is to promote brand awareness.

Enabling Site Targeting

To enable site targeting in your account, open the My Account tab. Click the User Preferences link. Under Campaign Types, click the Edit link. The Campaign Types window (Figure 10-28) will open.

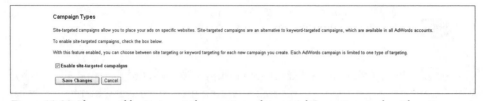

Figure 10-28. If you enable site-targeted campaigns, then an Ad Campaign can be either site- or keyword-targeted

Check the Enable site-targeted campaigns box, and click Save Changes.

Creating a Site-Targeted Campaign

Once site targeting has been enabled, when you create a new Ad Campaign, you can choose between Keyword-targeted and Site-targeted (Figure 10-29).

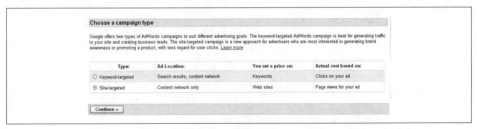

Figure 10-29. Just because you've enabled site targeting doesn't mean you're stuck with it—you can choose between keyword and site targeting on a per-campaign basis

Select Site-targeted, and click Continue. Next, create a text or image ad the way you would normally for a keyword-targeted campaign.

Once your initial AdGroup for the campaign has been created, you can start the process of site targeting, shown in Figure 10-30.

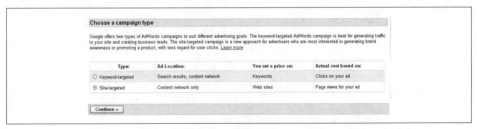

Figure 10-30. You provide a few sites and descriptive terms so Google can make suggestions of sites to target from its inventory

First add some sites where you'd like to see some ads in the Sites box on the left. Next, add a couple of descriptive phrases to the Descriptive Terms box on the right. Click Continue. As you can see in Figure 10-31, Google will come up with some suggestions from its available inventory of content sites that match your terms for you to choose from, along with traffic estimates for each of the sites that it has available.

Choose the sites that interest you from the Google-generated list of Candidate sites and add them to the list box shown at the bottom of Figure 10-31.

Figure 10-31. It's worth taking the time to investigate the Candidate sites that Google suggests to make sure that you really want your ad to appear on them

It's work taking the time to review any sites you don't know well to make sure they're really appropriate for your site targeting. Since the primary purpose of CPM advertising—and site-targeting is a form of CPM advertising—is promoting brand awareness, you should be careful about the context surrounding your ad (meaning the pages on which the ads appear). For example, it wouldn't do at all to have an ad for a prestigious car appear on a sleazy site.

Click Continue when you are satisfied with your site selection. The next window, shown in Figure 10-32, will let you set the maximum CPM, or cost per one thousand ad impressions, you are willing to pay for ads in your site-targeted campaign.

At this point, you can create another Ad Group for this site-targeted Ad Campaign or click Continue to set a budget for the campaign with the single initial ad. Figure 10-33 shows a setting for the daily budget for the campaign.

Once your daily budget has been set, click Continue to open the campaign review window, shown in Figure 10-34.

If all is in order, click Save Campaign to add the site-targeted campaign to your account. It will now appear in your account summary of campaigns (for example, the bottom campaign shown in Figure 10-35).

New Site-targeted Campaign Set-up

Target customers > Create ad > Target ad > **Set pricing** > Set daily budget > Review and save

selected sites	Max Impressions / Day:
2 Sites that allow image or text ads	0k-10k
4 Sites that allow text ads only	10k-100k
Total — All selected sites	**10k-100k**

These represent the impressions available to all advertisers, NOT your total impressions. We recommend that you set an affordable bid, run your ads for a few days, then adjust your sites and max CPM accordingly.

Set pricing: cost per thousand impressions (CPM)

The maximum CPM [?] is the top amount you'd like to spend for each 1000 impressions (or views) your ad receives. The higher your max CPM, the better the chance that your ad will show frequently. The minimum max CPM is $2.00.

Maximum CPM for sites in this Ad Group: $ 2.00

[« Back] [Create Another Ad Group] [Continue »]

Figure 10-32. The maximum CPM you enter amounts to a bid for placement on a site; your ad will appear if this bid makes it worthwhile for the site operator compared to CPC ads and other CPM bids

New Site-targeted Campaign Set-up

Target customers > Create ad > Target ad > Set pricing > **Set daily budget** > Review and save

Set your daily budget

Your daily budget is the amount you're willing to spend each day on your entire campaign. Your ad(s) will be shown as often as possible, based on your maximum CPM, while still keeping your total spend within your daily budget.

Daily budget: $ 30.00

[« Back] [Continue »]

Figure 10-33. Be careful when setting your daily budget that you enter an amount you can live with!

New Site-targeted Campaign Set-up

Target customers > Create ad > Target ad > Set pricing > Set daily budget > **Review and save**

Review your selections

Campaign name: site target #1   [Edit]

Language(s) that your customers speak: English   [Edit]
Location(s) of your customers: United States
[Edit]

Daily budget: USD $3.00   [Edit]

Ad Group name: Brainiac   [Edit]

Ads:

Digital Photography
Techniques & tips
Photos by Harold Davis
www.Photoblog2.com
Edit - Delete

Sites: [Edit]

digitalphotography.weblogsinc.com   photographyblog.com
photoshopcafe.com   treklens.com
digitalcamerainfo.com   shuttertalk.com

Maximum CPM: USD $2.00   [Edit]

[« Back] [Save Campaign]

Figure 10-34. AdWords always gives you plenty of chances to review your campaign choices to make sure your campaign will work for you

Campaign Name ▼	Current Status	Current Budget	Clicks	Impr.	CTR	Avg. CPC	Avg. CPM	Cost
DFG	Active	$7.00 / day	12	1,901	0.6%	$0.09	-	$1.13
Hot Feeds primary	Active	$3.00 / day	0	0	-	-	-	$0.00
Photo Blog	Active 3 Ad Groups Paused	$3.00 / day	3	1,273	0.2%	$0.12	-	$0.37
Sex Blogs	Active	$5.00 / day	12	539	2.2%	$0.09	-	$1.02
site target #1	Active	$3.00 / day	0	0	-	-	-	$0.00
Total - 5 active campaigns	-	$21.00 / day active campaigns	27	3,713	0.7%	$0.09	-	$2.52
Total - all 7 campaigns	-	$21.00 / day active campaigns	27	3,713	0.7%	$0.09	-	$2.52

Figure 10-35. The new site-targeted campaign appears in your account summary right along with more typical Google CPC campaigns

Getting a Client Manager Account

A *client manager* AdWords account is an umbrella account that allows you to access as many as 1,000 different AdWords accounts using a single window (Figure 10-36).

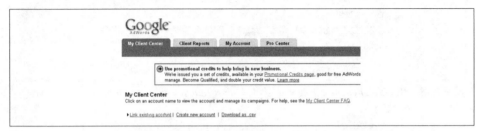

Figure 10-36. If you are responsible for managing multiple AdWords accounts, it's a great convenience to be able to link all the AdWords accounts in a single client manager account

Client manager accounts are primarily intended for advertising professionals who manage multiple AdWords accounts on behalf of clients, but Google also uses the client manager account window for other purposes. For example, the first step to getting a Google AdWords API developer key is to sign up for a client manager account (see Chapter 13).

To sign up for a client manager account, open the URL *https://adwords.google.com/ select/ProfessionalWelcome* in your browser. Next, click the Want to Become a Google Advertising Professional link. The Enrollment page will open.

In the Enrollment page, enter your existing AdWords logon information (Figure 10-37).

Click Continue Enrollment. In the next window (Figure 10-38), you provide an email address and password for managing accessing your My Client Center. The email address cannot be the same as the one for your existing AdWords account.

A client manager account acts as a container for multiple AdWords accounts (just as each AdWord client account is a container for Ad Campaigns, which in turn are containers for Ad Groups). Besides making it easier to manage multiple AdWords accounts, client manager accounts provide a number of other benefits, including the ability to enroll in the Google Advertising Professional program (see box below) and a special tab providing access to Google AdWords API developer key and quote information (see Chapter 13) once you've enrolled in the developer program.

Figure 10-37. To sign up for a client manager account, you need an existing AdWords account

Figure 10-38. The sign-up process emphasizes that you must provide an email address to access your client manager account that is different from the one used for your AdWords account

---

Becoming a Google Advertising Professional

Google Advertising Professionals is a program offering certifications, tools, training, and incentives for those who manage multiple AdWords accounts (and numerous AdWords Campaigns) on behalf of multiple clients. It is intended for professional advertising managers.

You can learn more about the program at the Google Advertising Professional's welcome page, *https://adwords.google.com/select/ProfessionalWelcome*. In order to enroll in the program, you'll need to first get a client manager account.

The benefits to advertising professionals include:

- A professional certification program for program members who pass an exam and spend at least $1000 per month on Google advertising
- Professional visibility for program members who are certified via a referral program
- Promotional goodies—including cash discounts—to give away to advertising clients
- Promotional materials that program members can use to help sell potential clients on the benefits of the AdWords program

---

Action Items

To start driving traffic to your web properties with AdWords, you should:

- Sign up for an AdWords account.
- Create an initial Ad Group and Ad Campaign.
- Create multiple campaigns for multiple web properties.
- Add variant text and image ads to your Ad Campaigns.
- Understand how to implement site targeting as opposed to keyword targeting and the implications of CPM advertising.
- If you manage multiple AdWords accounts, get a client manager account.

CHAPTER 11

Improving Campaign and Ad Group Performance

There's a great deal of information contained in the average AdWords account. This information—ads and keywords and the related performance data—is stashed away in Ad Groups. These Ad Groups are themselves contained in AdWords Campaigns.

To make effective use of AdWords, you need to be able to get at this information. In other words, drilling down into one Ad Group after another will only provide piecemeal data and usually won't give you the kind of picture you need to improve performance.

For CPC ads, an Ad Group consists of the text of an ad and its targeted keywords, along with budget choices. For CPM ads, an Ad Group consists of the creative for the ad or its text, the targeted domains, and budget choices.

It's pretty unlikely for an ad, or an ad campaign, to be perfect the first time round. A great part of the craft of creating effective campaigns is to see how your ads and campaigns are doing, tweak them, see how the improved ads and campaigns are doing, tweak again, and iterate the process.

This chapter explains how to monitor your AdWords Campaigns and AdWords Ad Groups performance, and how to use the tools that AdWords provides to improve ad and campaign performance.

Monitoring Your AdWords Activity

It's important to keep frequent track of the progress of your ads. The key high-level questions are:

- How much are you spending?
- How effective are your ads?

The AdWords Campaign Management Campaign Summary window (shown in Figure 11-1), which is the first thing you'll see when you log on to AdWords, gives you a pretty good idea of the answers to these questions.

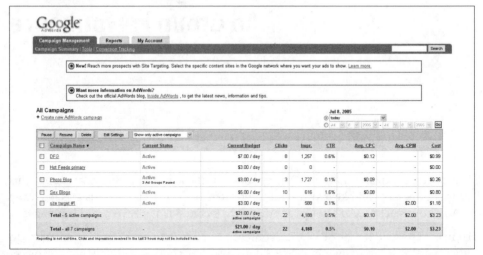

Figure 11-1. The opening AdWords Campaign Management window provides a great way to get a snapshot of your activity for the current day (or over any other time period)

Understanding Your Campaign Summary

You can set the Campaign Summary window to display information for the current day or for almost any date range after the beginning of your AdWords account. Pre-set time periods besides the current day include the current week, the current month, and all time (since you opened your AdWords account).

 For the purpose of monitoring your AdWords performance, you should check the current day's activity at least once a day before reviewing other time periods.

Here's what the columns in the Campaign Summary window tell you about each of your campaigns:

Status
> Campaign status can be Active, Paused, or Deleted. If a campaign is Active, AdGroups within the campaign can be paused. Paused campaigns are campaigns that are not running, but can be reactivated and set to Active. The number of paused Ad Groups within a campaign will be displayed below the campaign's status. Deleted campaigns cannot be reactivated. The historical data about deleted campaigns is still present, so you can use this information for the purposes of analysis.

Current Budget

This is the daily amount you've budgeted for each campaign.

Clicks

The aggregate number of times ads within a campaign have been clicked.

Impr.

The aggregate number of impressions, or times the ads within a campaign have been displayed.

CTR

The click-through rate, or ratio of clicks to impressions, for a campaign.

Avg. CPC

The average cost-per-click for the ads in a campaign (for CPC-based ads).

Avg. CPM

The average cost per thousand impressions for CPM-based ads.

Cost

The total cost for all the ads in a campaign.

Drilling Down into a Campaign

To get more detailed information about a specific campaign, click the campaign in the Campaign Summary window. A summary window, like the window shown in Figure 11-2, showing each Ad Group within the campaign, will open.

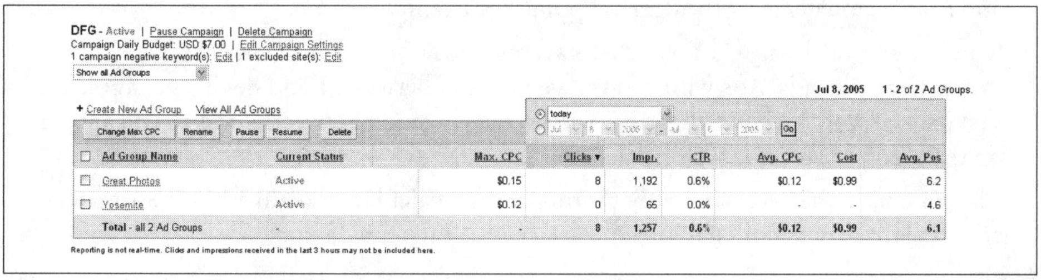

Figure 11-2. A summary is shown of each Ad Group within a campaign

Here's the information shown for each Ad Group within a campaign (in each case for the time period selected):

Status

Ad Group status can be Active, Paused, or Deleted.

Max. CPC

This is the maximum cost per click you are willing to pay for a particular ad. (For CPM ads, this column is maximum CPM rather than CPC.)

Clicks

The aggregate number of times an ad has been clicked.

Impr.

The aggregate number of impressions, or times an ad has been displayed.

CTR

The click-through rate, or ratio of clicks to impressions, for a campaign.

Avg. CPC

The average cost-per-click for an ad (for CPC-based ads).

Avg. CPM

The average cost per thousand impressions for CPM-based ads.

Cost

The cost of the ad.

Avg. Pos.

The average position in which, when there is a keyword search match, your ad is likely to be displayed.

 For CPM ads, the Avg. Pos. column does not appear.

Understanding Average Position

Average position is an integer that is 1 or greater, usually followed by a decimal point and a single integer after the decimal point, for example, 1.7.

Simply put, the closer to 1.0 your ad's average position, the more likely it is to appear in search results ads. Ads with an average position between 1 and 8 will appear on the first page of search results; those with an average position between 9 and 16 will appear on the second page of search results, and so on.

The reason for the decimal number is that it is the calculation of an average estimate—actual placement is not guaranteed and depends on many factors.

Understanding Ad Group Performance

The real information about ad performance comes at the granular level of the Ad Group. To see performance of an individual Ad Group, click on the Ad Group in the summary for a particular campaign. A window will open displaying the ad contained by the Ad Group and showing keyword statistics for the ad, like the one shown in Figure 11-3.

At first glance, the statistics for an Ad Group appear to be roughly similar to those presented for individual campaigns, and for the Ad Campaign summary, but there are some important differences:

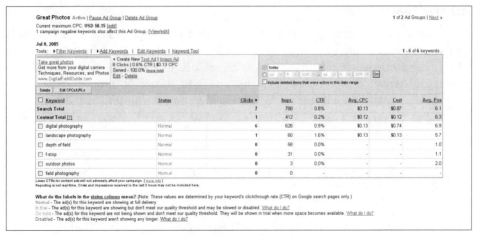

Figure 11-3. The Summary window for each Ad Group provides a detailed account of individual keyword performance

- Aggregate results are broken out by Search versus Content network.
- Results are broken out by individual keyword.
- Each keyword is assigned a status.

Properly understanding the statistics relating to the individual keywords associated with your ads can help you target ads better and improve your ad performance.

Search and content results

Statistics for a given ad are divided between Search—ads appearing on Google search results pages—and Content—ads appearing on Google's network of web sites affiliated via AdSense.

Google also contracts for its AdWords ads to appear on a number of networks besides AdSense, including those provided by America Online, Amazon, Ask Jeeves, and EarthLink, so there's no telling exactly where your ads may appear!

Search versus content statistics are significant because your ad may do better in one context than the other. If you learn that this is happening, you may decide to run your ad only in Search or only in Content.

It's normal to expect much lower CTR on content ads than on Google search results ads. This is so much the case that Google does not include content results when calculating keyword status.

Individual keyword results

Individual keyword results are important because they allow you to determine how well your ads are being targeted. For most CPC advertisers, the ultimate goal of an advertising campaign is customer conversion, that is, getting a site visitor to take an affirmative step such as joining or buying something. Clicking through is the single most significant thing someone on the Web can do on the journey towards customer conversion. If you don't get click throughs, your ad campaign is not working, at least if customer conversion is the goal.

Some ad campaigns don't have customer conversion as their primary goal. For these campaigns, created brand awareness might be the main purpose of an ad. Managers of these campaigns might be well advised to choose CMP rather than CPC advertising. In any event, they will pay less attention to CTR rates. They may also figure that CPC advertising with no click throughs is a good deal, because there are no costs associated with the advertising.

Assuming that your goals are like those of most advertisers on the Web—to drive traffic to your site with the hope of converting traffic into paying customers—you should monitor both absolute CTR and how your click-through rates are changing.

A CTR of 2% or better is extremely good.

By comparison, a direct mail campaign with a response rate of just 0.2%—an order of magnitude less than 2%—is considered successful.

On the other hand, if your absolute CTR for an ad is below 0.4% you should think about how to bring that rate up, by either:

- Improving your ad so that it is more compelling
- Improving your keywords, so they are more relevant to your ad

In a similar spirit, an increasing CTR for a keyword is a good thing, but a decreasing CTR is not and may mean that your ad has reached a saturation point for a specific keyword. If this is happening, you should think about alternative keyword targeting, starting with synonyms.

Keyword status

Google does not want ads to appear on its network that are targeted against keywords that it expects to have a CTR of less than 0.5%. So Google evaluates the keywords you've chosen for targeting based on their CTR with AdWords ads in general and on the CTR of similar keywords.

Keyword status is based on ads appearing on Google search results pages, not on ads appearing on content pages.

If one of your keywords falls below the minimum threshold in Google's estimating process, the keyword will be disabled, meaning your ad won't be targeted to that keyword. Glancing at the keyword status column in the statistics display for an ad is a good way to quickly make sure that your keywords are performing acceptably.

The possible keyword status labels and their meanings are shown in Table 11-1.

Table 11-1. Keyword status labels and meanings

Keyword status label	Meaning
Normal	Targeted keywords are above Google's minimum 0.5% CTR threshold; ads targeted to these keywords should display normally.
In trial	Keywords are below the minimum CTR threshold and under evaluation. Ads targeted to these keywords will continue to be served until Google is statistically confident that the keywords will deliver a CTR above or below the minimum—when the keyword will be moved to Normal or Disabled status, respectively. Each account has a limited (but unspecified) number of keywords that can be in trial at any one time.
On hold	The On hold status is assigned when an account's In trial limit has been exceeded and a keyword is slightly below the minimum threshold. When In trial space becomes available, On hold keywords are automatically moved up to In trial status.
Disabled	Keywords are disabled if they don't meet the minimum quality threshold (the 0.5% CTR) or if they haven't triggered a click through in 90 days. If you really think a disabled keyword is relevant to your ad, you can try turning the keyword into a descriptive phrase; for example, "yacht buying service" rather than "yacht."

Using the Ads Diagnostic Tool

Will my ad appear on a Google page that answers a specific search query? This is a question of vital importance to an ad campaign manager, who may care more about the answer to this practical issue than about the theoretical improvement of keywords.

The Ads Diagnostic Tool is intended to answer this question by telling you which of your ads are likely to appear on Google search results pages.

To open the Ads Diagnostic Tool, with the AdWords Campaign Management tab open, click the Tools link, and click Ads Diagnostic Tool. The Ads Diagnostic Tool, shown in Figure 11-4, will open.

The Ads Diagnostic Tool provides two different mechanisms, which come up with the same result provided you use the same search query with each option (see "Entering Search Queries or Search Results Page URLs," later in this chapter).

What Decides Whether Your Ad Will Appear?

Keyword selection—and performance—plays a crucial role in determining whether your ad will appear in response to a specific query, but so do other factors. For example, if you've used up your budget for the day for an Ad Group, your ad will probably not appear. (Note that this is not an absolute, because budgets are expressed as rolling 30-day averages; Google can overbudget on your behalf one day, and make up for it on another day.)

Additionally, if the maximum CPC you are willing to pay for a given ad is less than other advertisers are willing to pay for ads targeted to the same keyword, it becomes less likely that your ad will appear in response to a query for that keyword.

Figure 11-4. You can use the Ads Diagnostic Tool to see if your ad is targeted to a keyword on Google search results pages

Entering Search Queries or Search Results Page URLs

Option 1 and Option 2 shown in Figure 11-4 provide two different mechanisms that use the inputs and show the same results. If the keyword phrase you enter in the Option 1 box is the same as the search you used in Google prior to copying and pasting it into the Option 2 box, then the results will be the same.

However, if the keyword phrase you enter in the Option 1 box contains multiple terms, you must remember either to put plus symbols between the keywords or quote the phrase (in contrast, Google search will take care of this for you automatically with Option 2).

To use Option 1, enter a keyword or keyword phrase in the Keyword text box, as shown in Figure 11-5.

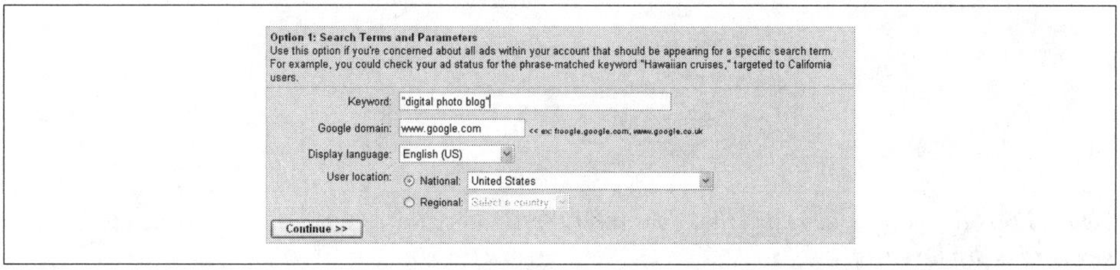

Figure 11-5. Enter a keyword or use the plus (+) operator or quotes to enter a multiword term

Next, click Continue. The Ad Diagnostics Results window will tell you if the ads in your account that are targeted to the keyword or keyword phrase you entered are likely to run on Google search pages (Figure 11-6).

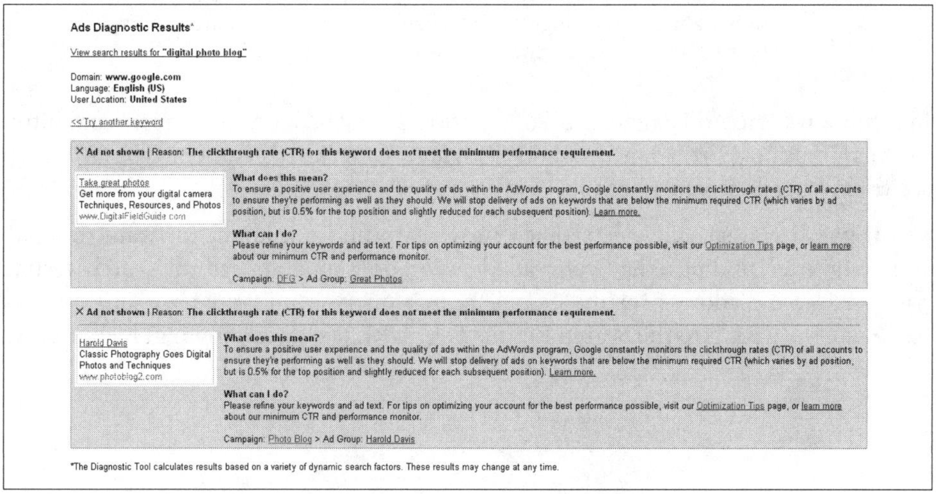

Figure 11-6. The tool displays your ads targeted to the keywords you are investigating and shows you if they fail to meet minimum CTR requirements

The ads shown in Figure 11-6 fail to meet minimum CTR requirements for the keywords under investigation. This means that they would be good candidates for keyword improvement, using the tools explained in "Optimizing Your Ads" next.

On the other hand, you can see if an ad is likely to be shown using another keyword targeted for the ad. If the ad will be shown, results like those shown in Figure 11-7 will be displayed.

Figure 11-7. *If you try a keyword that does meet threshold requirements, the ad targeted to the keyword is displayed*

The difference between the keyword targeted (and results shown) in Figures 11-6 and 11-7 lies in the broadness and lack of specificity of the terms ("digital photo blog" in Figure 11-6) versus the very precise and narrow term shown in Figure 11-7 ("f-stop," which refers to a photographic lens aperture). Narrow, precise, and technical terms will almost always have higher CTRs (although these searches will not come up as often as searches for broader terms).

In some ways, the Ad Diagnostics Tool Option 2 may be more convenient and intuitive than Option 1. You can search in Google to your heart's content (you may even see your own ads as you search!).

When you find a specific query that you want to find out about (or want to verify your empirical findings that your ad does or does not appear on search results pages), copy the address for the Google search query from your browser's address bar. Paste the URL into the Search Results Page URL text box, shown in Figure 11-8.

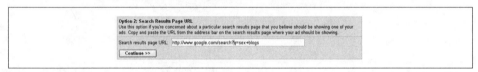

Figure 11-8. *You can alternatively search using a Google URL if you want to verify whether a particular search page will (or will not) display your ad*

The results from this procedure are exactly the same as if you used the query part of the Google search URL (the part after the q=sex+blogs in Figure 11-8) in Option 1.

The Ad Diagnostics Results will tell you if your ad should display (Figure 11-9) or provide diagnostic messages like the one shown in Figure 11-6 if it will not.

Figure 11-9. Google shows you when your keyword and related ad does meet minimum CTR thresholds (as in this case) and also when your ad and keyword do not

Optimizing Your Ads

Once you've determined that there are specific Ad Groups that need improvement, either by monitoring CTR statistics or by using the Ads Diagnostic Tool, Google provides a number of tools you can use. It's in your interest to try to improve your targeting, because more focused matching means that the most appropriate prospects see your ads and your CPC goes down. A good place to start honing your keywords is the Keyword Tool.

Keyword Tool

You can open the Keyword Tool in either of two ways:

- With the Content Management tab open, click the Tools link, followed by the Keyword Tool link (when the Keyword Tool opens, it won't have any keywords loaded, as shown in Figure 11-10, making this the best option for figuring out the keywords for a new Ad Group rather than clarifying an existing group).

- With the summary window for an Ad Group open, click the Keyword Tool link (when the Keyword Tool opens in a new window it will be preloaded with the existing keyword for the Ad Group, as shown in Figure 11-11).

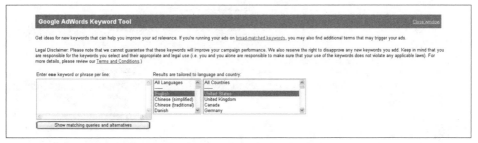

Figure 11-10. You can open the Keyword Tool from the Tools window to experiment with keywords generally

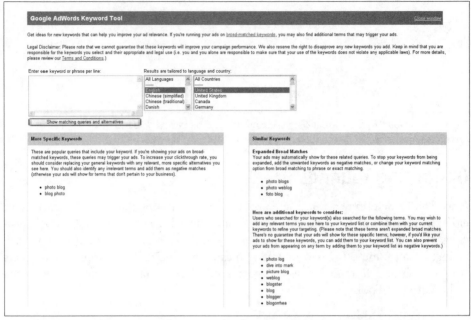

Figure 11-11. When you open the Keyword Tool from an existing Ad Group, more specific, similar, and additional keywords to the ones already targeted by the Ad Group are suggested

A goal of keyword optimization is to make sure that your ads will run according to the Ads Diagnostic Tool. For example, consider the ads shown in Figure 11-6 that were not displayed in response to the search query "digital photo blog". It makes sense to use the Keyword Tool to get these ads performing better.

You can run the poorly performing keywords for the ads that failed the Ads Diagnostic Tool through the Keyword Tool, as shown in Figure 11-12, to generate a long list of alternative suggestions.

Figure 11-12. Running failing keywords through the Keyword Tool is the best way to start coming up with better alternatives

 While the Keyword Tool comes up with a very extensive list of possibilities, ultimately it is up to an AdWords campaign manager—possibly by dint of trial and error—to come up with high-performing keywords.

Keyword Matching Options

AdWords offers a number of keyword matching options. Understanding these options can help to improve the relevancy of your ad placement, leading to fewer ad impressions but a higher CPC.

The keyword matching options are:

Broad match

> This is the default option. When you enter a phrase such as *sail boat*, ads will appear when a user's query contains *sail* and *boat* in any order in any part of a query, possibly along with other terms. In addition, broad-matched ads will also show for *expanded matches*, which are matches with plural (or singular) and other variant forms of the words in a phrase.

Phrase match

> When you enter your keywords in quotes—for example, *"sail boat"*—your ad will appear when a user enters the search phrase in order as it appears within the quotes, but possibly with other words as well, for example, *big sail boat*.

Exact match

> Exact matches are the least flexible kind of keyword matching. The term that users search for must exactly match the phrase you enter in brackets—for example, [sail boat]—in order, without any additional terms. Exact matching is the most targeted option among experienced AdWords managers because users searching for terms that make this kind of narrow match are more likely to be interested exactly in your business's offerings.

Negative keyword match

> Negative keywords are added to a search phrase, by adding a minus sign in front of the negative keyword, to make a search more precisely targeted. For example, if you target *sail boat -blue*, your ad will appear when a user searches for *sail boat*, but not *blue sail boat*. Negative keywords are an important mechanism for making targeting more precise.

The problem with the first ad shown as failing the Ad Diagnostics Tool in Figure 11-6 is a broad match with the phrase `digital photography`. Deleting digital photography and replacing it with exact matches [`digital photography tips`] and [`digital photography techniques`] improves the CTR for this ad.

The problem with the second ad shown in Figure 11-6 is the broad match targeting with `photo blog` and `photo blogging`. The Keyword Tool makes lots of suggestions, but most of them are not appropriate (for example, `erotic photo blog` or `blogspot`). CPC for this ad might be improved by dropping the keywords related to `blog` and focusing on keywords related to digital photography. However, that would actually diminish the relevancy of the advertisement, which is attempting to drive traffic to a photo blog. The recommendation here is to live with a low CTR and increase the likelihood of ad placement on search results pages by increasing the maximum CPC you are willing to pay.

Estimating Traffic

The Traffic Estimator is best used to get a quick idea of how keywords will perform and how that performance will impact the cost of running an Ad Group, without actually adding the new keyword(s).

To open the Traffic Estimator, with the Content Management tab open, click the Tools link, followed by the Traffic Estimator link. In the Traffic Estimator window, shown in Figure 11-13, enter the keywords you want to investigate, as well as a maximum CPC, language, location targeting method, and countries to target.

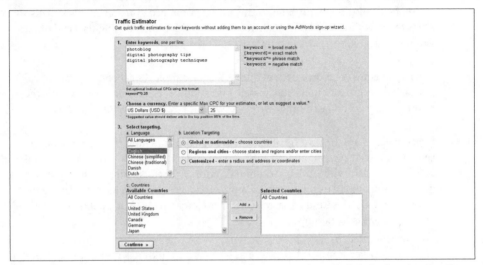

Figure 11-13. You can enter the amount you are willing to pay for a click through or let Google suggest a value, and Google will give you a traffic estimate for the keyword

 If you don't estimate a maximum CPC in the Traffic Estimator, Google will suggest one for you that will deliver ads in the top (1.0) position 85% of the time. As you can imagine, this is an expensive CPC choice, so to make the best use of the Traffic Estimator you should always enter your own, more realistic, maximum CPC.

Click Continue. The Traffic Estimator results screen, shown in Figure 11-14, gives you an idea of the average position, clicks per day, and cost per day you can expect, given the keywords you entered and the maximum CPC you specified.

Modifying Your Campaigns

If you are managing multiple Ad Campaigns, many of which contain multiple Ad Groups, it quickly gets tiresome to edit keywords, maximum CPC, and related

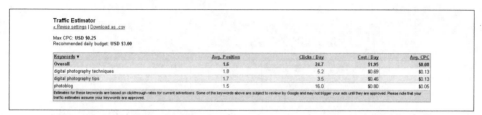

Traffic Estimator				
< Revise settings	Download as .csv				
Max CPC: USD $0.25				
Recommended daily budget: USD $3.00				
Keywords ▼	Avg. Position	Clicks / Day	Cost / Day	Avg. CPC
Overall	1.6	24.7	$1.95	$0.08
digital photography techniques	1.8	5.2	$0.69	$0.13
digital photography tips	1.7	3.5	$0.46	$0.13
photoblog	1.5	16.0	$0.80	$0.05

Estimates for these keywords are based on clickthrough rates for current advertisers. Some of the keywords above are subject to review by Google and may not trigger your ads until they are approved. Please note that your traffic estimates assume your keywords are approved.

Figure 11-14. You can use the estimates provided by the Traffic Estimator to see if you want to add keywords to an Ad Group

settings on an ad-by-ad basis. Fortunately, AdWords provides a number of tools that allow you to edit settings across Ad Groups and Campaigns at the account level.

 The tools for editing campaigns also allow you to edit on a per campaign or per Ad Group basis, depending on the filtering options you select.

These tools allow you to edit:

- Maximum CPCs
- Keyword matching options
- Ad text
- Keywords

Campaign editing tools are all accessed from the Tools window of the Campaign Management tab. Each of the editing applications explained in this section can be opened using a link in the Modify Your Campaigns section of the Tools window.

Editing Maximum CPC

In the Tools window, click the Find and Edit Max CPCs link to update single or multiple Max CPCs throughout your account all at once. The Find and Edit Max CPCs window is shown in Figure 11-15.

As you can see in Figure 11-15, the Find and Edit Max CPCs window provides a great deal of flexibility about which keyword CPCs will be modified and which Campaigns and Ad Groups they belong to. The simple example, shown in Figure 11-15, is to find all keywords containing *blog* across all campaigns. A further condition is that the current maximum CPC for any keyword matching this query should be less than $0.30. Anytime a keyword is found that meets these conditions, its CPC is modified by raising the maximum CPC for the keyword by 25%.

When you click Continue, each matching keyword will be shown (Figure 11-16), giving you the opportunity to apply the maximum CPC increase in a batch or individually.

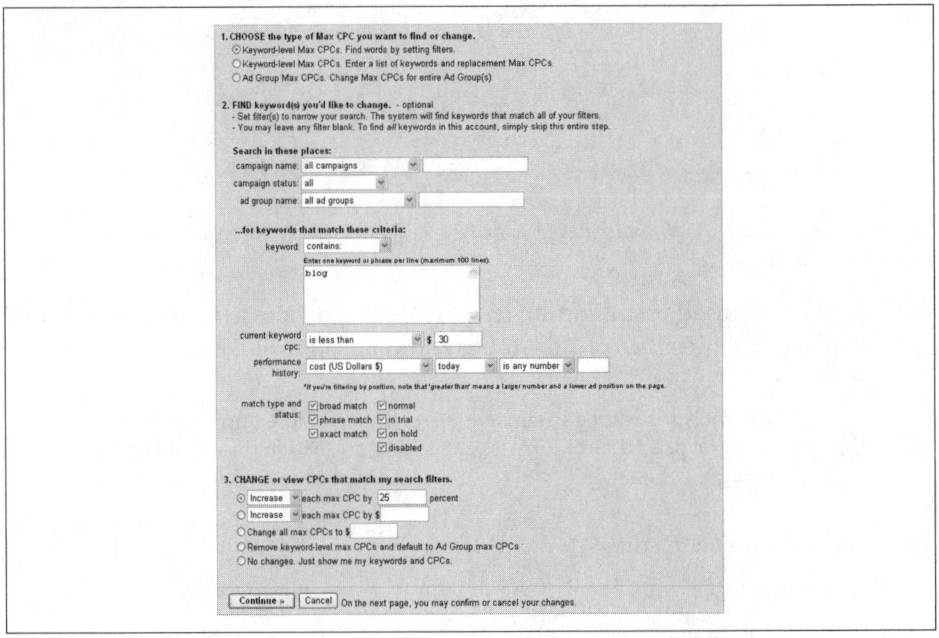

Figure 11-15. You can change the maximum CPC for keywords picked up by the filter across your account

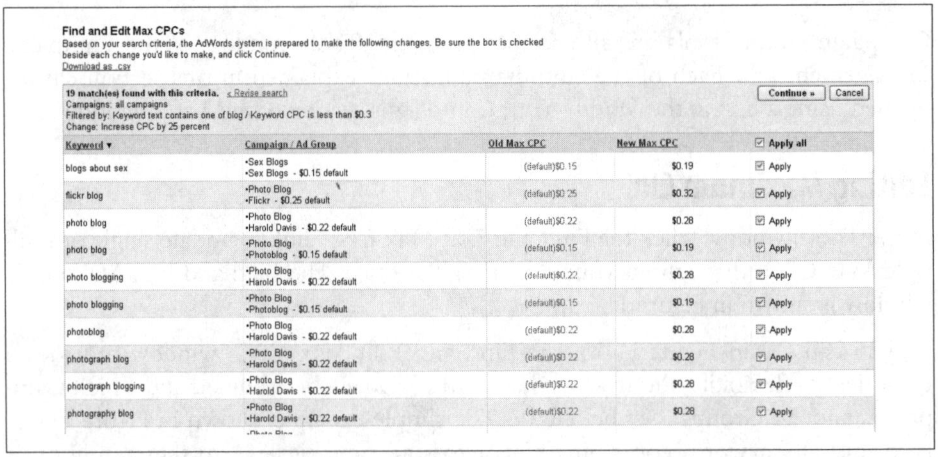

Figure 11-16. You can apply the changes to all matches or on an individual basis

Changing Keyword Matching Options

Keyword matches default to broad matching (see the "Keyword Matching Options" box earlier in this chapter). On a per campaign basis, or for more than one campaign in an account (by selecting multiple campaigns), you can change keyword matching options as shown in Figure 11-17.

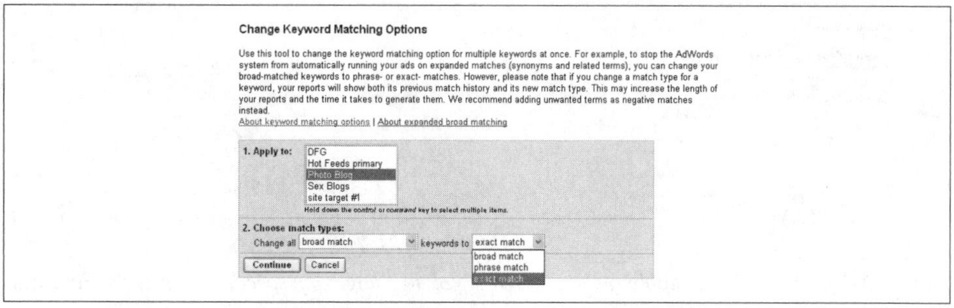
Change Keyword Matching Options
Use this tool to change the keyword matching option for multiple keywords at once. For example, to stop the AdWords system from automatically running your ads on expanded matches (synonyms and related terms), you can change your broad-matched keywords to phrase- or exact- matches. However, please note that if you change a match type for a keyword, your reports will show both its previous match history and its new match type. This may increase the length of your reports and the time it takes to generate them. We recommend adding unwanted terms as negative matches instead.
About keyword matching options | About expanded broad matching
1. Apply to:
DFG
Hot Feeds primary
Photo Blog
Sex Blogs
site target #1
Hold down the control or command key to select multiple items.
2. Choose match types:
Change all
broad match
keywords to
exact match
broad match
phrase match
exact match
Continue
Cancel

Figure 11-17. Changing the match type across campaigns saves you the work of drilling down into individual Ad Groups to make these changes

Editing Ad Text

It's not unusual to edit ad text across multiple ads in multiple campaigns. For example, the slogan you'd like to use for your company might change.

Fortunately, the Find and Edit Text window lets you easily make changes globally. The example shown in Figure 11-18 changes the ad text *Harold Davis* to *Yoda* in all ads in all campaigns in an account.

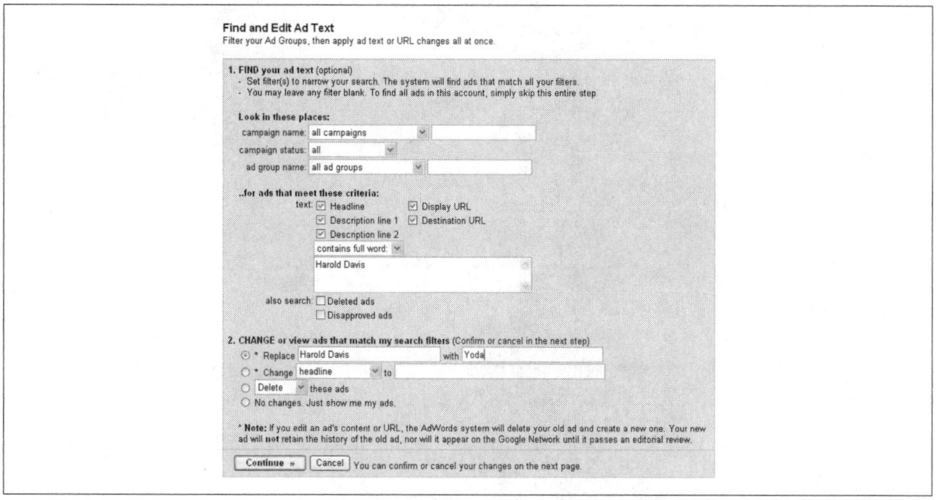
Find and Edit Ad Text
Filter your Ad Groups, then apply ad text or URL changes all at once.
1. FIND your ad text (optional)
- Set filter(s) to narrow your search. The system will find ads that match all your filters.
- You may leave any filter blank. To find all ads in this account, simply skip this entire step.
Look in these places:
campaign name: all campaigns
campaign status: all
ad group name: all ad groups
..for ads that meet these criteria:
text: Headline
Display URL
Description line 1
Destination URL
Description line 2
contains full word:
Harold Davis
also search: Deleted ads
Disapproved ads
2. CHANGE or view ads that match my search filters (Confirm or cancel in the next step)
* Replace Harold Davis with Yoda
* Change headline to
Delete these ads
No changes. Just show me my ads.
* Note: If you edit an ad's content or URL, the AdWords system will delete your old ad and create a new one. Your new ad will not retain the history of the old ad, nor will it appear on the Google Network until it passes an editorial review.
Continue »
Cancel
You can confirm or cancel your changes on the next page.

Figure 11-18. When something changes, such as a name or URL, that requires fixing a number of ads, you can make the edit globally

You can apply ad text changes to all ads that meet the criteria you supplied or make individual changes, as shown in Figure 11-19.

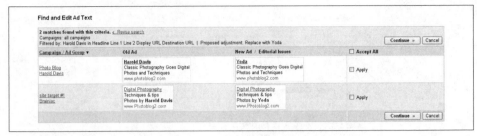

Figure 11-19. The ability to apply (or not apply) a global change to a specific ad gives the Find and Edit Ad Text feature great flexibility

Changing Keywords

Changing keywords works similarly to editing ad text. You use the Find and Edit Keywords window, shown in Figure 11-20, to filter for keywords across an account, in a Campaign that matches specified criteria, across all Ad Groups, or in an Ad Group that matches specified criteria.

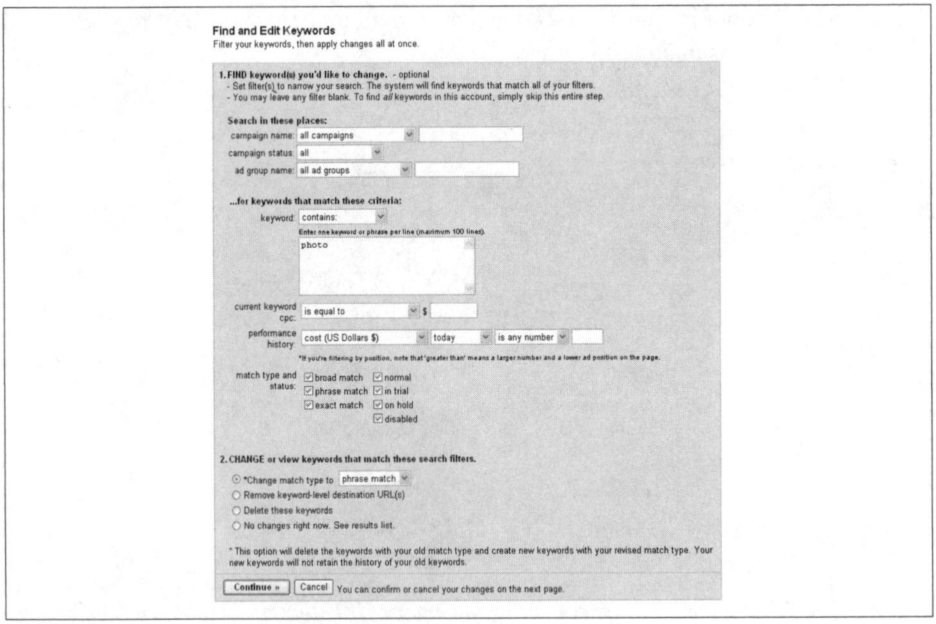

Figure 11-20. The ability to edit keywords globally using a variety of criteria, including the historical data of what a keyword has actually cost your account, makes it easy to experiment with keyword changes

In the example shown in Figure 11-20, all keywords containing *photo* are to be filtered and turned to a phrase match.

It's useful to list your keywords with the Find and Edit Keyword tool from time to time even if you don't want to edit the keywords. Given the large number of Campaigns, Ad Groups, and keywords many AdWords users are likely to work with, it's easy to forget the keywords you have enabled. Listing keywords that you have targeted helps to prevent your keywords from getting out of hand.

The Find and Edit Keywords tools offers you the choice to apply changes globally or to individual keywords that match the filter you specified, as shown in Figure 11-21.

Find and Edit Keywords

Based on your search criteria, the AdWords system is prepared to make the following changes. Be sure the box is checked beside each change you'd like to make, and click Continue.
Download as .csv

24 match(es) found with this criteria. x Revise search
Campaigns: all campaigns
Filtered by: Keyword text contains one of photo
Change: Change match type to Phrase

Keyword ▼	Campaign / Ad Group	Old Match Type	New Match Type	☑ Apply all
camping photo	DFG > Yosemite	Broad	Phrase	☑ Apply
digital photography resources	DFG > Great Photos	Broad	Phrase	☑ Apply
digital photography tips	DFG > Great Photos	Broad	Phrase	☑ Apply
field photography	DFG > Great Photos	Broad	Phrase	☑ Apply
landscape photography	DFG > Great Photos	Broad	Phrase	☑ Apply
outdoor photography	DFG > Yosemite	Broad	Phrase	☑ Apply
outdoor photos	DFG > Great Photos	Broad	Phrase	☑ Apply
photo blog	Photo Blog > Harold Davis	Broad	Phrase	☑ Apply
photo blog	Photo Blog > Photoblog	Broad	Phrase	☑ Apply
photo blogging	Photo Blog > Harold Davis	Broad	Phrase	☑ Apply
photo blogging	Photo Blog > Photoblog	Broad	Phrase	☑ Apply
photo flickr	Photo Blog > Flickr	Broad	Phrase	☑ Apply
photo yoda	Photo Blog > Yoda	Broad	Phrase	☑ Apply
photoblog	Photo Blog > Harold Davis	Broad	Phrase	☑ Apply

Figure 11-21. Applying a keyword change to all keywords can be a great timesaver, but it's nice to have the flexibility to apply (or not apply) keyword changes at the individual keyword level as well

Action Items

To improve the performance of your AdWord campaigns and groups, and more easily manage your AdWords account, you should:

- Monitor the overall Campaign Summary window for performance daily.
- Monitor the summary window for each active campaign daily.
- Monitor the summary window for each active Ad Group daily.
- Understand the meaning and implications of Ad Group performance.
- Learn to use the Ads Diagnostic Tool to see if your ads will run against specific search queries.
- Optimize ads using the Keywords Tool and the Traffic Estimator.
- Learn to use the tools available for modifying ads, keywords, and settings on an accountwide basis.

CHAPTER 12

AdWords Reporting and Conversion Tracking

If you have only a handful of Campaigns and Ad Groups to keep track of, the Campaign Summary window (explained in Chapter 11) should work fine. But once you are tracking a dozen or more Campaigns, each containing multiple ads and many keywords, in order to retain your sanity—and do a good job of tracking your spending and performance with the multiple campaigns and ads—you'll need to take advantage of the excellent AdWords reporting facility.

Conversion tracking means implementing a mechanism that tells you when visitors to your site perform a specified action. More specifically, if you are paying for advertising on a CPC basis, unless you are just interested in drawing eyeballs to your site, you'd probably like to know if this traffic brings you revenue.

Using AdWords conversion tracking, you can add code to your web pages that lets you determine if traffic generated by AdWords *converts*, to see if that traffic performs an action you want to have happen, such as making a purchase, leaving contact information, signing up for a subscription, or visiting a particular page.

This chapter explains how to use AdWords reports, and how to get started with AdWords conversion tracking.

Using AdWords Reports

To create a report, go to the Reports tab of the AdWords application. The Create Report window, shown in Figure 12-1, will open.

Kinds of Reports

There are seven kinds of prebuilt reports available, in addition to a custom report facility that lets you specify almost all aspects of what the custom report includes (see "Creating a Custom Report" later in this chapter for more on custom reports).

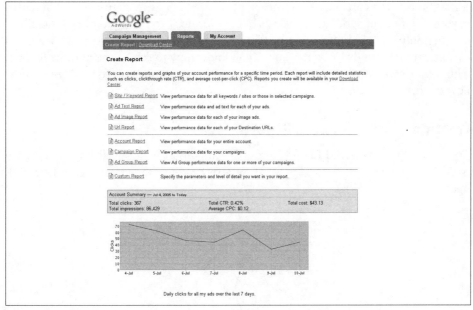

Figure 12-1. To create a report, click a link for the kind of report you want to generate in the Create Report window

The available prebuilt reports are:

Site / Keyword
> This report provides performance information for all sites and/or keywords in an account or in selected campaigns in an account.

Ad Text
> This report provides performance information for the text ads in an account or in selected campaigns in an account.

Ad Image
> This report provides performance information for the image ads in an account or in selected campaigns in an account.

Url
> This report provides performance information by destination URL for the ads in an account or in selected campaigns in an account.

Account
> This report provides aggregate performance information for your account.

Campaign
> This report provides aggregate performance information for one or more campaigns in your account.

Ad Group
> This report provides aggregate performance information for the Ad Groups in one or more campaigns in your account.

All of these reports are created in more or less the same way, with minor differences in your ability to include specific kinds of data (or not), so I'll show you the details of creating only one kind of report, the Site / Keyword report (and also how to create a custom report). But don't worry—once you know how to create one of these reports, with minor variations on the information you choose to display, you really do know how to create all of them!

Creating a Site / Keyword Report

To create a Site / Keyword Report, in the Create Report window click the Site / Keyword Report link. The Site / Keyword Report window, shown in Figure 12-2, will open.

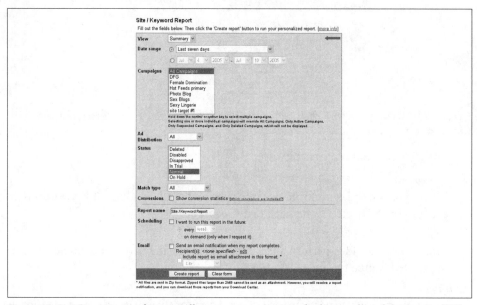

Figure 12-2. A Site / Keyword Report allows you to see activity for keywords and destination URLs across your campaigns

To create the Site / Keyword Report, make your selections from the drop-down lists shown in Figure 12-2 as follows:

View

The View setting lets you display data as an aggregated line of summarized information, or alternatively to display daily, weekly, monthly, or yearly data.

Date range

You can choose a preset period to be covered by the report or select your own date range.

Campaigns

You can choose to display information for all campaigns in your account or for one or more campaigns.

Ad Distribution

The Ad Distribution drop-down list lets you select AdWords Content, AdWords Search, or both programs for inclusion in the report.

Status

The Status list lets you choose the keyword delivery statuses you'd like to see in the report. You can multiselect statuses. For example, if you select only Normal, you will only see keywords in your report that are performing normally. See Chapter 11 for more information about keyword delivery status codes.

Match type

The Match type distribution box lets you choose the type of keyword matches you'd like to see in your reports. You can choose to see keywords matched using all matching criteria, or broad, phrase, exact, or web site targeted matches. See Chapter 11 for more information about keyword matching.

To show Conversions, enable the Show conversion statistics (see "Working with Conversion Tracking" later in this chapter for more information about conversion tracking).

> There's no convenient way to edit a report once you've created it. If you want to change something about a report, you'll need to create an entirely new report. You can then delete the first report from the Download Center window.

When you are satisfied with your choices, click Create Report.

Downloading Reports

Once you've created your report, it will be generated by the Google servers and then will be ready for you to view or download. It will take a few minutes to generate your report, and during this process, you will see a message like that shown in Figure 12-3.

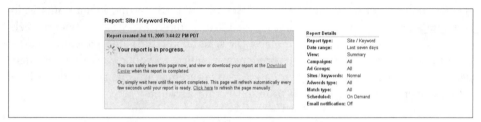

Figure 12-3. Depending on its size, it can take up to 15 minutes to generate a report

Once your report is complete, you will be shown a window with links that lets you view the report or download it (Figure 12-4).

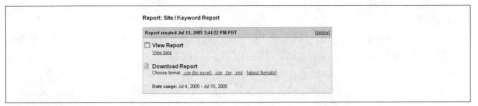

Figure 12-4. You can view your report or download it in one of several formats

This window, providing view and download links on a per report basis, can also be accessed by clicking the link for a specific report from the Download Center (shown in Figure 12-5), which shows all the reports you've created. The Download Center itself is accessed by clicking the Download Center link on the Reports tab.

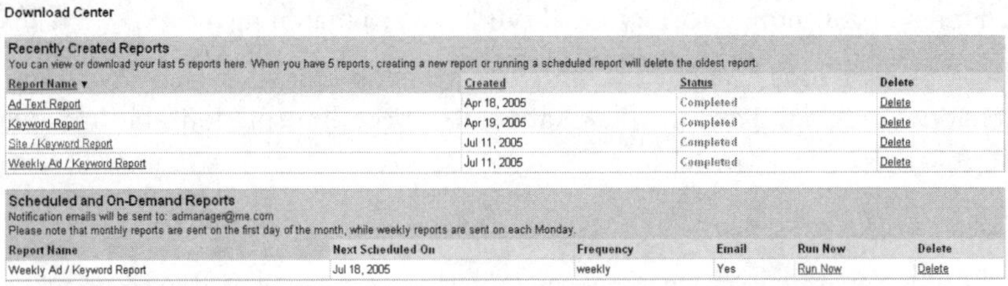

Figure 12-5. The Download Center provides links for viewing or downloading all the reports you have generated

If you decide to view your report by clicking the View data link, it will be displayed in chart format, as shown in Figure 12-6.

You don't have to open the Download Center window to open a report you recently created; when you open the main Create Report window you'll see a list of links to view (or download) reports at the upper right of the window (Figure 12-7).

Scheduling a Report

It's very convenient to schedule a report (see Figure 12-8) so that it is automatically run after a given amount of time has elapsed, for example, every day or once a week. The best part of this is that you can have the scheduled report automatically emailed to you. Scheduling reports and having them emailed to you means that the highlights of your AdWords activity will appear in your email in-box, so you don't have to remember to log into AdWords to monitor your account.

AdWords offers you four different formats for reports that you want to download. They are:

.csv (for Excel)
> This format uses comma-separated values encoded using the UTF-16LE character set and is a native Excel format.

.csv
> This format is plain text (using the UTF-8 character set) comma-separated values and is good choice if you will be loading the report into a database program. In addition, reports created in *.csv* are likely to produce smaller files than reports created in *.csv (for Excel)* and can probably still be read by Excel. So if your reports are large, you should experiment with using *.csv* rather than *.csv (for Excel)*.

.tsv
> A tab-separated value format using the UTF-8 character set.

.xml
> Reports are presented in XML, a good choice for publishing data to multiple formats. It's worth noting that reports downloaded in the *.xml* format feature more precision than the other formats—currency values are reported to one-millionth of a unit!

Reports that are over 100 megabytes in size can be downloaded only in *.xml* format. Google suggests splitting up reports that are this big into a number of smaller reports—for example, by covering fewer keywords or shorter date ranges—to view them in another format.

When you are creating a report, such as the Site / Keyword Report—in the area towards the bottom of the report creation window shown in Figure 12-8—take the following steps to schedule a report:

1. In the Report name box, give the report a name that identifies it as running periodically, for example, "My daily Site / Keyword report."

2. Check the I want to run this report in the future box.

3. Choose a time period from the drop-down list (day, week, or month) or select on demand.

> On demand reports are run only when the Run Now link for the scheduled report in the Download Center is clicked.

Showing rows 1 - 24 of 24.

Campaign ▼	Ad Group	Site / Keyword	Match Type	Status	Maximum CPC	Maximum CPM	Destination URL	Impressions	Clicks	CTR	Avg CPC	CPM	Cost	Avg Position
DFG	Great Photos	depth of field	Broad	Normal	$0.15	$0.00	default URL	523	5	1.0%	$0.05	$0.48	$0.25	1.0
DFG	Great Photos	digital photography resources	Broad	Normal	$0.25	$0.00	default URL	1	0	0.0%	$0.00	$0.00	$0.00	1.0
DFG	Great Photos	digital photography tips	Broad	Normal	$0.25	$0.00	default URL	2	0	0.0%	$0.00	$0.00	$0.00	4.5
DFG	Great Photos	f-stop	Broad	Normal	$0.15	$0.00	default URL	480	6	1.2%	$0.06	$0.79	$0.38	1.0
DFG	Great Photos	field photography	Broad	Normal	$0.15	$0.00	default URL	2	0	0.0%	$0.00	$0.00	$0.00	1.0
DFG	Great Photos	landscape photography	Broad	Normal	$0.15	$0.00	default URL	878	2	0.2%	$0.12	$0.26	$0.23	5.6
DFG	Great Photos	outdoor photos	Broad	Normal	$0.15	$0.00	default URL	38	0	0.0%	$0.00	$0.00	$0.00	2.5
DFG	Yosemite	Yosemite photo	Broad	Normal	$0.12	$0.00	default URL	242	8	3.3%	$0.06	$2.11	$0.51	4.2
DFG	Yosemite	Yosemite photography	Broad	Normal	$0.12	$0.00	default URL	64	1	1.6%	$0.05	$0.78	$0.05	3.8
DFG	Yosemite	camping photo	Broad	Normal	$0.12	$0.00	default URL	5	0	0.0%	$0.00	$0.00	$0.00	1.0
DFG	Yosemite	outdoor photography	Broad	Normal	$0.12	$0.00	default URL	304	0	0.0%	$0.00	$0.00	$0.00	4.7
Hot Feeds primary	Hot Feeds	variations	Broad	Normal	$0.15	$0.00	default URL	4	1	25.0%	$0.12	$30.00	$0.12	3.0
Photo Blog	Harold Davis	photo blog	Broad	Normal	$0.22	$0.00	default URL	1,315	2	0.2%	$0.14	$0.22	$0.29	5.4
Photo Blog	Harold Davis	photo blogging	Broad	Normal	$0.22	$0.00	default URL	99	0	0.0%	$0.00	$0.00	$0.00	6.9
Photo Blog	Harold Davis	photoblog	Broad	Normal	$0.22	$0.00	default URL	198	0	0.0%	$0.00	$0.00	$0.00	2.4
Photo Blog	Harold Davis	photography blog	Broad	Normal	$0.22	$0.00	default URL	24	0	0.0%	$0.00	$0.00	$0.00	2.0
Sex Blogs	Sex Blogs	blogs about sex	Broad	Normal	$0.15	$0.00	default URL	16	0	0.0%	$0.00	$0.00	$0.00	1.0
Sex Blogs	Sex Blogs	sex blog	Broad	Normal	$0.15	$0.00	default URL	4,656	66	1.4%	$0.08	$1.13	$5.27	1.1
Sex Blogs	Sex Blogs	sex blogging	Broad	Normal	$0.15	$0.00	default URL	59	5	8.5%	$0.10	$8.81	$0.52	1.4
Sex Blogs	Sex Blogs	sex blogs	Broad	Normal	$0.15	$0.00	default URL	4,441	98	2.2%	$0.08	$1.86	$8.27	1.2
Sex Blogs	Sex Blogs	sexlog	Broad	Normal	$0.15	$0.00	default URL	26	0	0.0%	$0.00	$0.00	$0.00	1.1
site target #1	Brainiac	photographyblog.com	WebSite	Normal	$0.00	$2.00	default URL	1,683	3	0.2%	$1.12	$2.00	$3.37	3.3
site target #1	Brainiac	photoshopcafe.com	WebSite	Normal	$0.00	$2.00	default URL	1,679	4	0.2%	$0.84	$2.00	$3.36	3.3
site target #1	Brainiac	shuttertalk.com	WebSite	Normal	$0.00	$2.00	default URL	644	2	0.3%	$0.84	$2.00	$1.29	2.2
Totals and Overall Averages								17,383	203	1.2%	$0.12	$1.38	$23.90	2.2

Figure 12-6. The Site / Keyword Report provides a summary for each keyword in your campaigns

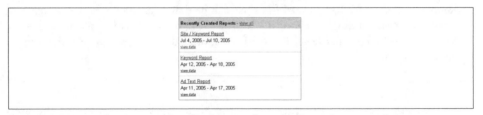

Figure 12-7. You can access recently related reports from the Create Report window

Figure 12-8. Automatically scheduling reports is a great way to stay on top of the data that AdWords creates

4. If you want an email notification when the report is ready, check Send an email notification.

  a. Click the edit link to provide an email address for the report. This link opens the Download Center window.

b. Enter your email address in the Email Preferences area, shown in Figure 12-9.

c. Click Update to return to report scheduling.

5. If you want the report emailed to you, check Include report as email attachment, and choose a report download format from the drop-down list. If you don't choose to have the report emailed to you, the email notification that the report has been created will provide a link you can use to view the report.

Figure 12-9. Enter one or more email addresses that reports are to be sent to in the Download Center

 Attachments are sent as ZIP archive files, and zipped files sent this way cannot be larger than 2 megabytes. If your attachment is larger than this size, Google will not send it, but will email a notification that your report has been created.

Creating a Custom Report

With a custom report, you specify exactly what information you want the report to show.

To create a custom report, in the Create Report window, click the Custom Report link. Next, in the Custom Report window (shown in Figure 12-10), make your selections:

View
The View setting lets you display data as summarized information, or alternatively to display daily, weekly, monthly, or yearly data.

Date range
You can choose a preset period to be covered by the report or select your own date range.

Values
Choose which of these metrics you want displayed.

Ad text
Choose which portion of the text of your ads you'd like displayed.

Give the report a name, schedule it (if you want), and click Create Report.

If you look closely at Figure 12-10, you'll notice that you can refine your custom choices by using the Show options link in the Detail level section. When you click

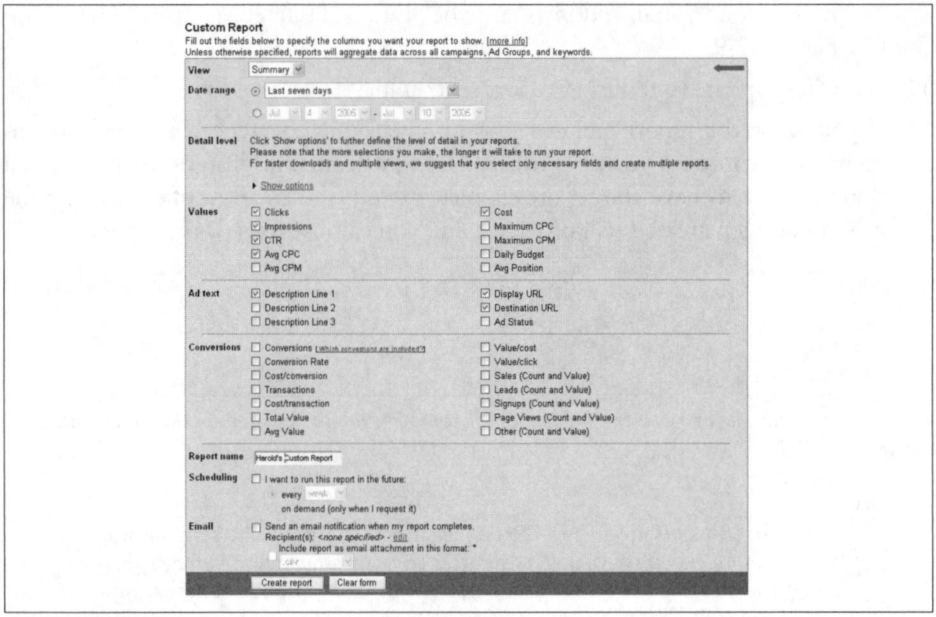

Figure 12-10. You can use a custom report to display only the information you care about, for example, only the actual cost of an ad and not its maximum theoretical CPC

this link, you can further define the elements in your custom report with the Detail Level window shown in Figure 12-11.

Once you are satisfied with your custom report selections using the Detail Level and Custom Report windows, you can create your report in the normal fashion to display your customized information (Figure 12-12).

> A good use for the adding specific keywords to the Detail Level of a custom report is to drill down into ads and keywords that you are particularly scrutinizing because performance may be borderline acceptable—not terrible and not great.

Working with Conversion Tracking

Conversion tracking is used to see whether the traffic that you've paid to drive to your site with AdWords actually does what you want it to do. If your site is in the business of selling widgets, then all the click throughs in the world don't do you any good unless your site visitors buy your widgets. So conversion tracking is a mechanism that helps you understand empirically whether site visitors coming via AdWords are converting (meaning performing the action you desire), and what percentage of the visitors sent to your site by AdWords do, in fact, convert.

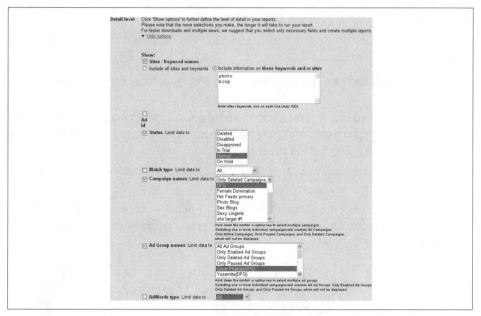

Figure 12-11. Using the Detail Level window, you can limit your report to specific keywords, sites, Campaigns, Ad Groups, and more

Campaign ▾	Ad Group	Site / Keyword	Status	Headline	Display URL	Destination URL	Impressions	Clicks	CTR	Avg CPC	Cost
DFG	Great Photos	landscape photography	Normal	Take great photos	www.DigitalFieldGuide.com	http://www.digitalfieldguide.com	878	2	0.2%	$0.12	$0.23
DFG	Great Photos	outdoor photos	Normal	Take great photos	www.DigitalFieldGuide.com	http://www.digitalfieldguide.com	38	0	0.0%	$0.00	$0.00
DFG	Great Photos	depth of field	Normal	Take great photos	www.DigitalFieldGuide.com	http://www.digitalfieldguide.com	523	5	1.0%	$0.05	$0.25
DFG	Great Photos	f-stop	Normal	Take great photos	www.DigitalFieldGuide.com	http://www.digitalfieldguide.com	480	6	1.2%	$0.06	$0.38
DFG	Great Photos	field photography	Normal	Take great photos	www.DigitalFieldGuide.com	http://www.digitalfieldguide.com	2	0	0.0%	$0.00	$0.00
DFG	Great Photos	digital photography tips	Normal	Take great photos	www.DigitalFieldGuide.com	http://www.digitalfieldguide.com	2	0	0.0%	$0.00	$0.00
DFG	Great Photos	digital photography resources	Normal	Take great photos	www.DigitalFieldGuide.com	http://www.digitalfieldguide.com	1	0	0.0%	$0.00	$0.00
Totals and Overall Averages:							1,924	13	0.7%	$0.07	$0.86

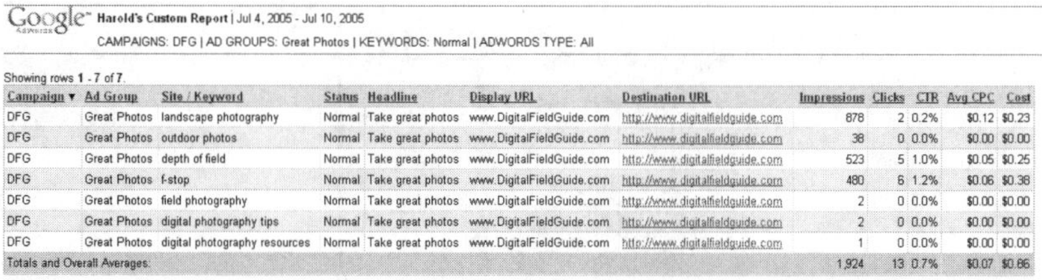

Figure 12-12. A custom report displays line by line the information you requested

ROI and Conversion Tracking

If you understand what a conversion is worth to you, in addition to the percentage of CPC AdWords visitors who convert (the *conversion ratio*), it is easy to calculate your *return on investment* (ROI) for an AdWords campaign. If the amount each conversion is worth multiplied times the conversion ratio is greater than your average CPC, then your AdWords campaign is producing a positive ROI, and probably makes sense.

You could state this as an equation. For an AdWords campaign to make sense, then the following should be true:

Conversion amount * Conversion Ratio > Average CPC

Understanding Conversion Tracking

Google's underlying conversion-tracking mechanism is fairly simple and works as follows:

- You add some special Google conversion-tracking code to a results page on your site.

- You make sure that the results page will be opened when a visitor is converted, for example, by buying something (in the case of a purchase, the results page usually doubles as an order confirmation).

- When a user clicks your AdWords ad, Google adds a cookie to the user's computer to track the user.

- When a user with the Google AdWords cookie on his computer opens the results page, a conversion is logged and a special tracking message is displayed to the user.

This process is shown in Figure 12-13.

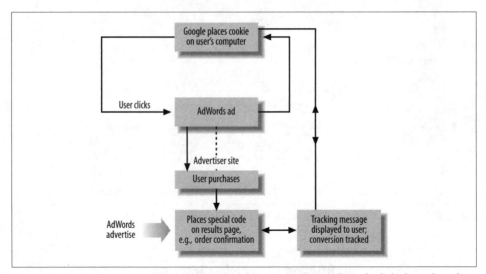

Figure 12-13. Conversion tracking is triggered when a user with an AdWords click-through cookie opens the results page

An interesting, and somewhat controversial, feature of Google AdWords conversion tracking is that as part of the tracking, Google notifies users that they are being tracked. This hard-to-notice message is produced by the Google-supplied code you add to the results page. A tracked user sees a message titled *Google Site Stats* with a "send feedback" link on the results page.

Although this notification is fairly unobtrusive, the look will vary depending upon the web page and the settings selected when the conversion tracking is set up. Figures 12-20 and 12-23 show fairly typical examples of the conversion-tracking notice.

Google explains that it prefers to be aboveboard about its actions, and that the send feedback link is a chance for users to understand Google's privacy policies and indeed to reject the Google tracking cookie if they wish.

However, most major advertising programs do provide conversion-tracking options, and other advertising programs that track users and conversions do not "brand" the process. Users who click through ads in these other programs never know they are being tracked.

The tracking message Google displays may make some users uneasy, and a few advertisers have therefore decided not to track AdWord conversions. That said, you have to admire the aboveboard aspect of Google's notification to users that they are, in fact, being tracked.

 If you see the Google Site Stats-send feedback message in the course of your web surfing, it means that a Google AdWords cookie on your computer has tracked a successful conversion.

You can define a conversion in any way you'd like, so long as you can put up a web page that the user opens when the conversion event takes place. But the most common conversions are:

Purchases
> The conversion occurs when the user makes the purchase, and the order confirmation page doubles as the results page.

Lead generation
> The conversion takes place when the user provides contact information, and the "a sales representative will be in touch with you shortly" page is also the results page.

Subscription sign-up
> The conversion takes place when the user signs up to join a community or subscribe to a newsletter; the membership or subscription confirmation page is also the tracking results page.

Viewing a key page
> If the point of your AdWords campaign is to subtly direct users to a specific, crucial page, then that important page can double as a tracking results page.

AdWords conversion tracking uses the same programmatic model as the Google AdSense program (and other contextual content ad programs). The code you embed in your results pages uses JavaScript to set some variables and then call a script on Google's servers.

By the very nature of conversion tracking, and the heterogeneous nature of development on the Web, conversion tracking has to coexist with a variety of technologies used for e-commerce and web deployment. The bottom line is that you can use Google's conversion tracking in any web page that will work with JavaScript, which is almost any web page (assuming the user hasn't turned off JavaScript in the browser). Essentially, the way conversion tracking works is more or less the same regardless of the technology that serves or generates the pages: you use Google AdWords to generate the conversion-tracking JavaScript code, which you embed in a results page on your site.

Google specifically expects conversion tracking to be used with sites that use the following technologies:

- Yahoo! stores
- Sites that enable users to purchase goods or services with PayPal
- Active Server Pages (ASP and ASPX)
- Java Server Pages (JSP)
- Sites written in Hypertext Preprocessor (PHP)
- Sites prepared using Macromedia Dreamweaver
- Sites prepared using Microsoft FrontPage

 As examples, I'm showing how to add conversion tracking to a PayPal Buy Now button for purchases and to a PHP page for users who open this key page. Implementing conversion tracking works comparably for these other technologies—just add the Google-generated JavaScript code to your results page.

It's up to you to create a results page and have it up on your site. Google will not do this for you. (Of course, if you are selling goods or services, you probably already have an order confirmation page!)

Tracking PayPal Purchases

A simple conversion event is a visitor to your site buying something by clicking a PayPal Buy Now button. You can easily track these conversions. This tracking can be enabled when you add a new Buy Now button to your web page or when you add a conversion-tracking mechanism to an existing Buy Now button.

You can track conversions made by purchases in a PayPal shopping cart in much the same fashion as with the PayPal Buy Now button.

Setting up a new PayPal button

The first part of the process of adding conversion-tracking code is to use AdWords to generate the JavaScript you'll need.

To get this code, in the AdWords Campaign Management tab, click the Conversion Tracking link. Next, choose Get Conversion page code. The Choose Conversion Types window, shown in Figure 12-14, will open.

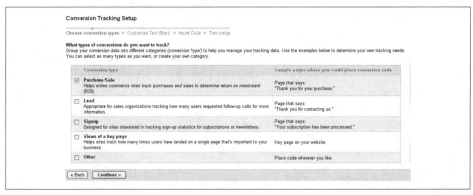

Figure 12-14. You can put conversion-tracking code on any results page, but conversion tracking usually works best with specific conversion events like buying something, leaving contact information for lead generation, or signing up for a site or subscription

For the PayPal button, you should check Purchase/Sale and click Continue. The Customize Text Block window, shown in Figure 12-15, will open.

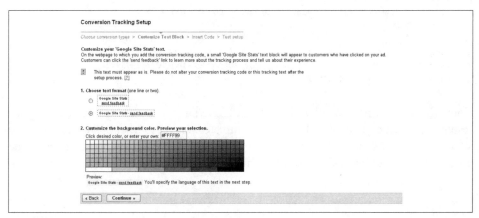

Figure 12-15. You can choose the background color for Google's notification to users and one of two formats for the notification's text format

The only significant choice in the Customize Text Block window is the background color. You should probably plan to select the background color used in the your web site's scheme as the general background color for web pages.

Once you've made your choices in the Conversion Tracking Setup window, choose Continue. The Insert Code page will open.

In the Insert Code page, specify your web site's language and whether the confirmation page is accessed via HTTPS (Secure Hyper Text Transport Protocol) or regular HTTP.

 You can recognize HTTPS pages because their URL begins *https://*. These pages are more secure than pages with a more typical URL beginning with *http://*, so they are often used for shopping applications.

Your JavaScript code is now ready for you to copy and paste. Here's what it looks like (the XXXXXXXXX in the code snippet is replaced with your actual conversion tracking ID):

```
<!-- Google Code for Purchase Conversion Page -->
<script language="JavaScript" type="text/javascript">
<!--
var google_conversion_id = XXXXXXXXX;
var google_conversion_language = "en_US";
var google_conversion_format = "2";
var google_conversion_color = "CCCCCC";
if (1) {
   var google_conversion_value = 1;
}
var google_conversion_label = "Purchase";
//-->
</script>
<script language="JavaScript"
src="http://www.googleadservices.com/pagead/conversion.js">
</script>
<noscript>
<img height=1 width=1 border=0
src="http://www.googleadservices.com/pagead/conversion/1070313714/?
value=1&label=Purchase&script=0">
</noscript>
```

Copy the JavaScript code that Google generated for you, and paste it into your results page, which I've named for this example confirmation.html. The Google code should go towards the bottom of the page, and not in a header or footer. It should be visible, but you probably don't want to make it too prominent.

Setting a Conversion Value

If you click the Advanced Option: conversion value link that you'll find to the right of your generated code before you copy the code, you can set a conversion value that AdWords will use to automatically compute your ROI for you.

You can enter this conversion amount as an absolute sum (each conversion is worth $5.00, for example). You'll need to take care to enter the amount and the currency that it is expressed in using the comma-delimited form that Google requires.

An absolute amount per conversion is unlikely to be very realistic, so Google gives you the option of entering server-side variables in this field rather than an amount. It makes sense to use the variables that will be available to the results page—for example, the total dollar amount in the user's shopping cart—but getting this to work will be a unique programmatic issue, depending on what variables are available and how they have been named.

As an example, when tracking conversions using a PayPal Buy Now button, you can enter the variable totalValue into the value field for the Advanced Option.

When the PayPal page opens your results tracking page following a successful transaction, PayPay does so using a CGI Post command, passing the transaction amount using a variable named amount. Provided your results tracking page is capable of dynamically processing the Post variable, you can set it equal to the Google AdWords totalValue variable and the actual total amount of the PayPal transaction will show up as the value of the conversion.

Make sure the results page has been loaded on your web server.

Next log onto your PayPal account. Go to the Merchant Tools tab. Click on the Website Payments Standard link in the Business Solutions area (shown on the left of Figure 12-16) to expand the link.

Click the Feature List link found under Website Payments Standard. The Complete Feature List window will open (Figure 12-16). Locate Buy Now Buttons in the Payment Processing section and choose the Set it up link.

Configure your button as you'd like, for example, by setting a price and choosing from the button graphics that PayPal makes available. Next, scroll to the bottom of the page and click Add More Options.

Go to the Customize Your Buyer's Experience area, shown in Figure 12-17.

Enter the full URL to your results tracking page (on your web site) in the Successful Payment URL text box.

Figure 12-16. PayPal account holders can use the payment resources their account provides to add Buy Now buttons to their web sites

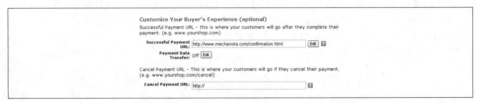

Figure 12-17. PayPal lets you specify a page that is opened immediately after the buyer successfully completes a purchase

Select Create Button Now, and the HTML form code for your PayPal button (including the reference to the tracking results page) will be generated for you as shown in Figure 12-18.

Figure 12-18. The HTML code generated by PayPal includes the page to be opened when the transaction is successfully completed

Copy and paste the PayPal code into your web page used to make purchases, and upload the page to your web server.

Depending on the graphics you chose for your Buy Now button and the layout for your page, your site visitors will see a page that looks something like the one shown in Figure 12-19.

Figure 12-19. The PayPal Buy Now button that will propel a user who makes a successful transaction to the results tracking page looks just like any other PayPal Buy Now button

When the user successfully completes a purchase using the PayPal Buy Now button, the results tracking page (`confirmation.html`) shown in Figure 12-20 opens.

Figure 12-20. The Google Site Stats text and link tells a savvy user that Google AdWords tracking is in use

The final step, of course, is to test that conversion tracking is actually working. You can wait for a user to click through from an AdWords ad and complete a transaction. You'll then see the conversion in your Campaign Summary (and your reports) with a time delay (of up to about 24 hours).

 See Figure 12-24 for a display of conversion tracking in the Campaign Summary window and Figure 12-26 to see conversion tracking in a report.

You can also initiate a conversion tracking test yourself, but it will cost you for the clicks you make. To do this, first search Google for one of your ads. Click through your own ad (this is not illegal, but you will have to pay Google for the click!).

Next, open the results page. Note that since you know the address for the results page, such as *http://www.mechanista.com/confirmation.html*, you don't have to actually use the Buy Now PayPal button—just open the results page.

Your actions will record a conversion, which will show up in the AdWords Campaign summary and AdWords reports after the time delay.

Modifying an existing PayPal button

You don't need to create a new PayPal Buy Now button to add conversion tracking. Suppose you have an existing page with a Buy Now button and HTML form code like this:

```
Pay for your purchase with any major credit card using PayPal:
<form action="https://www.paypal.com/cgi-bin/webscr" method="post">
<input type="hidden" name="cmd" value="_xclick">
<input type="hidden" name="business" value="admanager@me.com">
<input type="hidden" name="item_name" value="Calculator">
<input type="hidden" name="item_number" value="101">
<input type="hidden" name="amount" value="105.00">
<input type="hidden" name="currency_code" value="USD">
<input type="image" src="https://www.paypal.com/images/x-click-butcc.gif"
border="0" name="submit" alt="Make payments with PayPal -
it's fast, free and secure!">
</form>
```

To modify this code to track results, you simply need to add a hidden form field named value with a value of the tracking results page:

```
<input type="hidden" name="value"
value="http://www.mechanista.com/confirmation.html">
```

Here's the modified form code, which will track the results of your PayPal transaction:

```
Pay for your purchase with any major credit card using PayPal:
<form action="https://www.paypal.com/cgi-bin/webscr" method="post">
<input type="hidden" name="cmd" value="_xclick">
```

```
<input type="hidden" name="business" value="admanager@me.com">
<input type="hidden" name="value"
value="http://www.mechanista.com/confirmation.html">
<input type="hidden" name="item_name" value="Calculator">
<input type="hidden" name="item_number" value="101">
<input type="hidden" name="amount" value="105.00">
<input type="hidden" name="currency_code" value="USD">
<input type="image" src="https://www.paypal.com/images/x-click-butcc.gif"
border="0" name="submit" alt="Make payments with PayPal -
it's fast, free and secure!">
</form>
```

Tracking Visitors to a Crucial Page

Suppose you are not quite so concerned with whether visitors actually make a purchase, but rather want to determine whether site visitors are visiting a key page.

For example, part of the strategy of the AdWords campaign that sends traffic to the Photoblog 2.0 at *http://www.digitalfieldguide.com/blog/* is that some of this traffic will migrate along internal site links to the resources and equipment pages of the site, for example, *http://www.digitalfieldguide.com/resources.php*. This page provides links to high-ticket items such as digital cameras that provide substantial affiliate revenue when a site visitor makes a purchase. It would be nice to know how many of the AdWords-driven visitors to the photo blog actually "trickle down" into the affiliate sections of the site. Using AdWords conversion tracking, we can find this out.

The first step is to generate new conversion-tracking code, choosing Views of a key page as the conversion tracking type in the Choose conversion types window in AdWords Conversion Tracking Setup (Figure 12-21).

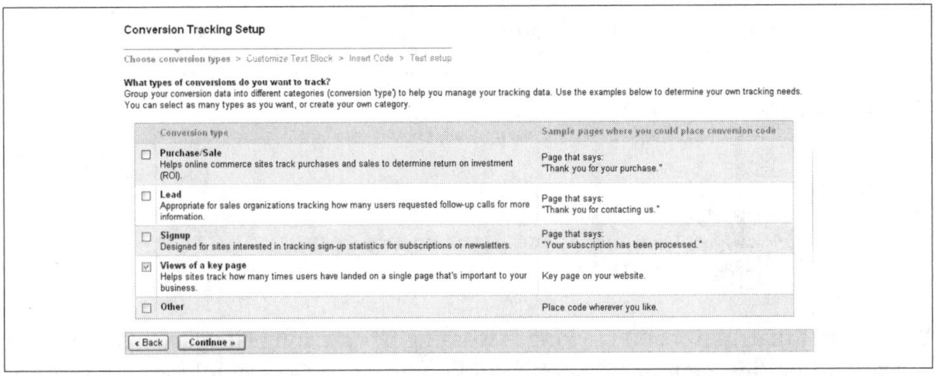

Figure 12-21. Choose Views of a key page if you want to track how many users migrate from an AdWords click through to a specific page on your site

In the Customize Text Block, be sure to choose a background color to match your key page (in the case of the Digital Field Guide site, this is "#CCCCCC", or light gray), as shown in Figure 12-22.

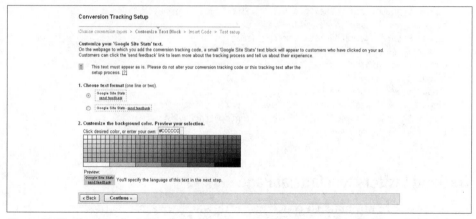

Figure 12-22. To make the AdWords tracking message as unobtrusive as possible, make sure that its background color matches your site's

Choose Continue, and copy and paste the conversion-tracking code into the key results page. Here's the code (with the actual conversion ID replaced by XXXXXXXXXXX):

```
<!-- Google Code for PageView Conversion Page -->
<script language="JavaScript" type="text/javascript">
<!--
var google_conversion_id = XXXXXXXXXXX;
var google_conversion_language = "en_US";
var google_conversion_format = "2";
var google_conversion_color = "CCCCCC";
if (1) {
  var google_conversion_value = 1;
}
var google_conversion_label = "PageView";
//-->
</script>
<script language="JavaScript"
src="http://www.googleadservices.com/pagead/conversion.js">
</script>
<noscript>
<img height=1 width=1 border=0
src="http://www.googleadservices.com/pagead/conversion/1070313714/?
value=1&label=PageView&script=0">
</noscript>
```

You can test that conversion tracking is working by searching Google for one of your keywords (for this example, "f-stop" works fine since the Photoblog 2.0 ad campaign is the only AdWords ad that matches this keyword). Click the link in the ad (yes, you do have to pay for the click through if you are unwilling to wait for a real site visitor to test conversion tracking). Navigate to the key results page, shown in Figure 12-23.

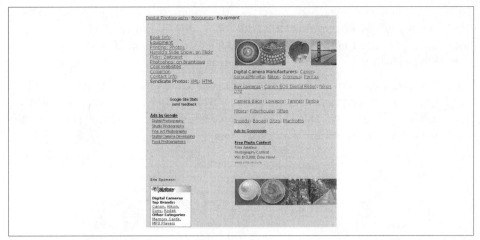

Figure 12-23. This key results page displays affiliate links used to purchase expensive camera gear

The Google Site Stats send feedback text and link in the middle of the page show that you've been spotted for conversion tracking. You can also spot your "conversion" after a time delay in the Campaign Summary screen (Figure 12-24).

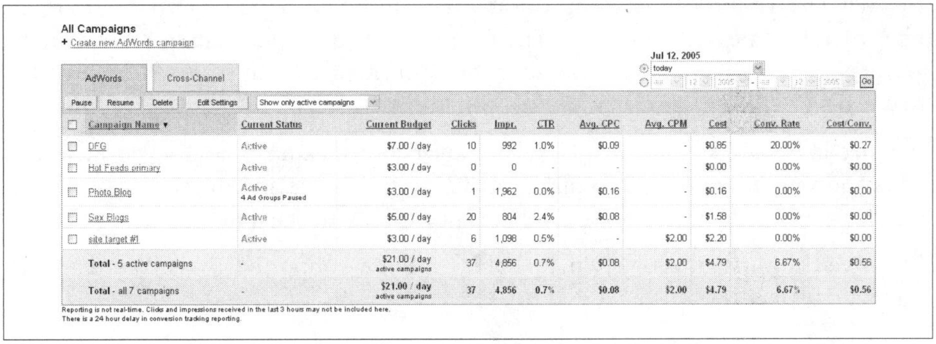

Figure 12-24. Conversion tracking metrics are shown on the first line for the DFG campaign, based on the number of site visitors who opened the key page

By the way, now that you've activated conversion tracking, you'll see its status as Active in the main Conversion Tracking window (reached by clicking Conversion Tracking from the Campaign Summary tab), as shown in Figure 12-25.

Figure 12-25. You can turn conversion tracking off, leaving conversion code in your pages in case you want to turn it back on later

There is a (minor) downside to conversion tracking, namely that to some degree it slows down your web pages (because additional code is now loading on the results page). So if you don't end up taking advantage of conversion tracking, you should turn it off by clicking the Stop AdWords tracking link.

Each AdWords report provides an option to include conversion information. Provided you select this option when you create your reports, they will show conversion-tracking information, such as the report in Figure 12-26 showing the conversion-tracking test for the key results page.

Campaign ▼	Ad Group	Ad Group Status	Impressions	Clicks	CTR	Avg CPC	CPM	Cost	Avg Position	Conversions	Conversion Rate	Cost / Conversion
DFG	Great Photos	Active	382	4	1.0%	$0.10	$1.05	$0.40	4.0	1	100.00%	$0.05
DFG	Yosemite	Active	610	6	1.0%	$0.08	$0.74	$0.45	3.1	0	0.00%	$0.00
Totals and Overall Averages:			992	10	1.0%	$0.08	$0.66	$0.85	3.5	1	20.00%	$0.27

Google Ad Group Report | Jul 12, 2005 - Jul 12, 2005
CAMPAIGNS: DFG | AD GROUPS: All | ADWORDS TYPE: All
Showing rows 1 - 2 of 2.

Figure 12-26. Assuming you checked Show conversion statistics when you created the report, your Ad Group report will also display conversion metrics

Cross-Channel Conversion Tracking

Cross-channel conversion tracking is a mechanism for tracking conversion from ads other than Google AdWords ads. The great benefit of implementing cross-channel conversion tracking is that you monitor the performance of all your ads from within AdWords.

The mechanics are similar to AdWords conversion tracking. You use the AdWords application to generate code to place in your landing page and in the cross-channel. In order to generate this code, you will need to specify the channel to track.

The advertising channels shown in Table 12-1 are supported by AdWords cross-channel tracking.

 In addition, it's possible to choose the Other PPC, Other Banner, and Other online ads and with a bit of tweaking adopt the tracking code generated to almost any conceivable ad program.

Table 12-1. Channels available for cross-tracking

CPC (cost-per-click programs)	CPM (banner ads)	Misc
Findwhat	MSN	Email
Looksmart	Yahoo!	
Lycos		
Overture		

For example, to implement conversion tracking within AdWords for an ad placed on the Overture content network, in the main Conversion Tracking window on the Campaign Management tab, under Cross-Channel Tracking click Create new campaign.

In the Choose channel window, shown in Figure 12-27, select Overture PPC.

PPC is short for "pay per click," which is another name for CPC.

Figure 12-27. You can target cross-channel conversion tracking at any one of the major ad networks

Next, name the cross-channel campaign and provide the destination URL for your Overture ads, as shown in Figure 12-28.

Overture cross-conversion tracking will work more smoothly, and provide information in greater detail, if you have Tracking URLs turned on in Overture.

Choose Continue. The Insert Code and URLs window, shown in Figure 12-29, provides:

- Code to copy and paste into your results page (called a *landing page* here)
- A special URL to copy and paste into the URL field of each Overture ad listing

Once you have cross-conversion tracking turned on and have implemented a cross-conversion tracking campaign, your cross-conversion data will show up on a new tab on the primary Campaign Summary window. This tab is shown in Figure 12-30.

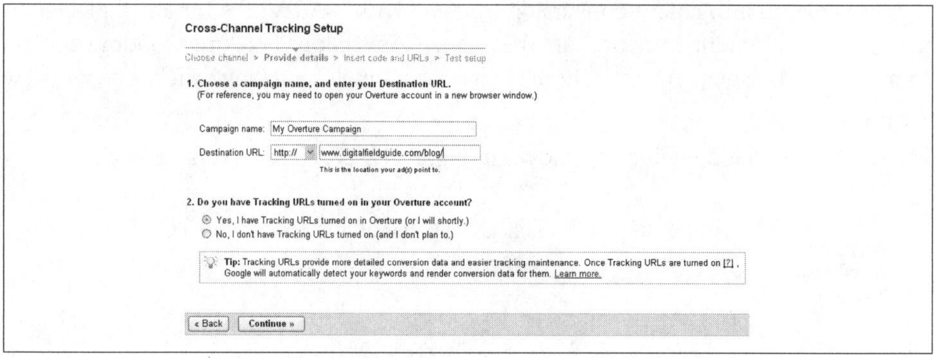

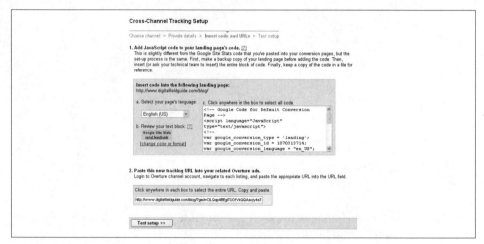

Figure 12-28. You'll need to provide the destination URL for your Overture ads

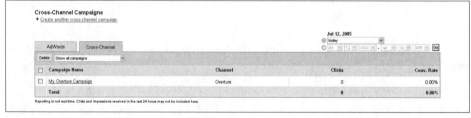

Figure 12-29. Cross-conversion tracking means adding a special URL to the ad listing as well as code to the results page

Figure 12-30. Your cross-channel campaign information is displayed on a new tab in the Campaign Summary window

Action Items

To monitor the performance of your ads and campaigns, you should:

- Customize, generate, and save reports.
- Schedule reports to be regularly emailed.
- Implement conversion tracking for purchases, key page views, and other events that are significant to your business model.
- Turn on cross-channel-conversion campaign tracking to keep track of performance in one place (AdWords) across all the networks in which your ads appear.

PART IV

Using the AdWords APIs

Chapters 13–16 are written for programmers who are interested in writing applications that take advantage of the Google AdWords API web services. This part explains what these web services are and how to write code that interacts with them.

CHAPTER 13

Understanding the AdWords API

You've seen in Part III of this book that the Google AdWords program provides a way for advertisers of any size to reach an audience consisting of most of today's Internet users. AdWords provides elaborate mechanisms and tools to help advertisers make sure that ads are published in a relevant context and viewed by those who are likely to be interested in these ads. In addition, AdWords provides sophisticated reporting and conversion-tracking tools so advertisers can easily figure out if they are getting their money's worth from their AdWords campaigns and modify their campaigns and ads for better performance.

But what happens when the number of ads, targeted keywords, and ad campaigns under management scales upwards? If you are managing multiple accounts with hundreds of ads in the aggregate, it becomes hard to manage AdWords using manual log ins into the AdWords Campaign Summary (and the other account management tools provided).

Google's AdWords API web service is intended to let programmers create software that interacts directly with the AdWords server. With custom applications created using the AdWords API, advertisers can (with some clever programming) efficiently manage their large AdWords accounts and campaigns.

This chapter introduces the AdWords API, explains the high-level process of working with a web service such as the AdWords API, tells you how to get a developer token, and explains the different services that comprise the AdWords API.

Introducing the AdWords API

Google is committed to making access to its software available programmatically. The mechanism for providing this access is to publish APIs (application program interfaces) that can be invoked remotely, as web services.

APIs aren't the only way to programmatically interact with Google applications. For example, you can create a plug-in for the Google Deskbar by writing an application using a .NET language such as C# and compiling it to a DLL (dynamic link library) file.

There are probably a number of good reasons for Google to make its APIs available, including the convenience it provides to major, technically sophisticated customers. But I think the most important reason that Google has opened up its software is to encourage innovation. The developer community may well come up with functionality that hasn't occurred to Google.

The Ecosystem of Google APIs

There seem to be more Google APIs every day. You should check the Google Code page, *http://code.google.com/apis.html*, which describes and provides links to the documentation for specific APIs; you never know what new API might pop up.

As of this writing, the following Google APIs are available to developers:

AdWords API
> The *Google AdWords API* lets programmers write code that interacts directly with all aspects of the AdWords program.

Blogger Atom API
> The *Blogger Atom API* can be used to programmatically interact with blogs using the Blogger Atom format, creating new posts, editing existing posts, and more.

Desktop Search API
> The *Google Desktop Search* API lets developers use Google Desktop Search in their own Windows applications. This API can also be used to add new file formats to Google Desktop Search for indexing.

Maps API
> The *Google Maps API* lets developers embed Google Maps in their own web pages and manipulate the maps programmatically using JavaScript.

Web Search API
> The *Google Web Search API*, also called the *Web APIs service*, is the first of the Google APIs, and arguably the most significant, as search is Google's most important function. This API allows you to search the Google index programmatically with a query generated in your code. You can find information about how to program with the Web Search API in my book *Building Research Tools with Google for Dummies* (Wiley).

> ### The Google API Application Mashup
>
> It's easy to think of creative applications that use multiple APIs. For example, an AdWords API application might also provide searching capabilities. You can also consider combining Google API applications with data from other kinds of programmatic access. Combining the strengths of several applications this way is sometimes called a *mashup*.
>
> For example, the most effective uses of the Google Maps API so far have combined Google maps with information obtained from other sources, for example, the locations of real estate classified advertisers.

Who Can Best Benefit from the AdWords API?

The AdWords API is intended to benefit organizations with considerable technical savvy and development expertise at their disposal. The AdWords program tools work pretty well without any programming. For example, using the AdWords report scheduling mechanism, you are already able to automate most reporting tasks. Since this is the case, why bother with a programmatic interface?

The time and expense involved in creating custom AdWords API applications begins to make sense for a couple of kinds of AdWords advertisers:

- Extremely large advertisers that are managing hundreds, thousands, or even tens of thousands of AdWords campaigns every day; for example, an auction site such as eBay or an online retailer such as Amazon with a huge number of inventory items

- Organizations that are involved in professional AdWords account management and are tasked with keeping AdWords campaigns optimal for many different clients, for example, an advertising agency that handles AdWords for many client accounts

In these kinds of situations, the large advertiser or third-party manager may well have developed a custom work flow that can be automatically integrated with AdWords using the API. In addition, ad text and keyword management may be optimized using proprietary methodology that can be usefully codified in an AdWords API application.

Working with the AdWords API Web Service

To program with the AdWords API, you need to have a basic understanding of how to work with a web service.

Web services are programs that are used to glue together disparate parts of applications across the far-flung Web. They often join together programs running on several servers, with each of the programs supplying a part of the larger software application. Web services constitute a safe and recognizable way to connect the parts of these programs so that they can be used by a wider population.

A web service exposes functions (also called *web methods*) over the Internet. These web methods are a kind of gating mechanism—they have to be called with the specified arguments, in some cases in a given order. Further, web services are designed to prevent an external programmer from harming the remote server via the methods the server exposes.

For example, an online comparison pricing service, such as CNET or BizRate, might make information about its data available via a web service and web methods. A hypothetical web method, getPrices, might return prices for an item when passed the item's product code. An external program could use this web method to display competitive pricing information to end users.

Of course, to use the web methods associated with a web service, you need to know that the service and methods exist. More specifically, in order to code a call to a web method and web service, you need to know an address for the web service, what the methods associated with the service are called, what kinds of values they take, and what kinds of values they return. In other words, to use the pricing web method example, you need to know that the method is called getPrices, that it takes a UPC product code, and returns an array of merchant IDs and prices.

As a programmer, how are you going to know this information so you can use the web service? Thankfully, there is a standard way to discover the crucial information about web methods and web services.

The AdWords API WSDL Files

Each web service provides a "contract" consisting of a WSDL (Web Services Description Language) file that provides information about the service and its methods. WSDL files describe a web service and its methods. If you have, or can find, a WSDL file, you know how to invoke the methods exposed by a web service, and you also know what types of values each web method will return. Using the WSDL file, some modern programming environments, such as Visual Studio.NET, automatically generate most of the code you need to use the web service and its methods.

Technically, a WSDL file is a text file written in XML following a schema specified for WSDL files by the W3C organization (see *http://www.w3.org/2002/ws/desc/* for more information about the W3C WSDL specification). The XML elements in the WSDL file correspond to programmatic methods that can be used to set values, call functions, and evaluate return values and error codes in a web service.

The AdWords API provides a separate WSDL file for each of the eight AdWords API services, which correspond to the organization of an AdWord account. You'll find a description of each of these services in "The AdWords API Services" later in this chapter, along with the address you'll need to access the corresponding WSDL file.

To get a taste of how the discovery and programming process works with one of the AdWord services and the related WSDL file, suppose you want to use Keyword Service to add a new keyword to an Ad Group. The method that adds a keyword is defined in the XML WSDL file for the Keyword web service like this:

```
<wsdl:operation name="addKeyword">
  <wsdlsoap:operation soapAction="" />
  <wsdl:input name="addKeywordRequest">
    <wsdlsoap:header message="impl:email" part="email" use="literal" />
    <wsdlsoap:header message="impl:clientEmail" part="clientEmail" use="literal"
    />
    <wsdlsoap:header message="impl:password" part="password" use="literal" />
    <wsdlsoap:header message="impl:useragent" part="useragent" use="literal" />
    <wsdlsoap:header message="impl:token" part="token" use="literal" />
    <wsdlsoap:body namespace="https://adwords.google.com/api/adwords/v2"
        use="literal" />
  </wsdl:input>
<wsdl:output name="addKeywordResponse">
  <wsdlsoap:header message="impl:responseTime" part="responseTime" use="literal" />
  <wsdlsoap:header message="impl:operations" part="operations" use="literal" />
  <wsdlsoap:body namespace="https://adwords.google.com/api/adwords/v2"
      use="literal" />
</wsdl:output>
```

If you were to make use of this WSDL method definition in a program, you would need to know the meaning of the arguments you need to pass to the method. These are the request headers, which must be sent to all AdWords API method requests and are shown in Table 13-1.

Table 13-1. AdWords API web services request headers

Argument	Meaning
clientEmail	This is an optional field used when you are managing multiple AdWords accounts through a My Client Center account. If you supply a client email, you still must supply your own email and password, and you can only manage the account referenced by the client email.
email	Email for the AdWords account being accessed.
password	Password for the AdWords account being accessed.
token	Your AdWords API developer token.
useragent	You can put anything you want in the useragent field. It's good form to use this field to identify the purpose of your request.

See Chapters 14 and 15 for examples using the AdWords API web services request headers.

Besides the request headers, which must be used for all calls to the AdWords services, the addKeyword method needs to be passed the keyword information as a Keyword type. Here's the XML definition of the Keyword complex type in the Keyword Services WSDL file:

```
<complexType name="Keyword">
    <sequence>
    <element name="type" nillable="true" type="impl:KeywordType" />
    <element name="maxCpc" type="xsd:long" />
    <element name="adGroupId" type="xsd:int" />
    <element name="language" nillable="true" type="xsd:string" />
    <element name="status" nillable="true" minOccurs="0"
        type="impl:KeywordStatus" />
    <element name="negative" type="xsd:boolean" />
    <element name="destinationUrl" nillable="true" type="xsd:string" />
    <element name="text" nillable="true" type="xsd:string" />
    <element name="id" type="xsd:long" />
    <element name="exemptionRequest" nillable="true" type="xsd:string" />
    </sequence>
</complexType>
```

Table 13-2 shows the meaning of the elements passed as part of a Keyword object and returned by the KeywordService API.

Table 13-2. Elements of a Keyword

Element	Type	Meaning	Comment
adGroupID	Integer	AdGroup associated with the keyword.	Required.
destinationURL	String	Destination URL for the keyword.	Optional. If omitted, the destination URL for the ad is used.
exemptionRequest	String	Reason for allowing a text ad or creative that violates Google editorial policy.	Optional. Specifying exemptionRequest makes sure that your API call will not throw an exception, but does not guarantee that the related ad will run.
id	Long integer	The numeric ID associated with the keyword.	Provided when the keyword is created.
language	String	Language for the keyword.	Optional.
maxCpc	Long integer	Maximum CPC for the keyword.	Optional. If 0 is given as the value for maxCPC, then the maximum CPC for the related AdGroup is used.
negative	Boolean	A true value means that this keyword is used for a negative match.	Optional.

Table 13-2. Elements of a Keyword (continued)

Element	Type	Meaning	Comment
status	KeywordStatus enumeration	Corresponds to the status assigned by AdWords for keywords.	Returned by system; possible values for this enumeration are: Normal, InTrial, OnHold, Disabled, Disapproved, Deleted.
text	String	The text of the keyword.	Required. 80 characters maximum.
type	KeywordType enumeration	Kind of targeting.	Required. Possible values for this enumeration are: Broad, Phrase, Exact.

The return value for a successful call to addKeyword is your Keyword object with the fields, such as id and status, filled in.

SOAP

Web services, specified by a WSDL file, can be published using a SOAP (Simple Object Access Protocol) mechanism running over HTTP (or some other transport protocol) or using HTTP Get requests.

Some web services are designed to use SOAP over HTTP but also can run as an HTTP request. The advantage of using HTTP requests is that it is simple to test web services (you just issue a request as a URL). However, using SOAP to encapsulate web service requests from the underlying transport mechanism (such as HTTP or HTTPS) is probably a more robust and secure architecture.

The Google AdWords API web services are implemented using SOAP over HTTPS. Requests are sent as an HTTP POST request with a special SOAPAction header; the response is sent back as the response to the POST.

All AdWords API calls are encrypted with SSL (that is, via HTTPS) for increased security.

The SOAP standard (see *http://www.w3.org/TR/SOAP/* for details) defines three parts used for communication between web service publishers, such as Google AdWords, and programs that use the methods exposed by the web service:

- An envelope that defines a framework for describing what is in a message
- Encoding and decoding rules for types of data used in the message
- A way of expressing remote calls to methods (also called *remote procedure calls*, or RPC) and the method response

As a general matter, to use the AdWords API web services—or any other web service—you don't need to know much about SOAP encoding or the specific XML specified by the WSDL file.

Depending on the programming language and development environment you are using, many of these lower-level details are taken care of by tools built into your development environment or by a toolkit you can download. These tools know how to interpret WSDL files and how to encode and decode XML request and response messages. When an AdWords API web service receives a request, it sends back the response as an XML message. The web service toolkits know how to parse the response and return a data structure or object back to the caller that can easily be used in your programming environment.

Table 13-3 shows the most commonly used SOAP toolkits.

Table 13-3. Common SOAP toolkits

Language	Toolkit	Where to get
Java	Apache Axis	*http://ws.apache.org/axis/*
.NET (C#, VB, etc.)	n/a	Built into Visual Studio .NET
Perl	SOAP::Lite	*http://www.soaplite.com/*
PHP	Pear	*http://pear.php.net/*
	NuSOAP	*http://cvs.sourceforge.net/viewcvs.py/ nusoap/lib/nusoap.php*
Python	SOAPPy	*http://pywebsvcs.sourceforge.net/*

Choosing a Programming Language

You can create programs that interact with the AdWords API in any language that can use a SOAP-based web service, which is most languages. So the choice of language and development environment should largely depend on the standards of your organization and what your organization's programmers are familiar with.

That said, the following languages are a particularly good place to start creating AdWords API applications, because Google provides sample code in these languages and they also have easily available tools for working with SOAP:

- C# .NET
- Java
- Perl
- PHP

The AdWords API Services

The AdWords API services have the same relationship to each other as the objects you can manipulate from a regular AdWords account.

Most importantly, an AdWords Campaign contains Ad Groups, which in turn contain keywords and creatives. To modify keywords associated with an ad, you'll need to start with the Campaign Service (using the client information for the account the campaign is part of) and drill down to an Ad Group via the Ad Group Service and from there to the Keyword Service. This containment relationship is shown in Figure 13-1.

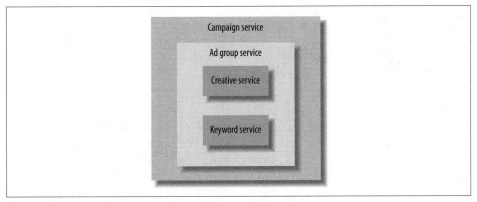

Figure 13-1. Manipulating granular information, such as the keywords associated with an ad, involves drilling down through the AdWords API services

Here's some more information about the purpose and role of each of the AdWords API services and where to find the service's WSDL file:

Account Service
> The Account Service lets you create and modify information associated with AdWords accounts, such as billing information. The WSDL file for the services is located at *https://adwords.google.com/api/adwords/v2/AccountService?wsdl*.

Ad Group Service
> The Ad Group Service lets you create ad groups, list Ad Groups, associate Ad Groups with a Campaign, and perform actions on a per group basis. For example, you can set the cost per click for all keywords in a particular Ad Group. The WSDL file for the services is located at *https://adwords.google.com/api/adwords/v2/AdGroupService?wsdl*.

Campaign Service
> The Campaign Service lets you create, list, and modify Campaigns. For example, you can change the name, set the daily budget, and define the end date of a

Campaign. This service also lets you perform actions on a Campaign, such as pausing it. The WSDL file for the services is located at *https://adwords.google. com/api/adwords/v2/CampaignService?wsdl*.

Creative Service

The Creative Service lets you create and modify creatives and associate them with an Ad Group. The WSDL file for the services is located at *https://adwords. google.com/api/adwords/v2/CreativeService?wsdl*.

Info Service

The Info Service lets you get basic information about how much you have used the AdWords API and how many operations you have left. The WSDL file for the services is located at *https://adwords.google.com/api/adwords/v2/InfoService?wsdl*.

Keyword Service

The Keyword Service lets you get information about keywords. For example, you can get the keywords in an Ad Group and create and modify keywords. The WSDL file for the services is located at *https://adwords.google.com/api/adwords/ v2/KeywordService?wsdl*.

Report Service

The Report Service lets you generate reports on the performance of your AdWords campaigns. For example, you can get reports on the daily number of impressions, clicks, and click-through rate. The WSDL file for the services is located at *https://adwords.google.com/api/adwords/v2/ReportService?wsdl*.

Traffic Estimator Service

The Traffic Estimator Service lets you estimate the performance of keywords, Ad Groups, and Campaigns. You can estimate data, such as the cost per click, click through rate, and average position of your ads. The WSDL file for the services is located at *https://adwords.google.com/api/adwords/v2/TrafficEstimatorService?wsdl*.

Signing up for a Developer Token

As Google puts it, all you need to develop AdWords API applications is a developer token—and some good programming chops.

The starting place for signing up for the developer token, and for getting good technical information about the AdWords services, is the AdWords API beta center, which can be opened at *http://www.google.com/apis/adwords/*, shown in Figure 13-2.

To get a developer token, click the Register as a developer link shown in the upper left of Figure 13-2.

Accessing Your Own My Client Center

In order to get a developer token, and to sign on as an AdWords developer, you'll need a My Client Center.

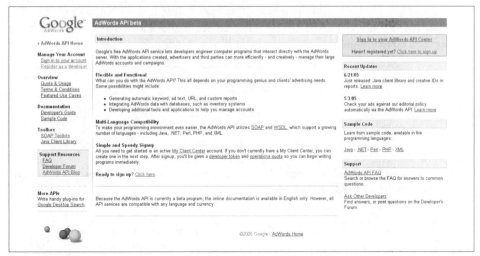

Figure 13-2. The AdWords API beta center is packed with information and is the starting place to register as an AdWords developer

 See Chapter 11 for more information about the AdWords My Client Center.

The primary purpose of a My Client Center is to manage multiple AdWords accounts from one window. When you get an AdWords developer token, a special tab is added to your My Client Center.

If you have already signed up for a My Client Center, use that for the AdWords API Developer Signup (shown in Figure 13-3). Otherwise, use your AdWords logon.

Figure 13-3. Log on to you're My Client Center (if you don't have a My Client Center yet, use your AdWords logon)

Click Continue, check the box to accept terms and conditions, and then click Continue again.

If you don't already have a My Client Center, you'll now be prompted to create one, using an email address that must be different from the address you used for your AdWords account (Figure 13-4).

Figure 13-4. Google won't let you create a My Client Center account using the same email address as you used for your AdWords account

> Once you've signed up, Google AdWords will email your developer token to the address you used to create you're My Client Center.

It's not as off-the-wall as it might seem to associate a My Client Center with the AdWords API developer program, because Google expects many API developers to be businesses involved in professionally managing AdWords accounts. If you are, in fact, a lone-wolf solo practitioner, the only real implication is that you'll need a second working email address to complete the registration process.

Getting Your AdWords API Developer Token

The first time you log onto your My Client Center after registering with the AdWords API Developers Program, the welcome screen will display your developer token (Figure 13-5).

You can find your developer token on your My Account tab. It's still a good idea to copy and paste it into a text file so it's handy when you need to use it in your code.

AdWords API Quotas and Usage

Open the My Account tab followed by the AdWords API Center link to see the AdWords API Center (Figure 13-6), which displays your API usage, your developer token, and a link to the program terms and conditions.

> Don't click the reset link (shown next to Your Developer Token in Figure 13-6) lightly. Opening this link deletes your developer token. There's no getting it back, and you'll have to reapply to the program—and modify all your code that uses the deleted token!

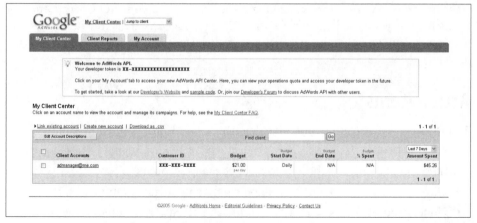

Figure 13-5. Your AdWords API developer token is displayed the first time you log onto My Client Center; subsequently you can find it on the My Account tab

Figure 13-6. Your API quote depends on your AdWords budget; it is displayed along with your developer token

Each AdWords API developer is assigned a monthly operations quota, based on the total spent in the developer's My Client Center.

Google's rationale for the quota system is to protect the integrity of AdWords operations from getting too much traffic. It probably also wants to make sure that the large-scale businesses that the AdWords API program is targeting get the benefit from the program, rather than "Jane Six-Pack" individual developers.

Updating individual bids on 1000 keywords equates to 1000 operations, so the developer with the 25,000 operations shown in Figure 13-5 could theoretically perform 25,000 keyword updates and stay within quota. Once you've used your quota for the month, your API calls will return a quota exceeded error code (fault code 43) until the next month.

You can increase your quota by linking more accounts to your My Client Center or by increasing your total monthly spend (Google suggests that you don't raise an account spend without the permission of the client who pays the bills for the account).

Action Items

To prepare to start creating programs that use the AdWords API, you should:

- Understand what kind of AdWords client the AdWords API is intended to benefit (large customers or those who manage many accounts).
- Have a look at the AdWords API home page and documentation center.
- Understand the purpose of a WSDL file and at least scan some of the AdWords API services WSDL files.
- Choose a development language and SOAP toolkit.
- Understand the purpose of the eight different AdWords API services.
- Obtain a developer token and a My Client Center logon (if you don't already have one).

CHAPTER 14

Programming the AdWords API

In this chapter you'll learn how to use the AdWords API web services to program a web application that allows users to create a campaign, an ad, and keywords in their Google AdWords account.

From a high level, you'll need to:

Get Google's ID for a campaign
> One way to accomplish this (shown in this chapter) is to successfully create a new campaign; the ID is part of the return value when the campaign is created.

Use the campaign's ID to create an ad group, and get the ID for the ad group
> When you create a new ad group, its ID is part of the return value from the call to the web service that creates the ad group.

Add a creative (a creative is a text or graphical ad) to the ad group
> You need the ad group ID to do this.

Add keywords, used for contextual targeting, to the ad
> This also requires the Ad Group ID.

Along the way, add various optional and required pieces of information
> For example, you can't create a campaign without providing a budget for the campaign, and you can't create an ad group without providing the maximum CPC (cost per click) you are willing to pay for the keywords in the ad group.

 It's a good idea to understand how AdWords works before attempting to program with the AdWords API. See Part III for more information about working with AdWords.

If you think these steps sound like a lot of trouble for re-creating functionality that you can find in the Google AdWords application, you are right. There's not much reason for creating a standalone replica of the user interface that Google already provides. Most applications that take advantage of the AdWords API will integrate with other applications, such as a company's internal inventory program, to create a unified system that provides custom functionality beyond what you find in AdWords.

The point of the application in this chapter is to show how to manipulate the objects that make up the AdWords application. Many of the most important of these objects—campaigns, ad groups, creatives, and keywords—are used in the example programs in this chapter. When you understand how to program these objects, you'll be able to code with them in your own custom applications.

You can run the web application in this chapter, and download its source code, at *http://www.braintique.com/ad/*.

Using the AdWords API with PHP

The web application in this chapter is programmed using PHP. PHP is most commonly used for programming in web applications. PHP pages on the Web are HTML pages with PHP code embedded in the HTML. This makes PHP great for web programming—after all, it is used by more than 20 million web domains—but not always the best language choice for all applications.

When the first version of PHP was created by Rasmus Lerdorf in the early 1990s, PHP was short for "Personal Home Page." As PHP has become a tool used by serious programmers on the Web, the meaning of the acronym has also changed; PHP now stands for "PHP: Hypertext Preprocessor."

Case in point: as you'll come to understand as you follow along with the code listings in this chapter, PHP does not interact easily with the document literal style of SOAP web services offered by the Google AdWords API. This means you'll have to go through some contortions to make PHP play nicely with the AdWords API.

Document Literal Versus RPC SOAP

The web services that make up the AdWords API are *document literal* web services, meaning that they work by processing XML documents. Formally, the input and output of a document literal web service is defined by an XML schema, and the body of the SOAP message (the input or output) can be any XML document that will validate with the schema.

In contrast, the body of an RPC (remote procedure call) SOAP message contains an element with the name of the method or remote procedure being invoked. This element in turn contains an element for each argument of that procedure.

Several other languages and development environments do a good job of encapsulating the messiness of document literal SOAP from programmers who are writing applications that consume these web services. Specifically, Visual Studio.NET—and one of the .NET languages such as VB or C#—or Java (combined with the Apache Axis library) make it very easy to program with the Google AdWords API. These tools hide the details of the SOAP interaction by generating proxy classes. The programmer can focus on working with the high-level objects instantiated from these classes, rather than worrying about the details of the SOAP handshake.

 Document literal SOAP support is baked into Visual Studio.NET. For information about document literal SOAP support with Axis, see *http:// ws.apache.org/axis/*. If you plan to work with Java/Axis, you should know that Google makes available a client library in a single JAR file that contains all the Axis JARs and precompiled stub classes needed to write Java clients. You can download this library from *http:// sourceforge.net/projects/goog-ad-api-cli/*.

To summarize, if .NET or Java/Axis works well with your other systems, perhaps because you or your business is already programming in one of these environments, then these languages would be the best choice for working with the Google AdWords API.

Despite the ease of using these other languages with AdWords, I've chosen to show the examples in this book in PHP, which is a nice language for web development, even if it's not so good for working with the AdWords API. If I had written the examples using C# .NET or Java, it wouldn't have been as useful to readers unfamiliar with these languages and their development environments. PHP is accessible to almost any programmer. It's free (well, so is Java!) and it runs on every flavor of operating system, so no one is ruled out. And PHP is as good as any other environment for learning about the different services that comprise the AdWords API, the classes that comprise the services, and how they interact.

SOAP Libraries for PHP

SOAP libraries, also called SOAP toolkits, are used to interpret WSDL files (see Chapter 13 for information about WSDL files). These libraries also provide tools that help encode and decode XML request and response messages.

The two SOAP libraries available for use with PHP are PEAR and NuSOAP (both are free to use). PEAR generates RPC-encoded XML as its output message, whereas NuSOAP can be made to generate document literal XML to be used with SOAP, making NuSOAP the better choice for working with the Google AdWords API web services.

PHP Resources

If you need some more background with PHP to understand the code in this chapter, there are a number of good resources available.

The PHP books on my shelf that I refer to most often are *Programming PHP* (Lerdorf and Tatroe) and *PHP Cookbook* (Sklar and Trachtenberg), both published by O'Reilly Media, Inc. The PHP language web site is *http://www.php.net/*. You'll find a basic PHP tutorial on the site at *http://us3.php.net/tut.php*, an online PHP manual at *http://us3.php.net/manual/en/index.php*, and a catalog of online PHP references at *http://us3.php.net/links.php*.

The Open Directory Project categorizes more than 1500 PHP resources at *http://dmoz.org/Computers/Programming/Languages/PHP/*.

 NuSoap does not take care of all the details of using document literal SOAP. Specifically, you have to generate the XML in your code used to wrap elements that are used when NuSOAP generates an input message to one of the AdWords API web services.

Downloading and Installing NuSOAP

The NuSOAP toolkit consists of a primary file, *nusoap.php*, and 12 supporting files, all containing PHP code. You must have all these files in order to use NuSOAP. You can download a zipped archive containing the complete NuSOAP files, documentation, and samples from *http://sourceforge.net/projects/nusoap/*.

 Beware of the NuSoap download link provided in the Google AdWords API document, which will lead you to separately download each NuSOAP file, which is not necessarily a problem, but certainly a nuisance.

It's most common to write PHP code to a file on your local computer, using a text editor or an editor specifically intended for programming, and then upload the file to your web server and run it from that server.

Assuming this is the approach you're taking, follow these steps to get NuSOAP working with your PHP installation and development environment:

1. Extract the contents of the NuSOAP zipped archive to your local computer.
2. Use FTP to copy the PHP files in the NuSOAP lib directory from your local computer to a location on your web server where they will be accessible to your PHP programs. I created a folder named *NuSOAP* for these files immediately beneath the folder used for my PHP program files.

3. Include the *nusoap.php* library file in each of your PHP code pages that will need to invoke the NuSOAP toolkit, using the PHP require_once( ) function. For example, if the NuSOAP files are located like mine in relationship to the program files:

```
require_once('NuSOAP/nusoap.php');
```

Creating the Campaign Web Service Client

In order to use one of the Google AdWords API web services, you need to:

- Use the WSDL file for the service to create a new SOAP client object
- Set the authentication headers for the SOAP service

The authentication headers require the same information for all of the AdWords API web services, so once you've generated this information, you can use it in repeated calls to the AdWords API web services.

The information required for the authentication headers is shown in Table 14-1.

Table 14-1. Authentication headers required for making a request

XML wrapper	Value required
<email>...</email>	Email address associated with AdWords account.
<password>...</password>	Password associated with AdWords account.
<useragent>...</useragent>	This is an arbitrary string you can use as you like. It bears no relationship to the *UserAgent* you may have seen associated with web browsers.
<token>...</token>	AdWords API developer key.

You must pass the actual values for each field required for authentication wrapped in the XML shown in Table 14-1. The values themselves go between the XML tags, for example, <email>me@me.com</email>.

In a real program in the real world you probably won't let users enter the header authentication information; it will be programmatically generated. But in this situation, I've set things up so that the user enters authentication information, as well as the information to create a campaign, as shown in Figure 14-1.

Example 14-1 shows *authenticate.php*, which contains the HTML for the form depicted in Figure 14-1; the form allows a user to input authentication and campaign information.

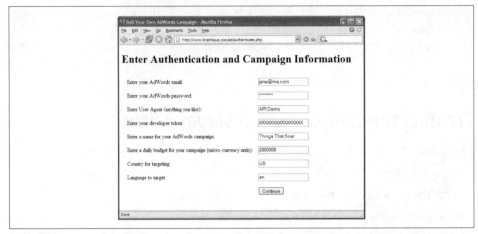

Figure 14-1. The authentication information—the first four items requested—are used for all the different services

Example 14-1. HTML form for entry of authentication and campaign information (authenticate.php)

```
<!DOCTYPE html PUBLIC "-//W3C//DTD XHTML 1.0 Transitional//EN"
   "http://www.w3.org/TR/xhtml1/DTD/xhtml1-transitional.dtd">
<html xmlns="http://www.w3.org/1999/xhtml">
<head>
<title>Roll Your Own AdWords Campaign</title>
</head>
<body>
<h1>Enter Authentication and Campaign Information</h1>
<form action="campaign.php" method="POST">
<table cellspacing=15>
<tr><td>
Enter your AdWords email:
</td><td>
<input type="text" name="email" value="you@email.com">
</td></tr><tr><td>
Enter your AdWords password:
</td><td>
<input type="password" name="password">
</td></tr><tr><td>
Enter User Agent (anything you like):
</td><td>
<input type="text" name="useragent" value="API Demo">
</td></tr><tr><td>
Enter your developer token
</td><td>
<input type="text" name="token">
</td></tr><tr><td>
Enter a name for your AdWords campaign:
</td><td>
<input type="text" name="name">
</td></tr><tr><td>
```

```
Enter a daily budget for your campaign (micro-currency units):
</td><td>
<input type="text" name="dailyBudget">
</td></tr>
<tr><td>
Country for targeting:
</td><td>
<input type="text" name="countries" value="US">
</td></tr>
<tr><td>
Language to target
</td><td>
<input type="text" name="languages" value="en">
</td></tr><tr><td></td><td>
<input type="submit" name"Continue" value="Continue">
</td></tr>
</table>
</form>
</body>
</html>
```

> The HTML form shown in Example 14-1 uses the form POST rather than GET so that the AdWords email address, password, and developer key don't appear as part of the browser address field when the next page (*campaign.php*) is opened.

The General Pattern

Within the AdWords API web services, there's a fairly generic set of steps to follow. This pattern works the same way at all levels of the hierarchy of AdWords objects. You need a client object based on a particular AdWords API web service.

Each time you invoke a new client object, you need to authenticate it. You need to wrap your parameters in XML, and you need to use the identification of the containing object (unless you are at the top of the object hierarchy, as with a campaign).

Here are the steps:

1. Create a client object.
2. Authenticate.
3. Obtain parameters, including the identification for the containing object.
4. Wrap the parameters in XML.
5. Use the client object to add the wrapped parameters and create a specified entity within AdWords.

Creating the Authentication Headers

You need authentication information (email, password, user agent, and developer token) to create the authentication headers.

The email, password, user agent, and token are passed to *campaign.php* using HTTP POST, so these can be read in PHP easily:

```
$email = $_POST['email'];
$password = $_POST['password'];
$useragent = $_POST['useragent'];
$token = $_POST['token'];
```

Next, these values need to be wrapped in the appropriate XML element tags. To simplify this a bit, here's a utility function that accepts plain text representing the contents of an element and creates an element with that content (using the supplied element name):

```
function makeDocLit($xml, $var) {
    return '<' . $xml . '>' . $var . '</' . $xml . '>';
}
```

The function is in the library file and needs to be included in each PHP module that uses it, like this:

```
require_once('hd_lib.inc');
```

This code then wraps the authentication headers in the appropriate XML:

```
$email = makeDocLit ("email", $email);
$password = makeDocLit ("password", $password);
$useragent = makeDocLit ("useragent", $useragent);
$token = makeDocLit ("token", $token);
```

The header consists of the four XML-wrapped values concatenated:

```
$header = $email . $password . $useragent . $token;
```

 The PHP string concatenation operator is represented by a period (.).

This header will be used to authenticate each of the AdWords API web services used. To make it available in other PHP modules in the application besides the current one, it's easy to use PHP's session-tracking facility. To implement session tracking, put a directive in the file before any HTML has been generated:

```
<?php session_start( ) ?>
```

With that directive in place at the beginning of the file, it's easy to save a variable so it can be used across a multipage application:

```
session_register('header');
```

PHP normally uses cookies to track sessions. If PHP finds it can't use cookies on a specific computer—perhaps because the user has turned them off in their browser—PHP adds session identification strings to the URLs that it generates.

Connecting to the WSDL File and Creating a Client Object

Creating a client object for one of the Google AdWords API web services gives you programmatic access to the members of that web service, meaning its properties and methods. So the next step is to use the URL for the WSDL file to create a client object based on the web service:

```
$campaignwsdl = "https://adwords.google.com/api/adwords/v2/CampaignService?wsdl";
$campaignclient = new soapclient($campaignwsdl, 'wsdl');
```

Setting the Authentication Headers for the Clients

Once the web service has been instantiated in your code, Google needs to know that your program has a legitimate right to use the web service to create (and set) AdWords objects. To accomplish this, set the authentication header that was created in code:

```
$campaignclient->setHeaders($header);
```

 -> is PHP's object membership operator, so this line of code calls the setHeaders() method of the web service client object. Other SOAP toolkits provide different mechanisms for setting the authentication headers.

Here's what the script looks like so far (leaving the HTML out of it):

```
...
<?php
require_once('NuSOAP/nusoap.php');
require_once('hd_lib.inc');
...
$email = $_POST['email'];
$password = $_POST['password'];
$useragent = $_POST['useragent'];
$token = $_POST['token'];
...

// Set up the authentication headers
$email = makeDocLit ("email", $email);
$password = makeDocLit ("password", $password);
$useragent = makeDocLit ("useragent", $useragent);
$token = makeDocLit ("token", $token);
$header = $email . $password . $useragent . $token;
session_register('header');
```

```
// Connect to the WSDL file for the CampaignService
$campaignwsdl = "https://adwords.google.com/api/adwords/v2/CampaignService?wsdl";
$campaignclient = new soapclient($campaignwsdl, 'wsdl');

// Set the headers for the client
$campaignclient->setHeaders($header);
```

Creating a Campaign

The HTML form that lets a user provide authentication information also lets the user provide campaign information. You can pick these values up easily in PHP:

```
$name = $_POST['name'];
$dailyBudget = $_POST['dailyBudget'];
$languages = $_POST['languages'];
$countries = $_POST['countries'];
```

The only one of these values that is required is dailyBudget, which is specified in microunits of currency. Table 14-2 shows the default values used for optional campaign information.

Table 14-2. If you don't provide campaign information, here are the values Google will supply

Information	Default value
name	A name of the form *Campaign #N*, where N is an ordinal number
languages	All languages
countries	All locations

Microunits of Currency

Within the AdWords API, the daily budget for a campaign and the maximum CPC for an ad group (the most you are willing to pay when someone clicks on your ad) are specified in microunits, or *micros*, of currency. A micro is defined as one-millionth of the fundamental currency unit.

The specific currency used depends on the currency selection for the AdWords account involved. If the AdWords account uses U.S. dollars, then $1.00 is 1,000,000 micros. The least amount you can specify for the maximum CPC is $.05; expressed as micros this is 50,000 micros.

The maximum CPC you enter must be expressed in legitimate, billable units; in U.S. dollars, all CPC bids must be in round pennies. This means that the value for the maximum CPC must be a multiple of 10,000 micros (which equals 1 cent).

Campaign Settings

Once you've instantiated an object based on the `CampaignService` web service, using the code I showed you earlier:

```
$campaignwsdl = "https://adwords.google.com/api/adwords/v2/CampaignService?wsdl";
$campaignclient = new soapclient($campaignwsdl, 'wsdl');
```

and have sent it authentication information as I showed you:

```
$campaignclient->setHeaders($header);
```

you can go about the business of configuring a new campaign.

Configuring the campaign involves these steps:

1. Create a new, empty campaign.
2. Construct XML-wrapped entries for the campaign parameters you want to set (`dailyBudget` is required).
3. Put the parameters together in one string.
4. Wrap the parameter string in XML.

First, create an empty campaign element:

```
$campaign = "<campaign></campaign>";
```

Construct the campaign name and `dailyBudget` values:

```
$campaignName = makeDocLit ("name", $name);
$dailyBudget = makeDocLit ("dailyBudget", $dailyBudget);
```

Construct the targeted language(s):

```
$languages = "<languageTargeting>" . makeDocLit ("languages", $languages)
    . "</languageTargeting>";
```

> The languages are specified within `<languageTargeting>` tags, which contain one or more language codes wrapped within `<languages>` tags. You can find the language codes you can use at this address: *http://www.google.com/apis/adwords/developer/adwords_api_languages.html*.

Construct the geotargeting:

```
$geotargets = "<geoTargeting>" . makeDocLit ("countries", $countries)
    . "</geoTargeting>";
```

> The countries, regions, and cities for geotargeting are specified within `<geoTargeting>` tags, which contain one or more country codes wrapped within `<countries>` tags. GeoTargeting tags can also contain metros, cities, and regions in addition to countries. You can find the country codes you can use at this address: *http://www.google.com/apis/adwords/developer/adwords_api_countries.html*.

Put together the campaign parameters:

```
$campaignparams = "<campaign> $campaignName $dailyBudget $languages
    $geotargets</campaign>";
```

Add an XML wrapper:

```
$campaignparamsxml = "<addCampaign> $campaignparams </addCampaign>";
```

Web service operations take place within a namespace. The AdWords API web services all use the same namespace, *https://adwords.google.com/api/adwords/v2*. You don't have to specify this namespace, because it is the default, but you could if you wanted to:

```
$campaignparamsxml = "<addCampaign
    xmlns='https://adwords.google.com/api/adwords/v2'>
    $campaignparams </addCampaign>";
```

Here's the complete code for generating the campaign in its XML wrapper (assuming the actual values were input by the user and omitting the namespace reference):

```
$campaign = "<campaign></campaign>";
$campaignName = makeDocLit ("name", $name);
$dailyBudget = makeDocLit ("dailyBudget", $dailyBudget);
$languages = "<languageTargeting>" . makeDocLit ("languages", $languages)
    . "</languageTargeting>";
$geotargets = "<geoTargeting>" . makeDocLit ("countries", $countries)
    . "</geoTargeting>";
$campaignparams = "<campaign> $campaignName $dailyBudget $languages
    $geotargets</campaign>";
$campaignparamsxml = "<addCampaign> $campaignparams </addCampaign>";
```

If you were to hand construct the XML that this code will generate using arbitrary actual values, the XML would look like this:

```
<addcampaign>
    <campaign>
        <name>myCampaign</name>
        <dailyBudget>2000000</dailyBudget>
        <languageTargeting>
            <languages>EN</languages>
        </languageTargeting>
        <geoTargeting>
            <countries>US</countries>
        </geoTargeting>
    </campaign>
</addcampaign>
```

Adding the Campaign

So far, none of the campaign settings have been sent to Google. Sending these settings to Google is where "the rubber meets the road"; the campaign actually gets added only if the authentication headers check out and everything else was done right.

Now that the values for the campaign have been constructed, the campaign can be added using the web service client that was created earlier:

```
$campaign = $campaignclient->call("addCampaign", $campaignparamsxml);
$campaign = $campaign['addCampaignReturn'];
```

If there are no SOAP errors, a campaign is successfully created; rather than just assume that things will go well, you need to handle errors and ensure that's what actually occurs.

Handling Errors

If the fault property of the web service client object is not null, then there is a SOAP error. A message generated by the web service will be displayed, and the process of adding objects to AdWords can't continue. Here's the code to check for an error:

```
if($campaignclient->fault) {
    showErrors($campaignclient);
    echo '<a href="authenticate.php">Try again</a>';
}
...
```

The showErrors( ) function, part of the hd_lib, is called:

```
function showErrors($client) {
    echo "FAULT: {$client->fault}<br>\n";
    echo "Code: {$client->faultcode}<br>\n";
    echo "String: {$client->faultstring}<br>\n";
    echo "Detail: {$client->faultdetail}<br>\n";
}
```

As mentioned before, you'll need to include this library to take advantage of showErrors( ):

```
require_once('hd_lib.inc');
```

If there is a problem, this code will generate a display like that shown in Figure 14-2.

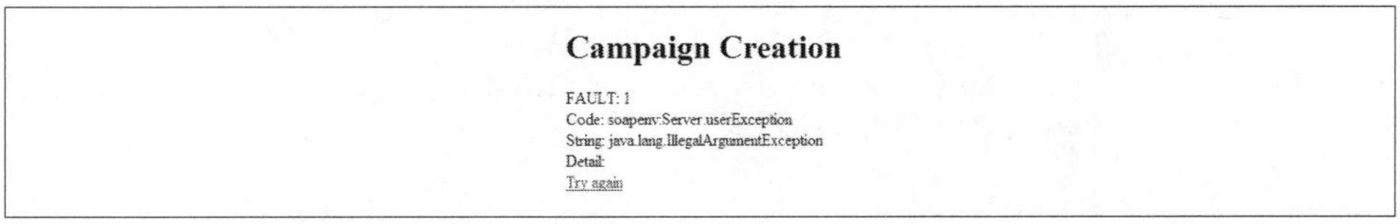

Campaign Creation

FAULT: 1
Code: soapenv:Server userException
String: java.lang.IllegalArgumentException
Detail:
Try again

Figure 14-2. Error-handling leaves something to be desired, but it's better than nothing and helps to give the developer a clue about the cause of problems

This error handling will help developers by giving them a clue about the cause of a problem when their code isn't correctly creating objects. However, it is not the kind of thing you'd want an end user to see. In an end-user application, great care should be taken to validate user input, and error messages should be encapsulated to be more user-friendly.

Getting the Campaign ID

If there are no faults, then the campaign has been created and added to the AdWords account, and a campaign ID is generated. The campaign ID is the crucial value you need to programmatically move down the chain of AdWords objects. Essentially, obtaining a valid campaign ID is the point of all the code up to this point.

This information can be displayed and saved via PHP session tracking for use in other modules:

```
...
else{
    $campaignId = $campaign['id'];
    echo "Your new campaign has been created! <br>\n";
    echo "The id of the new campaign is " . $campaign['id'] .
        " and the name is " .
    $campaign['name'] . ".<br>\n<br>\n";
    session_register('campaignId');
```

The code can also dynamically generate an HTML form for the user to input the name of an AdGroup to create and its maximum CPC.

Example 14-2 shows the complete code for creating authentication headers, connecting to the campaign service WSDL file, creating a campaign, checking for errors, and (upon success) displaying the campaign ID, and a form for ad group information.

Example 14-2. Creating the campaign and getting input for AdGroup creation (campaign.php)

```
<?php session_start( ) ?>
<!DOCTYPE html PUBLIC "-//W3C//DTD XHTML 1.0 Transitional//EN"
    "http://www.w3.org/TR/xhtml1/DTD/xhtml1-transitional.dtd">
<html xmlns="http://www.w3.org/1999/xhtml">
<head>
<title>Campaign Creation</title>
</head>
<body>
<?php
require_once('NuSOAP/nusoap.php');
require_once('hd_lib.inc');
echo "<h1>Campaign Creation</h1>";
$email = $_POST['email'];
$password = $_POST['password'];
$useragent = $_POST['useragent'];
$token = $_POST['token'];
$name = $_POST['name'];
```

```php
$dailyBudget = $_POST['dailyBudget'];
$languages = $_POST['languages'];
$countries = $_POST['countries'];

// Set up the authentication headers
$email = makeDocLit ("email", $email);
$password = makeDocLit ("password", $password);
$useragent = makeDocLit ("useragent", $useragent);
$token = makeDocLit ("token", $token);
$header = $email . $password . $useragent . $token;
session_register('header');

// Connect to the WSDL file for the CampaignService
$campaignwsdl = "https://adwords.google.com/api/adwords/v2/CampaignService?wsdl";
$campaignclient = new soapclient($campaignwsdl, 'wsdl');

// Set the headers for the client
$campaignclient->setHeaders($header);

// First create the campaign
$campaign = "<campaign></campaign>";
$campaignName = makeDocLit ("name", $name);
$dailyBudget = makeDocLit ("dailyBudget", $dailyBudget);
$languages = "<languageTargeting>" . makeDocLit ("languages", $languages)
   . "</languageTargeting>";
$geotargets = "<geoTargeting>" . makeDocLit ("countries", $countries)
   . "</geoTargeting>";
$campaignparams = "<campaign> $campaignName $dailyBudget $languages
   $geotargets</campaign>";
$campaignparamsxml = "<addCampaign> $campaignparams </addCampaign>";

// Add the campaign
$campaign = $campaignclient->call("addCampaign", $campaignparamsxml);
$campaign = $campaign['addCampaignReturn'];

// Handle any SOAP errors
if($campaignclient->fault) {
   showErrors($campaignclient);
   echo '<a href="authenticate.php">Try again</a>';
}
else{
   $campaignId =  $campaign['id'];
   echo "Your new campaign has been created! <br>\n";
   echo "The id of the new campaign is " . $campaign['id'] .
      " and the name is " .
   $campaign['name'] . ".<br>\n<br>\n";
   session_register('campaignId');
   echo '<form action="adgroup.php" method="POST">
   <table cellspacing=15>
   <tr><td>
   Enter the name for your new AdGroup:
   </td><td>
```

Example 14-2. Creating the campaign and getting input for AdGroup creation (campaign.php) (continued)

```
    <input type="text" name="name" value="AdGroup 1">
    </td></tr><tr><td>
    Enter your Max CPC for the AdGroup (micro-currency units):
    </td><td>
    <input type="text" name="maxcpc">
    </td></tr><tr><tr><td></td><td>
    <input type="submit" name"Continue" value="Create AdGroup">
    </td></tr>
    </table>
    </form>';
}
?>
</body>
</html>
```

Figure 14-3 shows the ID for the newly created campaign and the form that is dynamically generated in PHP for the user to name an AdGroup within the campaign and provide a maximum CPC for that campaign.

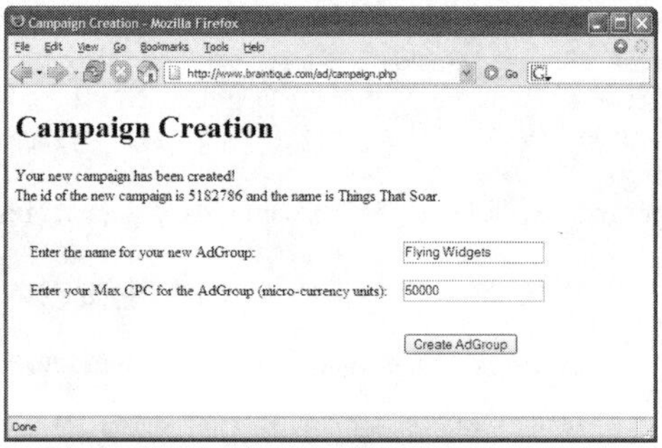

Figure 14-3. Once the new campaign has been created, you can use its ID to create an AdGroup within it

Example 14-3 shows the XML wrapper function and the error-handling function, both in a library file (both functions are used by the code in the example).

Example 14-3. Handling errors and adding XML wrappers (hd_lib.inc library file)

```
<?php
function makeDocLit($xml, $var) {
    return '<' . $xml . '>' . $var . '</' . $xml . '>';
}
function showErrors($client) {
    echo "FAULT: {$client->fault}<br>\n";
    echo "Code: {$client->faultcode}<br>\n";
    echo "String: {$client->faultstring}<br>\n";
    echo "Detail: {$client->faultdetail}<br>\n";
}
?>
```

Creating an AdGroup

With the Campaign ID (generated by Google), an AdGroup name, and the ad group's maximum CPC (both provided by a user), you can next create an AdGroup.

> The AdGroup name is optional. If a name is not provided, Google will name it for you: *AdGroup #1*, and so on. The only required setting for an AdGroup is the maximum CPC, the maximum cost per click you are willing to pay (sometimes referred to in the AdWords API reference documentation as your *bid*).

Creating a Client Object and Setting Headers

In order to create an ad group, it's necessary to create a client web service object based on the AdGroupService web service. To do this, use the URL for the WSDL file to create a client object based on the AdGroupService web service:

```
$adgroupwsdl = "https://adwords.google.com/api/adwords/v2/AdGroupService?wsdl";
$adgroupclient = new soapclient($adgroupwsdl, 'wsdl');
```

Since the authentication header has already been put together, this doesn't have to be done again. But the authentication header does have to be sent to the service each time a new client object is created. To do this, set the authentication header, using the $header variable that was previously constructed:

```
$adgroupclient->setHeaders($header);
```

> The $header variable can be accessed in the new module because PHP session tracking is engaged. The variable is used just like any other PHP variable.
>
> If these two PHP programs were not running in the same session, though, you would need to re-create the headers manually.

Creating the AdGroup

The process of creating the ad group involves the following steps:

1. Obtain values for AdGroup parameters you want to supply (the maximum CPC is required).
2. Wrap the values in XML.
3. Construct a string combining the values.
4. Wrap the parameter string in XML.
5. Use the XML-wrapped parameter string to add the AdGroup.

Here's the process put into practice. First, grab the AdGroup name and `maxcpc` using HTTP Post:

```
$maxcpc = $_POST['maxcpc'];
$name = $_POST['name'];
```

Wrap these values in XML:

```
$maxcpc = makeDocLit ("maxCpc", $maxcpc);
$name = makeDocLit ("name", $name);
```

 The value for the maximum CPC is wrapped in XML using the tag maxCpc, for example, `<maxCpc>50000</maxCpc>`.

Construct the XML string for the new AdGroup using the values and the Campaign ID (accessed via session tracking):

```
$adgroupParams = "<newdata> $maxcpc $campaignId $name</newdata>";
$campaignidparam = "<campaignID> $campaignId </campaignID>";
$adgroupParamsxml = "<addAdGroup> $campaignidparam $adgroupParams  </addAdGroup>";
```

Now add the AdGroup:

```
$adgroup= $adgroupclient->call("addAdGroup", $adgroupParamsxml);
$adgroup = $adgroup['addAdGroupReturn'];
```

Getting the AdGroup ID

If there are any errors, they should be displayed. The program will stop processing, and a link will be provided for the user to start over again (all using the `showErrors()` method again).

Otherwise, an AdGroup ID has been created by Google. This internal identification for an AdGroup is what is needed to add creatives and keywords to the AdGroup. The AdGroup ID can be displayed and saved via session tracking for use in other modules (another module adds the creative and keyword to the AdGroup in this example):

```
if($adgroupclient->fault) {
    showErrors($adgroupclient);
    echo '<a href="authenticate.php">Try again</a>';
}
else{
    echo "<P>Ad Group " . $adgroup['name'] .
        " was created successfully.<br>\n<br>\n";
    $adgroupid = "<adGroupId>" . $adgroup['id'] . "</adGroupId>";
    session_register('adgroupid');
    ...
```

If the AdGroup is successfully created, a form is dynamically generated for the user to enter an ad and the related keywords (as shown in Figure 14-4).

Figure 14-4. *Once an AdGroup has been created, you can ad keywords and creatives to it*

Example 14-4 shows the complete code for creating an AdGroup, as well as the form that is generated when the AdGroup is successfully created.

This form, as was the case with earlier examples, uses HTTP POST to open *create_ad.php*.

Example 14-4. Adding an AdGroup and getting input for an ad and keywords (adgroup.php)

```php
<?php session_start( ) ?>
<!DOCTYPE html PUBLIC "-//W3C//DTD XHTML 1.0 Transitional//EN"
   "http://www.w3.org/TR/xhtml1/DTD/xhtml1-transitional.dtd">
<html xmlns="http://www.w3.org/1999/xhtml">
<head>
<title>AdGroup Creation</title>
</head>
<body>
<?php
require_once('NuSOAP/nusoap.php');
require_once('hd_lib.inc');
echo "<h1>AdGroup Creation</h1>";

// Connect to the WSDL file for the AdGroupService
$adgroupwsdl = "https://adwords.google.com/api/adwords/v2/AdGroupService?wsdl";
$adgroupclient = new soapclient($adgroupwsdl, 'wsdl');

$adgroupclient->setHeaders($header);

$maxcpc = $_POST['maxcpc'];
$name = $_POST['name'];

$maxcpc = makeDocLit ("maxCpc", $maxcpc);
```

Example 14-4. Adding an AdGroup and getting input for an ad and keywords (adgroup.php) (continued)

```
$name = makeDocLit ("name", $name);

// Add an AdGroup
$adgroupParams = "<newdata> $maxcpc $campaignId $name</newdata>";
$campaignidparam = "<campaignID> $campaignId </campaignID>";
$adgroupParamsxml = "<addAdGroup> $campaignidparam $adgroupParams  </addAdGroup>";

$adgroup= $adgroupclient->call("addAdGroup", $adgroupParamsxml);
$adgroup = $adgroup['addAdGroupReturn'];

// Handle any SOAP errors
if($adgroupclient->fault) {
    showErrors($adgroupclient);
    echo '<a href="authenticate.php">Try again</a>';
}
else{
    echo "<P>Ad Group " . $adgroup['name'] .
        " was created successfully.<br>\n<br>\n";
    $adgroupid = "<adGroupId>" . $adgroup['id'] . "</adGroupId>";
    session_register('adgroupid');
    echo '<form action="create_ad.php" method="POST">
    <table cellspacing=15>
    <tr><td>
    Enter ad Headline:
    </td><td>
    <input type="text" name="headline">
    </td></tr><tr><td>
    Enter first description line:
    </td><td>
    <input type="text" name="description1">
    </td></tr><tr><td>
    Enter second description line:
    </td><td>
    <input type="text" name="description2">
    </td></tr><tr><td>
    Enter display URL:
    </td><td>
    <input type="text" name="displayUrl">
    </td></tr><tr><td>
    Enter destination URL:
    </td><td>
    <input type="text" name="destinationUrl">
    </td></tr><tr><td>
    Enter keyword:
    </td><td>
    <input type="text" name="keyword1">
    </td></tr><tr><td>
    Enter keyword:
    </td><td>
    <input type="text" name="keyword2">
    </td></tr><tr><td>
    Enter keyword:
    </td><td>
```

```
   <input type="text" name="keyword3">
   </td></tr><tr><td></td><td>
   <input type="submit" name"Continue" value="Create Ad and Keywords">
   </td></tr>
   </table>
   </form>';
}
?>
</body>
</html>
```

Adding an Ad

The CreativeService Google AdWords API web service is used to add an ad to an AdGroup. It works in much the same way as the other Google AdWords API services, such as the AdGroupService and the CampaignService web services.

Here are the steps you need to follow to create an ad:

1. Create a client object.
2. Use the header information to authenticate the client object.
3. Generate (or retrieve) the fields of the ad, including the identification for the ad group, and wrap the fields in appropriate XML.
4. Make the request to add the creative.

Creating a Client Object and Setting Headers

Once again, the WSDL file is used to create a new SOAP client object, this time using the CreativeService:

```
$creativewsdl = "https://adwords.google.com/api/adwords/v2/CreativeService?wsdl";
$creativeclient = new soapclient($creativewsdl, 'wsdl');
```

The authentication header that was constructed and saved via session tracking is used to set the header for the service:

```
$creativeclient->setHeaders($header);
```

Generating the Creative and Making the Request

In a real-life application, you might get a fair amount of whiz-bang functionality out of generating portions of a creative programmatically. For example, the text of an ad could respond to internal inventory conditions and be automatically generated.

For this example, to keep things relatively simple, the creative is generated from the user's input in the form shown earlier. It can be picked up using HTTP POST:

```
$headline = $_POST['headline'];
```

The other elements of the ad are obtaining similarly (see Example 14-5) and each element in the creative is then wrapped in XML. For example:

```
$headline = makeDocLit ("headline", $headline);
```

The creative is then constructed by putting all the elements together along with the AdGroup ID, which is retrieved using session tracking:

```
$creative1 = "<creative>$adgroupid $headline $description1 $description2
    $destinationUrl $displayUrl </creative>";
$creativeparamsxml = "<addCreative> $creative1 </addCreative>";
```

The creative is next added to the AdGroup:

```
$creativesarray = $creativeclient->call("addCreative", $creativeparamsxml);
$creativesarray = $creativesarray['addCreativeReturn'];
```

If there are any errors, they should be displayed and the program halted:

```
if($creativeclient->fault) {
    showErrors($creativeclient);
echo '<a href="authenticate.php">Try again</a>';
exit;
}
```

Otherwise, if there are no errors, the keywords can be added to the AdGroup.

Adding Keywords

The KeywordService is used to ad keywords to an AdGroup and works in what should by now be a familiar fashion:

1. The client object is created and authenticated.
2. The keywords are obtained and wrapped in XML.
3. The entire parameter string is wrapped in XML.
4. A request is made to the KeywordService to add the parameterized string of keywords, using the AdGroup ID.

Creating a Client Object and Setting Headers

The WSDL file is used to create a new SOAP client object for the KeywordService web service:

```
$keywordwsdl = "https://adwords.google.com/api/adwords/v2/KeywordService?wsdl";
$keywordclient = new soapclient($keywordwsdl, 'wsdl');
```

The authentication header that was constructed and saved via session tracking is used to set the header for the service:

```
$keywordclient->setHeaders($header);
```

Stringing Together the Keywords

Effective keyword targeting is the essence of getting the most out of a CPC marketing program like AdWords. In the real world, keywords might be autogenerated using internal data. Sophisticated organizations can probably come up with proprietary algorithms based on their own historical sales and conversion information to help determine cost-efficient keywords and phrases.

To keep things simple in this example, a keyword list, consisting of one or more keywords, is constructed based on the user input of keywords (an input form for the keywords is shown back in Figure 14-4).

Each "keyword" can actually contain multiple words. For example, "digital photography tips" can be entered as one keyword.

The keywords are wrapped in XML and next put together:

```
$keyword1 = $_POST['keyword1'];
$keyword2 = $_POST['keyword2'];
$keyword3 = $_POST['keyword3'];

$keyword1 = "<newKeywords><text>$keyword1</text><type>Broad</type></newKeywords>";
$keyword2 = "<newKeywords><text>$keyword2</text><type>Broad</type></newKeywords>";
$keyword3 = "<newKeywords><text>$keyword3</text><type>Broad</type></newKeywords>";

$keywordlist = "$keyword1 $keyword2 $keyword3";
```

Each keyword has a type attribute. The possible values for this attribute are Broad, Phrase, and Exact (see Chapter 10 for more information about these matches).

Making the Request

Once the keyword list has been constructed, the AdGroup ID (retrieved using PHP session tracking) is used to make the request (along with the XML-wrapped parameter list):

```
$keywordparamsxml = "<addKeywordList> $adgroupid $keywordlist </addKeywordList>";
$keywordarray = $keywordclient->call("addKeywordList", $keywordparamsxml);
$keywordarray = $keywordarray['addKeywordList'];
```

First check to see if this causes an error:

```
if($keywordclient->fault) {
    showErrors($keywordclient);
}
```

If adding the keyword list doesn't cause a SOAP fault, then all the operations have been successful and a message to that effect can be displayed (Figure 14-5).

Figure 14-5. The program has successfully created an ad, and associated keywords with it, using the AdWords API

Example 14-5 shows the complete code for adding creatives and keywords to an AdGroup.

Example 14-5. Creating the ad and related keywords (create_ad.php)

```php
<?php session_start( ) ?>
<!DOCTYPE html PUBLIC "-//W3C//DTD XHTML 1.0 Transitional//EN"
   "http://www.w3.org/TR/xhtml1/DTD/xhtml1-transitional.dtd">
<html xmlns="http://www.w3.org/1999/xhtml">
<head>
<title>Ad and Keyword</title>
</head>
<body>
<?php
require_once('NuSOAP/nusoap.php');
require_once('hd_lib.inc');
echo "<h1>Ad and Keyword</h1>";

// Connect to the WSDL file for the CreativeService
$creativewsdl = "https://adwords.google.com/api/adwords/v2/CreativeService?wsdl";
$creativeclient = new soapclient($creativewsdl, 'wsdl');

$creativeclient->setHeaders($header);

$headline = $_POST['headline'];
$description1 = $_POST['description1'];
$description2 = $_POST['description2'];
$destinationUrl = $_POST['destinationUrl'];
$displayUrl = $_POST['displayUrl'];

$headline = makeDocLit ("headline", $headline);
$description1 = makeDocLit ("description1", $description1);
$description2 = makeDocLit ("description2", $description2);
$destinationUrl = makeDocLit ("destinationUrl", $destinationUrl);
$displayUrl = makeDocLit ("displayUrl", $displayUrl);

$creative1 = "<creative>$adgroupid $headline $description1 $description2
   $destinationUrl $displayUrl </creative>";
$creativeparamsxml = "<addCreative> $creative1 </addCreative>";
$creativesarray = $creativeclient->call("addCreative", $creativeparamsxml);
$creativesarray = $creativesarray['addCreativeReturn'];
```

Example 14-5. Creating the ad and related keywords (create_ad.php) (continued)

```php
// Handle any SOAP errors
if($creativeclient->fault) {
    showErrors($creativeclient);
echo '<a href="authenticate.php">Try again</a>';
exit;
}

// The creative was created
// Connect to the WSDL for the KeywordService
$keywordwsdl = "https://adwords.google.com/api/adwords/v2/KeywordService?wsdl";
$keywordclient = new soapclient($keywordwsdl, 'wsdl');

$keywordclient->setHeaders($header);

$keyword1 = $_POST['keyword1'];
$keyword2 = $_POST['keyword2'];
$keyword3 = $_POST['keyword3'];

$keyword1 = "<newKeywords><text>$keyword1</text><type>Broad</type></newKeywords>";
$keyword2 = "<newKeywords><text>$keyword2</text><type>Broad</type></newKeywords>";
$keyword3 = "<newKeywords><text>$keyword3</text><type>Broad</type></newKeywords>";

$keywordlist = "$keyword1 $keyword2 $keyword3";
$keywordparamsxml = "<addKeywordList> $adgroupid $keywordlist </addKeywordList>";
$keywordarray = $keywordclient->call("addKeywordList", $keywordparamsxml);
$keywordarray = $keywordarray['addKeywordList'];

// Handle any SOAP errors
if($keywordclient->fault) {
    showErrors($keywordclient);
}
else {
    echo 'Your ad and keyword have been successfully added.<br>
    Please login to your <a href="https://adwords.google.com/">AdWords</a>
    account to review.';
}
?>
</body>
</html>
```

Verifying Your Creation

You should log on to AdWords to make sure that your campaign, ad group, ad, and keywords have been created. (Also, charges for the ad within the limits of the budget and maximum CPC that you set will start.)

Figure 14-6 shows a campaign, Things That Soar, created using the code in this chapter.

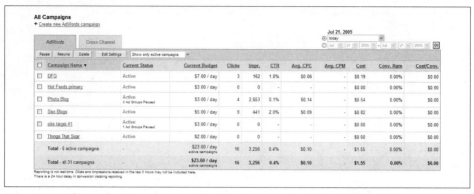

Figure 14-6. Things That Soar, the campaign that was created with the AdWord API, appears in the list of campaigns

The budget of $2.00 per day shown for the campaign corresponds to 2,000,000 micros.

If you drill down by clicking Things That Soar, you'll see the Flying Widgets ad group (Figure 14-7).

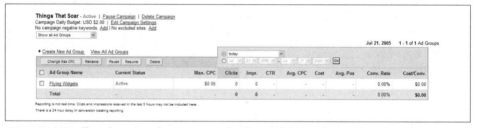

Figure 14-7. Drilling down into the campaign, the Flying Widgets ad group appears

The $.05 maximum CPC shown for the Flying Widgets ad group corresponds to 50,000 micros.

By clicking on the Flying Widgets ad group, one can verify in Figure 14-8 that the ad elements and keywords were entered in the demonstration program.

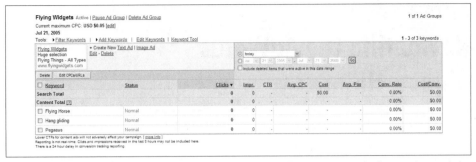

Figure 14-8. The Flying Widgets ad is active and ready for placement using the keyword provided in the program

Action Items

If you want to use the AdWords API to programmatically interface with AdWords, you should:

- Consider which programming languages and development environments best suit your needs.

- Download and experiment with the appropriate SOAP toolkit.

- As you create your programs, understand the hierarchy of AdWords API objects: keywords require AdGroups, AdGroups require campaigns, and so on.

- Create one authentication header to use with all the AdWords API web services you call.

- Encapsulate as much code as you can in functions placed in library files that can be shared between modules so that you can reuse code.

- Make sure to carefully validate user input before submitting values to the AdWords API web services.

CHAPTER 15

Navigating the AdWords Objects Hierarchy

In the real world, the most sensible use for the AdWords API is to integrate with systems that manage massive amounts of advertising. It makes sense to create custom AdWords API web service code if you are managing thousands of campaigns, ads, and keywords—on your own account or as an ad agency on behalf of clients.

Complex inventory systems that automatically publish AdWords ads when inventory items meet certain criteria—and revise these ads when an item goes out of stock—are also good candidates for automated interaction with the AdWords API.

In either of these cases, or to program any application that interacts with existing AdWords objects, you need to know how to navigate the hierarchy of existing AdWords objects in code. Starting with the authentication information for an account, you can programmatically access campaigns, ads, and the elements that make up ads (such as keywords).

This chapter shows you how to work your way from account information to campaign to AdGroup level, getting as granular as you'd like, all using C# and Visual Studio.NET.

 C# .NET is appropriate to a technique that is most likely to be used in larger shops and allows a focus on the relationship of the AdWords classes and objects, rather than the XML of the AdWords API web services.

Working with the AdWords API Web Services

Visual Studio.NET provides excellent tools for working with web services. When you reference a web service in Visual Studio, Visual Studio generates a *proxy class*. The proxy class for the web service uses the information provided by the WSDL file to encapsulate the XML SOAP input and output messages provided by the web service. You can use the members of this proxy class in your code just as you would the members of any other class, without having to know anything much about SOAP or web services.

Drilling Down

The application in this chapter displays all the campaigns associated with an account in a tree. Each campaign node on the tree can be expanded to show the AdGroups that are part of the campaign. You need to use a separate web service first to access an account, next to display the campaigns in the account, and finally to show the AdGroups within the campaigns.

Each of these three different web services need to be authenticated. In addition, a web service not at the top of the hierarchy needs an ID from the object that is above it to return values. For example, to access an AdGroup, your code needs to know the campaign ID of the campaign that contains the AdGroup. Similarly, to access keywords, your code needs to know the AdGroup ID of the AdGroup that contains the keywords. This relationship between objects and their containers is shown in Figure 15-1.

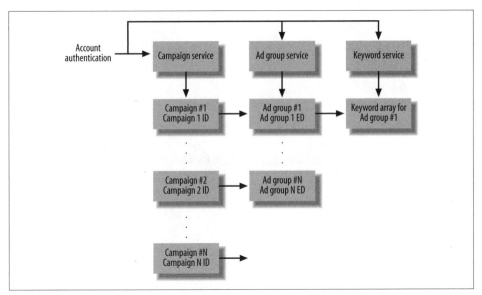

Figure 15-1. Objects need both account authentication and the identification code from an object in the hierarchy

The AdWords API web services used in this chapter, and their WSDL files, are as follows:

CampaignService
    https://adwords.google.com/api/adwords/v2/CampaignService?wsdl

AdGroupService
    https://adwords.google.com/api/adwords/v2/AdGroupService?wsdl

KeyWordService
    https://adwords.google.com/api/adwords/v2/KeywordService?wsdl

Adding Web References

To add a web reference to one of the Google AdWords API web services, open a project I Visual Studio and choose Add Web Reference from the Project menu. The Ad Web Reference window, shown in Figure 15-2, will open.

Figure 15-2. When the Add Web Reference window opens, you can enter the URL for a web service WSDL file

Next, enter the address of the WSDL file for the web service in the URL box at the top of the window (the URL for the CampaignService WSDL is shown in Figure 15-3). Click the Go icon (to the right of the WSDL URL).

Figure 15-3. When Visual Studio connects to the WSDL file, the available web methods are displayed

When Visual Studio finds the WSDL file, it will parse it and display the methods associated with the web service in the Add Web Reference window. You can now add a proxy class that encapsulates the web service to your project by clicking Add Reference.

You should change the name of the web service reference in your project to something intelligible, rather than Visual Studio's suggestion. You can change this name in the Add Web Reference dialog (using the Web reference name text box) or after the web service reference has been added in Solution Explorer.

To drill down through the Google AdWords hierarchies, references must be added to multiple AdWords API web services. It's particularly important to change the names of the references to these web services, because if you let Visual Studio name them, it will attempt to name each the same thing—com.google.adwords—which will cause errors, confusion, and delay.

Once the web service reference has been added to your project, you can see the web reference and its supporting files in Solution Explorer (Figure 15-4).

Figure 15-4. You can see the web reference files in Solution Explorer, including the Reference.cs file containing the actual proxy class code

To see all the supporting files for the web service reference and proxy class, you may need to click the Show All Files button in Solution Explorer.

You can repeat the process of entering the URL for the WSDL file for a web service to add references to the AdGroupService (Figure 15-5) and the KeywordService.

As the web service references are added to your project, and proxy classes generated, these appear in Solution Explorer (Figure 15-6).

With the web references added, and the proxy classes generated, you can also use Visual Studio's Object Browser to have a look at the proxy class members (Figure 15-7). This is a great way to easily find out about the facility that a web service makes available—much easier than reading the XML in the WSDL file, or even the documentation provided by Google with its web services.

Figure 15-5. *If you look through the list of web methods, getAllAdGroups should return information about all AdGroups*

Figure 15-6. *It helps to name the web services intelligibly, rather than accepting Visual Studio's default name*

Figure 15-7. *You can find information about arguments and return values by using the Object Browser to inspect the proxy class for a web service*

Using the Object Browser, you can easily see the methods available in the web service's proxy class. You can also find out the arguments each method takes, the type of the argument, and what the method returns.

Creating Objects Using the Proxy Classes

To use the members provided by a web service proxy class, an object based on the class must be instantiated.

First, as a convenience, include the namespace for each web service proxy class with a using directive:

```
using AccountInfo.CampaignService;
using AccountInfo.AdGroupService;
using AccountInfo.KeywordService;
```

 AccountInfo is the name of the project containing the web services.

Next, declare variables typed as each web service. These variables should be declared with sufficient scope so that you'll be able to use them when you need them (for example, in a Windows form class at the form class level). Use the new keyword to assign an object instance to each variable:

```
CampaignServiceService service = new CampaignServiceService();
AdGroupServiceService ag = new AdGroupServiceService();
KeywordServiceService ks = new KeywordServiceService();
```

Creating Authentication Information

To use an instance of a Google AdWords API web service, the web service must be authenticated. The required authentication information is:

- Email address associated with an AdWords account
- Password associated with the AdWords account
- UserAgent (this can be any arbitrary string you'd like)
- Developer Key

In an example Windows application, these values are entered by the user into Text-Box controls named as shown in Table 15-1.

Table 15-1. You need to provide a mechanism for the developer to enter information associated with the account (and the developer key)

Control name	Contains
txtEmail	Email address for AdWords account
txtPassword	Password for AdWords account
txtUserAgent	UserAgent string
txtSecret	Developer key

To add the email authentication value to the service object (instantiated from the CampaignService), create a new emailValue object within the service object:

```
service.emailValue = new CampaignService.email();
```

Next, use the string object constructor to assign the value of the Text property of textEmail (entered by the user) to the new value:

```
service.emailValue.Text = new String[] {txtEmail.Text};
```

 You need to qualify emailValue (and other authentication values) with the name of the object that is being authenticated; otherwise, the reference would be ambiguous (it could refer to the emailValue associated with any AdWords web service object).

Create authentication value objects, and assign text based on user input, for the rest of the required authentication information in the CampaignService:

```
service.passwordValue = new CampaignService.password();
service.passwordValue.Text = new String[] {txtPassword.Text};
service.useragentValue = new CampaignService.useragent();
service.useragentValue.Text = new String[] {txtUserAgent.Text};
service.tokenValue = new CampaignService.token();
service.tokenValue.Text = new String[] {txtSecret.Text};
```

Repeat the process for other AdWords API web services you'd like to authenticate, for example, the AdGroupService and KeywordService services:

```
ag.emailValue = new AdGroupService.email();
ag.emailValue.Text = new String[] {txtEmail.Text};
ag.passwordValue = new AdGroupService.password();
ag.passwordValue.Text = new String[] {txtPassword.Text};
ag.useragentValue = new AdGroupService.useragent();
ag.useragentValue.Text = new String[] {txtUserAgent.Text};
ag.tokenValue = new AdGroupService.token();
ag.tokenValue.Text = new String[] {txtSecret.Text};

ks.emailValue = new KeywordService.email();
ks.emailValue.Text = new String[] {txtEmail.Text};
ks.passwordValue = new KeywordService.password();
ks.passwordValue.Text = new String[] {txtPassword.Text};
ks.useragentValue = new KeywordService.useragent();
ks.useragentValue.Text = new String[] {txtUserAgent.Text};
ks.tokenValue = new KeywordService.token();
ks.tokenValue.Text = new String[] {txtSecret.Text};
```

Iterating Through the AdWords Hierarchy

With each proxy class for the various AdWords API web services instantiated and authenticated, it is time to use these classes to interact with AdWords information.

It's good practice in a real application to place code within try...catch...finally blocks (which I've omitted here in the interests of simplicity). In particular, calls to web services should always be placed using the try syntax, because so many things can go wrong with remote calls. In addition, good code includes exception handling (once again omitted here in the interests of simplicity).

It's worth bearing in mind that an actual application would probably do more than simply iterating through the AdWords objects. Your code could compare values retrieved from the AdWords objects to find specific items and then update the values associated with these items using criteria generated by your internal systems.

Displaying Campaign Information

With the preliminaries accomplished, the getAllAdWordsCampaigns() method of the CampaignService web service can be called:

```
Campaign[] campaignList = service.getAllAdWordsCampaigns(42);
```

The method assigns the information about all the campaigns in an account into an array of Campaign objects named campaignList. (The Campaign class is defined in the web service proxy class.)

The getAllAdWordsCampaigns() method is passed an integer argument. However, this argument is referred to by the Google documentation as "dummy" information—it is never used and can be any positive integer.

Next, for every Campaign in the campaignList array, add the internal identification for the related campaign to a node in a TreeView control:

```
foreach (Campaign c in campaignList)
{
    TreeNode c_node = treeView1.Nodes.Add("Campaign " +
        c.id.ToString() + ": " + c.name);
    ...
}
```

Displaying AdGroup Information

For each campaign, you can display the AdGroups that are part of the campaign using the ID for the specific campaign.

Within the foreach loop that adds each campaign to a node in the TreeView control, you can add subnodes for each AdGroup using the campaign ID:

```
//add a campaign node
...
AdGroup[] agList = ag.getAllAdGroups(c.id);
```

```
foreach(AdGroup a in agList)
    // now add the AdGroup info nodes
```

It turns out, however, that this code fails. It works fine on campaigns that contain one or more AdGroups, but returns an object reference error when it encounters a campaign without AdGroups.

 Deleted campaigns hang around. Even once you've deleted a campaign in AdWords, it will still be returned by the APIs (with a Deleted status).

Most AdWords users will have campaigns without AdGroups, particularly if you consider deleted campaigns. So it's necessary first to test for the existence of AdGroups (before one can attempt to display them):

```
if (ag.getAllAdGroups(c.id) != null)
```

Here's the code snippet that checks to make sure that there is at least one AdGroup for a specific campaign ID. It then cycles through all the AdGroups in the campaign, adding the ID and a human-readable name to a subnode on the TreeView:

```
if (ag.getAllAdGroups(c.id) != null)
{
    AdGroup[] agList = ag.getAllAdGroups(c.id);
    foreach(AdGroup a in agList)
    {
        TreeNode ag_node = c_node.Nodes.Add("AdGroup "
            + a.id.ToString() + ": " + a.name);
        ...
```

Showing Keywords Associated with an Ad

Using the ID returned for an AdGroup, the same technique works to access keywords associated with the AdGroup.

 You could also use the AdGroup ID to retrieve the creative (and its elements) associated with an AdGroup.

The first step is to check to see that there is at least one keyword to retrieve:

```
if (ks.getAllKeywords(a.id) != null)
```

Next, cycle through the Keywords array to retrieve the text of individual keywords and display them as third-level nodes:

```
if (ks.getAllKeywords(a.id) != null)
    foreach (KeywordService.Keyword k in keywordList)
    {
        ag_node.Nodes.Add(k.text);
    }
```

Displaying Results

The Windows application shown in Figure 15-8 can now be used to display the AdWords objects as nodes, with three levels of depth: campaigns, ads, and keywords.

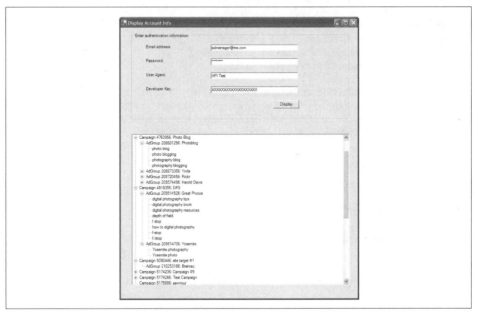

Figure 15-8. It's useful to be able see the keywords you have in place across campaigns and ad groups

The user enters authentication information for the AdWords account and clicks Display. The initial display will show campaign IDs and names. Expanding the campaign node, by clicking the plus icon (+) to the left of the node, will show the AdGroups it contains, and expanding an AdGroup node will show the keywords associated with that ad.

Example 15-1 shows the complete code from a Windows form project that displays AdWords API nodes using a TreeView control.

Example 15-1. Displaying account information using a TreeView control; navigating the hierarchy of information provided by the various Google ad web services allows you to drill down to specific ads you want to manipulate

```
using System;
...
using AccountInfo.CampaignService;
using AccountInfo.AdGroupService;
using AccountInfo.KeywordService;

namespace AccountInfo
{
```

Example 15-1. Displaying account information using a TreeView control; navigating the hierarchy of information provided by the various Google ad web services allows you to drill down to specific ads you want to manipulate (continued)

```csharp
public class Form1 : System.Windows.Forms.Form
{
  private System.Windows.Forms.TreeView treeView1;
  private System.Windows.Forms.GroupBox groupBox1;
  private System.Windows.Forms.TextBox txtEmail;
  private System.Windows.Forms.TextBox txtPassword;
  private System.Windows.Forms.TextBox txtUserAgent;
  private System.Windows.Forms.TextBox txtSecret;
  ...
  private System.Windows.Forms.Button btnDisplay;
  CampaignServiceService service = new CampaignServiceService( );
  AdGroupServiceService ag = new AdGroupServiceService( );
  KeywordServiceService ks = new KeywordServiceService( );
  ...
  public Form1( )
  {
    ...

    static void Main( )
    {
        Application.Run(new Form1( ));
    }

    private void btnDisplay_Click(object sender, System.EventArgs e)
    {
        service.emailValue = new CampaignService.email( );
        service.emailValue.Text = new String[] {txtEmail.Text};
        service.passwordValue = new CampaignService.password( );
        service.passwordValue.Text = new String[] {txtPassword.Text};
        service.useragentValue = new CampaignService.useragent( );
        service.useragentValue.Text = new String[] {txtUserAgent.Text};
        service.tokenValue = new CampaignService.token( );
        service.tokenValue.Text = new String[] {txtSecret.Text};

        ag.emailValue = new AdGroupService.email( );
        ag.emailValue.Text = new String[] {txtEmail.Text};
        ag.passwordValue = new AdGroupService.password( );
        ag.passwordValue.Text = new String[] {txtPassword.Text};
        ag.useragentValue = new AdGroupService.useragent( );
        ag.useragentValue.Text = new String[] {txtUserAgent.Text};
        ag.tokenValue = new AdGroupService.token( );
        ag.tokenValue.Text = new String[] {txtSecret.Text};

        ks.emailValue = new KeywordService.email( );
        ks.emailValue.Text = new String[] {txtEmail.Text};
        ks.passwordValue = new KeywordService.password( );
        ks.passwordValue.Text = new String[] {txtPassword.Text};
        ks.useragentValue = new KeywordService.useragent( );
        ks.useragentValue.Text = new String[] {txtUserAgent.Text};
        ks.tokenValue = new KeywordService.token( );
```

Example 15-1. Displaying account information using a TreeView control; navigating the hierarchy of information provided by the various Google ad web services allows you to drill down to specific ads you want to manipulate (continued)

```
            ks.tokenValue.Text = new String[] {txtSecret.Text};

            treeView1.Visible=false;

            // retrieve all campaigns and display the data
            Campaign[] campaignList = service.getAllAdWordsCampaigns(42);
            foreach (Campaign c in campaignList)
            {
                // Display a wait cursor while the TreeNodes are being created.
                Cursor.Current = Cursors.WaitCursor;
                TreeNode c_node = treeView1.Nodes.Add("Campaign " +
                c.id.ToString() + ": " + c.name);
                if (ag.getAllAdGroups(c.id) != null)
                {
                    AdGroup[] agList = ag.getAllAdGroups(c.id);
                    foreach(AdGroup a in agList)
                    {
                        TreeNode ag_node = c_node.Nodes.Add("AdGroup "
                            + a.id.ToString() + ": " + a.name);
                        if (ks.getAllKeywords(a.id) != null)
                        {
                            KeywordService.Keyword[] keywordList =
                                ks.getAllKeywords(a.id);
                            foreach (KeywordService.Keyword k in keywordList)
                            {
                                ag_node.Nodes.Add(k.text);
                            }
                        }
                    }
                }
                // Reset the cursor to the default.
                Cursor.Current = Cursors.Default;
            }
            treeView1.Visible=true;
        }
    }
}
```

Action Items

To create effective applications in .NET that take advantage of Visual Studio and the AdWords API web services:

- Use .NET to generate a proxy class to easily access the functionality of the Google web services.

- Understand how to drill down the hierarchy of AdWords objects; for example, using campaign IDs to access AdGroups, and AdGroup IDs to access keywords.
- Expect to implement applications that use the AdWords API across a wide range of AdWords objects.
- Plan to test for specific values in objects within the AdWords hierarchy, such as Keyword text, and take actions (such as replacing that text) when there is a match.

CHAPTER 16

Keyword Estimation

As you create systems that use the AdWords API to automate the creation and modification of campaigns, ads that target specific keywords, and keywords themselves, it's important to know how these created keywords are likely to perform. If you have good reason to believe that a keyword will not deliver many impressions, or if the keyword will produce a low click-through rate (CTR), your system should not target the keyword. Conversely, if a high cost per click (CPC) is estimated for a keyword, your system might decide not to run the keyword, or to assign a low maximum CPC to the keyword.

The KeywordEstimatorService AdWords API web service provides keyword traffic estimates for new or existing keywords, ad groups, and campaigns. This chapter shows you how to use the service in a simple way to get a traffic estimate for a keyword, assuming a broad match, and taking into account a maximum CPC specified along with the keyword. In a "real" application that integrated with the AdWords API, these results could be used as the basis for deciding whether to target a keyword.

KeywordEstimatorService Messages and Responses

The KeywordEstimatorService will provide traffic estimates for campaigns, AdGroups, and keywords. Table 16-1 shows the request objects, requests, and responses used for each of these types of estimates.

Table 16-1. Messages and responses for different kinds of estimates

AdWords object	Request object	Request message	Output response
Campaign	CampaignRequest	estimateCampaignList	CampaignEstimate
AdGroup	AdGroupRequest	estimateAdGroupList	AdGroupEstimate
Keyword	KeywordRequest	estimateKeywordList	KeywordEstimate

With an AdWords API client authenticated and instantiated, your code needs to:

1. Create a request object.
2. Provide the request object in a request message (which can contain multiple request objects).
3. Obtain estimate information from the response message.

These steps are illustrated in Figure 16-1.

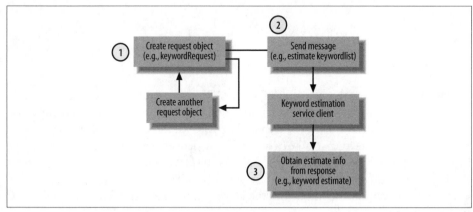

Figure 16-1. Working with the KeywordEstimatorService

Keyword Requests and Estimates

The Keyword request, message, and response are probably the most useful of the KeywordEstimatorService methods; it is much more common to change a keyword than an ad or an entire campaign based on performance estimates.

To make a keyword request, the required information about the keyword must be put together in the right format. Then one or more keywords are assembled into a request message. The fields of the response to the message contain the estimate information.

The Request Object

A KeywordRequest object represents a keyword to be estimated. The six fields of the KeywordRequest object are shown in Table 16-2.

Table 16-2. You use a KeywordRequest object to specify the details of the keyword you want to estimate

Field	Type	Comments
id	Long integer	If the `id` is omitted, then a new keyword is being estimated.
maxCpc	Long integer	Value in micros of the maximum you are willing to pay for a click; required field unless the `id` refers to an existing keyword. The minimum bid is 50,000 micros ($.05 in U.S. dollars). Entering a `maxCPC` of less than 50,000 throws an error.
negative	Boolean	Optional. If this field is True (the default is False), then a negative match is indicated.
text	String	The text of a keyword or phrase; can be omitted if the request concerns an existing keyword and its `id` was supplied.
type	KeywordType (enumeration)	Match type. The possible values of this enumeration are `Broad`, `Phrase`, and `Exact`. Required unless the request refers to an existing keyword by `id`.

 For more information about micros as a unit of currency, see Chapter 14. Match types are explained in Chapter 11.

The Response Object

A KeywordEstimate contains the actual estimate information that is returned once a request message that contains one or more KeywordRequest objects has been sent. The fields of a KeywordEstimate are shown in Table 16-3.

Table 16-3. The details of the results of a keyword traffic estimation are shown in the fields of a KeywordEstimate object

Field	Type	Comments
avgPosition	Float	Estimated average position for an ad that targets this keyword
cpc	Long integer	Estimated cost per click (CPC) in micros of an ad targeting this keyword
ctr	Float	Estimated click-through rate (CTR)
id	Integer	ID of a keyword contained in an existing AdGroup; -1 if the keyword is new
impressions	Integer	Estimated number of impressions for an ad targeted to this keyword
notShownPerDay	Integer	Estimated number of times an ad targeted to this keyword will not be shown despite a keyword match

If you raise the maxCpc input in an estimate request and keep everything else the same, the notShownPerDay will go down in the response, because the more you are willing to pay, everything else being equal, the more your ad will be shown.

Getting User Information

It's fairly easy to construct an example in PHP that uses the KeywordEstimatorService to allow a user to enter a keyword and a maximum bid for that keyword, and get traffic estimates for ads targeted to that keyword.

Obtaining Authentication Headers

The first step is to get the user to input the information required for authentication:

- Email address associated with an AdWords account
- Password for the account
- UserAgent (an arbitrary string)
- AdWords Developer key

An interface like that shown in Figure 16-2 can be used to get this information.

Enter Account Information

Enter your AdWords email: `wants2@know.com`

Enter your AdWords password: `••••••••`

Enter User Agent (anything you like): `No_Muggles`

Enter your developer token: `XXXXXXXXXXXXXX`

[Next]

Figure 16-2. For this application, the user enters authentication information, but when keyword automation is used as part of an automated ad placement program this information would be provided by the system

Example 16-1 shows the HTML for the form that lets the user enter information about a keyword to be estimated. The form posts the user input to *estimate_keyword. php*, which does the actual estimation.

Example 16-1. Obtaining authentication information from the user (account.php)

```
<!DOCTYPE html PUBLIC "-//W3C//DTD XHTML 1.0 Transitional//EN"
    "http://www.w3.org/TR/xhtml1/DTD/xhtml1-transitional.dtd">
<html xmlns="http://www.w3.org/1999/xhtml">
<head>
<title>Enter Account Info</title>
</head>
<body>
<h1>Enter Account Information</h1>
```

Example 16-1. Obtaining authentication information from the user (account.php) (continued)

```
<form action="estimate_keyword.php" method="POST">
<table cellspacing=15>
<tr><td>
Enter your AdWords email:
</td><td>
<input type="text" name="email" value="">
</td></tr><tr><td>
Enter your AdWords password:
</td><td>
<input type="password" name="password" value=" ">
</td></tr><tr><td>
Enter User Agent (anything you like):
</td><td>
<input type="text" name="useragent" value="Keyword Estimatation Demo">
</td></tr><tr><td>
Enter your developer token:
</td><td>
<input type="text" name="token" value=" ">
</td></tr>
<tr><td></td><td>
<input type="submit" name"Continue" value="Next">
</td></tr>
</table>
</form>
</body>
</html>
```

Getting a Keyword and Maximum CPC

The next form, shown in Figure 16-3, is used to get a keyword and maximum CPC for the keyword.

> A keyword can be a multiple-word phrase. In fact, the best keywords usually consist of several words, because longer phrases generally produce more pinpointed results.

Enter a Keyword for Estimation

Enter the keyword to estimate:	digital photo
Enter the maximum CPC you are willing to pay in micro-units:	500000
	Estimate

Figure 16-3. The user enters the keyword (or phrase) for estimation along with a maximum CPC

The code in Example 16-2 shows gathering the authentication information that was previously posted, adding XML and combining it to make a header, and saving the header using PHP's session-tracking facility (see Chapter 14 for a detailed explanation of this process). Next, in Example 16-2, a form that allows the user to enter the keyword and bid is displayed, and the form is posted to *show_estimate.php*.

Example 16-2. Getting a keyword and maximum CPC (estimate_keyword.php)

```php
<?php session_start( ) ?>
<!DOCTYPE html PUBLIC "-//W3C//DTD XHTML 1.0 Transitional//EN"
"http://www.w3.org/TR/xhtml1/DTD/xhtml1-transitional.dtd">
<html xmlns="http://www.w3.org/1999/xhtml">
<head>
<title>Enter Keyword for Estimation</title>
</head>
<body>
<?php
require_once('NuSOAP/nusoap.php');
require_once('hd_lib.inc');
echo "<h1>Enter a Keyword for Estimation</h1>";
$email = $_POST['email'];
$password = $_POST['password'];
$useragent = $_POST['useragent'];
$token = $_POST['token'];

// Set up the authentication headers
$email = makeDocLit ("email", $email);
$password = makeDocLit ("password", $password);
$useragent = makeDocLit ("useragent", $useragent);
$token = makeDocLit ("token", $token);
$header = $email . $password . $useragent . $token;
session_register('header');

echo '<form action="show_estimate.php" method="POST">
<table cellspacing=15>
<tr><td>
Enter the keyword to estimate:
</td><td>
<input type="text" name="keyword" value="digital photo">
</td></tr><tr><td>
Enter the maximum CPC you are willing to pay in micro-units:
</td><td>
<input type="text" name="maxCpc" value="500000">
</td></tr><tr><td></td><td>
<input type="submit" name"Continue" value="Estimate">
</td></tr>
</table>
</form>';
?>
</body>
</html>
```

Returning the Keyword Estimate

The information returned from a keyword estimate can be pretty valuable for making decisions about whether you want to target a keyword or whether you want to raise your bid for the keyword. All the example in this chapter does is display the raw data, but it's easy to see how this data could be used to provide intelligence for a business application that divides resources among different keywords.

 Using the other estimation capabilities of the KeywordEstimatorService, similar kinds of decisions about campaigns and AdGroups could also be automated.

If you want to do something with the information that the response to a keyword estimate request provides, you need to follow a number of steps to retrieve the data. These steps are not that complex, although it is a bit tricky to construct XML-wrapped keyword requests and request messages that don't cause the NuSOAP library to generate a SOAP error.

 The proxy class generated by Visual Studio.NET or the Axis SOAP library for Java makes programming the KeywordEstimatorService and the other AdWords API web services much simpler than in PHP.

To return a keyword estimate:

1. Connect to the WSDL file for the Google API web service.
2. Instantiate a client web service object.
3. Use the header information to authenticate the web service object.
4. Construct a keyword request.
5. Use one or more keyword requests to construct a request message.
6. Send the request message to the web service object.
7. Display the estimate information using the service's response (the Keyword-Estimate).

Creating a Service Object

You can use the NuSoap `soapclient` class to create a new client service object by supplying the WSDL file for the web service. Once you have instantiated the client object, you can authenticate it and then send it messages and use the responses.

Here's the code for creating a new client object based on the WSDL file:

```
$wsdl =
    "https://adwords.google.com/api/adwords/v2/TrafficEstimatorService?wsdl";
$client = new soapclient($wsdl, 'wsdl');
```

Using the Header Information for Authentication

Authentication works the same way for all of the AdWords API web services, but it must be done each time a new client based on one of the services is created.

The header information consists of the email address for an AdWords account, the password for the account, an arbitrary UserAgent string, and a developer key. In this example, the user has supplied all this information.

The $header variable stores the authentication information supplied by the user, wrapped in XML, and concatenated together. The $header variable is used to authenticate the service:

```
$client->setHeaders($header);
```

You should check to see that this worked by checking for SOAP errors:

```
if($client->fault) {
    showErrors($client);
    echo '<a href="estimate_keyword.php">Try again</a>';
}
else{
    // construct the keyword request
    ...
```

If there are no SOAP faults displayed, the program can move on and construct the keyword request.

Constructing the Keyword Request

To construct the keyword request, the fields of the request need to be wrapped in XML to meet the requirements of the NuSOAP library and document literal SOAP (see Chapter 14 for details):

```
$keyword = makeDocLit ("text", $keyword);
$maxCpc = makeDocLit ("maxCpc", $maxCpc);
```

In addition, information that in this case was not requested of the user (the type of match) needs to be added:

```
$otherinfo = $maxCpc . "<type>Broad</type>";
$keywordRequest = $keyword . $otherinfo;
```

Then the entire request is, itself, wrapped in XML:

```
$keywordxml = makeDocLit ("KeywordRequest", $keywordRequest);
```

Send a Request Message

To send the request message, wrap the keyword requests (in this case, there is only one keyword request) in XML as an estimateKeywordList object:

```
$param = makeDocLit ("estimateKeywordList", $keywordxml);
```

Call the web service client estimateKeywordList method:

```
$response = $client->call("estimateKeywordList", $param);
```

The response will contain the estimate information:

```
$response = $response['estimateKeywordListReturn'];
```

Displaying Information Using the Keyword Estimate

Before attempting to display the estimate information, check to see if there were any SOAP faults:

```
if($client->fault) {
    showErrors($client);
    echo '<a href="estimate_keyword.php">Try again</a>';
}
else{
    // display estimate information
    ...
```

If there are no errors, go ahead and display the results element fields:

```
echo "<h2>Here is your keyword estimate:</h2>";
echo "<h3>" . $keyword . "</h3>";
printResults($response);
...
function printResults ($estimate) {
    echo "\n<br>cpc = " . $estimate['cpc'] . " in micro-units";
    echo "\n<br>clicks = " . $estimate['ctr'] * $estimate['impressions'];
    echo "\n<br>ctr = " . ($estimate['ctr'] * 100) . "%";
    echo "\n<br>impressions = " . $estimate['impressions'];
    echo "\n<br>notShown = " . $estimate['notShownPerDay'];
    echo "\n<br>position = " . $estimate['avgPosition'];
}
```

When this code is run, depending on the keyword entered, the display will look like that shown in Figure 16-4.

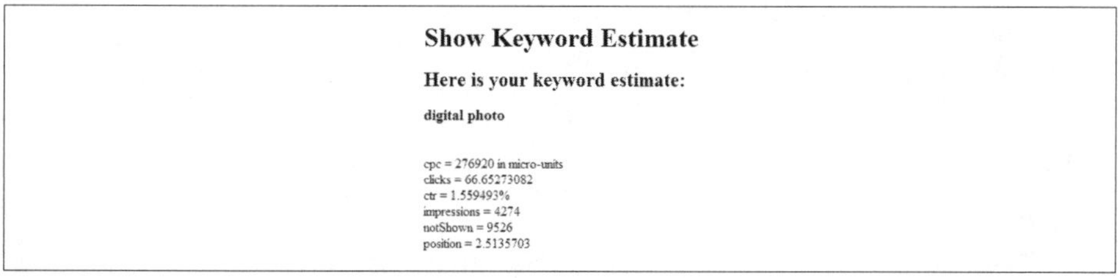

Show Keyword Estimate

Here is your keyword estimate:

digital photo

cpc = 276920 in micro-units
clicks = 66.65273082
ctr = 1.559493%
impressions = 4274
notShown = 9526
position = 2.5135703

Figure 16-4. Keyword estimation statistics, simply displayed here, can be used as part of an automated keyword selection process

 If you enter a keyword for estimation that doesn't generate much traffic, the estimate won't have as much statistical validity as for a higher traffic keywords, and fields such as clicks and impressions may show zero as their value.

Example 16-3 shows the library functions that add XML to a variable, required by the NuSOAP library and document literal SOAP, and the function that displays errors (see Chapter 14 for a detailed explanation).

Example 16-3. Adding XML and Displaying Errors (hd_lib.inc)

```php
<?php
function makeDocLit($xml, $var) {
    return '<' . $xml . '>' . $var . '</' . $xml . '>';
}
function showErrors($client) {
    echo "FAULT:  {$client->fault}<br>\n";
    echo "Code: {$client->faultcode}<br>\n";
    echo "String: {$client->faultstring}<br>\n";
    echo "Detail: {$client->faultdetail}<br>\n";
}
?>
```

Example 16-4 shows the code required to construct the request object and request message, and then to display the fields of the request response.

Example 16-4. Constructing the Request and Displaying the Response (show_estimate.php)

```php
<html xmlns="http://www.w3.org/1999/xhtml">
<head>
<title>Show Keyword Estimate</title>
</head>
<body>
<?php
require_once('NuSOAP/nusoap.php');
require_once('hd_lib.inc');
echo "<h1>Show Keyword Estimate</h1>";
$keyword = $_POST['keyword'];
$maxCpc = $_POST['maxCpc'];
if ($keyword == null){
    echo 'You must enter a keyword to estimate it! <br>
    <a href="estimate_keyword.php">Try again</a>';
}
else {
    // Connect to the WSDL for the TrafficEstimatorService
    $wsdl =
        "https://adwords.google.com/api/adwords/v2/TrafficEstimatorService?wsdl";
    $client = new soapclient($wsdl, 'wsdl');

    // Set the headers for the client
    $client->setHeaders($header);

    // Handle any SOAP errors
    if($client->fault) {
        showErrors($client);
        echo '<a href="estimate_keyword.php">Try again</a>';
    }
    else{
        $keyword = makeDocLit ("text", $keyword);
        $maxCpc = makeDocLit ("maxCpc", $maxCpc);
        $otherinfo = $maxCpc . "<type>Broad</type>";
        $keywordRequest = $keyword . $otherinfo;
```

```php
        $keywordxml = makeDocLit ("KeywordRequest", $keywordRequest);
        $param = makeDocLit ("estimateKeywordList", $keywordxml);
        // Make the request to estimate the keyword
        $response = $client->call("estimateKeywordList", $param);
        $response = $response['estimateKeywordListReturn'];
        if($client->fault) {
            showErrors($client);
            echo '<a href="estimate_keyword.php">Try again</a>';
        }
        else{
            echo "<h2>Here is your keyword estimate:</h2>";
            echo "<h3>" . $keyword . "</h3>";
            printResults($response);
        }
    }
}
function printResults ($estimate) {
    echo "\n<br>cpc = " . $estimate['cpc'] . " in micro-units";
    echo "\n<br>clicks = " . $estimate['ctr'] * $estimate['impressions'];
    echo "\n<br>ctr = " . ($estimate['ctr'] * 100) . "%";
    echo "\n<br>impressions = " . $estimate['impressions'];
    echo "\n<br>notShown = " . $estimate['notShownPerDay'];
    echo "\n<br>position = " . $estimate['avgPosition'];
}
?>
</body>
</html>
```

Action Items

If you are constructing custom applications that interact automatically with the Google AdWords API web services:

- Use the KeywordEstimatorService to estimate traffic for campaigns, ads, and keywords.
- Estimate traffic for new keywords before adding the keywords to an AdGroup.
- Consider raising and lowering your bids (maximum CPC) in code until you reach the desired level of impressions.
- Consider using CPC, CTR, impressions, position, and not-shown data as input to a business intelligence module that makes automated decisions about what ads to run.

Glossary

Above the fold
Positioning an ad so that it is viewed on a web page without the need for horizontal scrolling.

Ad unit
A group of from one to six ads, displayed by a single call to the ad program's server (typically via a program such as Google's AdSense).

Affiliate
A virtual online sales agent for an online merchant, sometimes also called an associate. Affiliates make money when visitors to the affiliate site click through to the merchant's site, and then make a purchase.

Affiliate aggregator
A business that manages the relationships between online merchants and their affiliates.

Associate
See *affiliate*.

Authentication headers
Information required by an AdWords API web service to validate access to the service.

Blog
An online dated chronicle, usually in reverse chronological order.

Blogging
The act of creating a blog entry.

Blogosphere
The online world of blogs and blogging.

Bot
Software that automatically searches the web for sites and pages to index (also called a *robot*, *web crawler*, or *spider*).

Channel
Used to track advertising results from different portions of a site (or sites).

Click fraud
A click made without actual interest in the product or services offered.

Click-through
The act of clicking on a link (or linked ad) on a web page and opening the target of that link or ad.

Competitive filter
Used to block ads that link to specific domains; often used to block competitor's ads from appearing on a site.

Contextually relevant ad
An ad whose content is relevant to the context in which the ad is placed; placing ads in a contextually relevant fashion is the goal of the Google AdSense for Content program.

Conversion
A conversion occurs when a site visitor performs a defined action, such as buying something.

Conversion ratio
The percentage of site visitors who convert.

Conversion tracking

A mechanism used to track the number of site visitors who convert.

Cookie

A piece of information sent by a web server to a web browser; the browser saves the cookie and sends it back to the server on request.

CPC

Cost Per Click; the amount paid by an advertiser when an ad—such as a Google AdWords ad—is clicked.

CPM

Cost Per Thousand; advertising paid for per thousand impression without regard to the number of click-throughs (in contrast to CPC ads).

Crawler

See *Bot*.

Creative

A text or graphical ad.

Cross links

Links between the pages on a site.

CTR

Click Through Rate; the percentage of ad click-throughs per ad impressions.

Developer token

A Google AdWords developer token (also called a *developer key*) is used to programmatically access the Google AdWords API web services.

Dynamic URL

A web address of a program, often followed by a question mark (?) and name=value pairs.

Dynamic web site

A web site whose content frequently changes, probably in response to user actions; dynamic web sites often using a database to supply content.

eCPM

effective Cost Per Thousand Impressions; a way to compare revenue from different kinds of advertising. eCPM is calculated by dividing the total earnings from an ad by its impressions in thousands. You can use this calculation to compare CPC revenue with its CPM equivalent.

Elevator pitch

Summary of a business idea, or of the content on a web site.

Imposition

The placement of ads in traditional print media.

Impressions

The number of times a page, or an ad, is displayed.

Inbound links

Links to a site

Include

See *server-side include*.

Keyword

(1) A word used as part of a search query; (2) A word or phrase used for targeting an ad in a program such as Google AdWords.

Link farm

A site that exists for the sole purpose of providing inbound links to better a page's search ranking.

Link unit

Displays links to pages containing ads.

Meta information

Information used to describe and categorize content such as a web page; for example, meta tag keyword and description data can help search engines properly categorize a site.

Meta tag

A mechanism used to provide information about a web page.

Micro-unit

A micro-unit, or micro, is used by the Google AdWords APIs to express monetary amounts. A micro is defined as one millionth of the fundamental currency unit, with the fundamental currency unit depending on the AdWords account involved. For example, with an AdWord account using U.S. dollars, 1,000,000 micros equals $1.00, and 10,000 micros = $.01.

MovableType

Leading blogging software, particularly appropriate for managing multiple blogs and authors.

No robots protocol

Used to exclude bots from searching a site.

ODP

Open Directory Project; an open source taxonomy and directory of web content.

Outbound links

Links leading off a web site.

Page CTR

The CTR for an individual web page.

PageRank

The algorithm used by Google to determine a web page's ranking, and hence the order it will be returned as part of a given search result set.

PHP

PHP Hypertext Processor; a popular server-side programming language used mostly for web pages

PPC

Pay Per Click, an ad that is paid for on a per-click basis, in other words, using a CPC ad program.

Proxy class

A class used to encapsulate remote interactions for another class, such as a web service.

Public Service Ad (PSA)

Public Service Ads are run by an advertising broker such as Google in the public interest. No fees are paid for click throughs of PSAs. PSAs will often appear before a site has been contextually profiled.

Robot

See *Bot*.

ROI

Return On Investment the financial benefit, usually expressed in terms of an annual percentage, of making a particular investment.

SOAP

Simple Object Access Protocol; a mechanism for publishing and invoking web services.

SEO

Search Engine Optimization; tuning web pages and sites so they will appear higher in the ranks of search engine results.

Server-side include

A mechanism used to place content from a file on the web inside a web page or file.

Skyscraper

A vertical ad block.

Spider

See *Bot*.

Static web site

A static web site provides content that doesn't change frequently, in contrast to a dynamic web site.

Syndication

The mechanism of distributing a feed of information in XML format, including information derived from blog entries.

Taxonomy

A system used to categorize knowledge and information.

Templating system

Uses templates and special tags to manage the display of content, often derived from a database, on the Web.

TOS

Terms of Service; the conditions to which you must agree to join a program.

Trackback

A trackback is a comment recorded in a blog indicating that another blog has referenced the current entry.

Tracking cookie

In some circumstances, placed on an end-user's computer to help keep track of the user's actions; used by the Google AdWords program to track conversions.

Tracking ID

In affiliate programs, used to track the source of the customer so a sales commission can be paid.

URL

Uniform Resource Locator; a web address. The typical URL specifies the method used to access the resource (a protocol such as HTTP or HTTPS), the name of the host computer on which the resource is located, and the path of the resource, e.g., *http://www.braintique.com/ad/index.php*.

WCM

Web Content Management; software used to manage content and display it on the Web.

Webalizer

Popular software used on Linux servers for showing information about visitors to a site.

Webmaster

The person responsible for creating and administering a web site.

Webmaster program

A webmaster program pays a fee for referring webmasters (rather than end-users).

Workflow

On the web, workflow usually means the process of managing, editing, approving, and displaying content.

WordPress

Open source blogging software created using the PHP programming language.

WSDL file

A Web Services Description Language file provides information about a web service and its members.

Index

We'd like to hear your suggestions for improving our indexes. Send email to *index@oreilly.com*.

AND operator, 142
APIs (application program
      interfaces), 273–275
architecture, 22–26
articles, Google Scholar and, 151
ASACP (Association of Sites Advocating
      Child Protection), 125
Ask Jeeves, 32
ASP/ASPX (Active Server Pages), conversion
      tracking and, 256
associates, 81, 103
Association of Sites Advocating Child
      Protection (ASACP), 125
Atom feeds, 48
audiences, 30
authentication headers, 291–296, 330, 333
authentication information, creating for web
      services, 319

B

bad neighborhoods, 78
banners, 9, 82, 86
   (see also creatives)
bcc (blank copy) senders, 53
beta software, Google and, 147
biometric measuring hardware/software, 126
BirthDateVerifier Age Verification
      System, 125
blank copy (bcc) senders, 53
blocking competitors' ads, 169
blog content management software, 7
blog templates, 49
Blogger, 7, 148
Blogger Atom API, 274
blogging services, 148
blogosphere, 7–8
blogs, 7–8
   Googleplex Blog and, 7
   templating and, 19
bold text, optimizing keyword placement
      and, 73
books, Google Print and, 150
boring pages, placing ads on, 22
bots, 31, 56–62
   database of excludable, 62
   excluding from your site, 59–62
   text-only browsers and, 58
Braintique.com, 15
BrightAds, 114
broad matches, 237
broad-site approach, 113
broad traffic, 3

broken links, 68, 88
browsers, 58
budgets
   Ad Campaigns, displaying for, 226
   currency and, 296
businesses, Google Local and, 149
buttons, 86
   (see also creatives)

C

Cached link, 145
calendars, 10
Campaign IDs, 287, 300–302
Campaign report (Ad Words), 245
Campaign Summary window
      (AdWords), 210, 215, 225–228
   conversions and, 262
   cross-channel tracking and, 267
Campaign Web Service client, 291–296
CampaignService (AdWords API), 281, 315,
      321
case sensitivity, Google searches and, 143
catalogs, Google Catalogs and, 149
categories (see taxonomies)
celebrities, adult content and, 124
channels, 163, 168
   cross-channel tracking and, 266
   displaying top-performing, 177
   generating reports and, 180
   search boxes and, 172
channels link, 176
Channels page (AdSense), 168
chatrooms, 10
checklists, 30
Child Internet Protection Act, 126
child pornography, reporting, 125
children, protecting from adult
      content, 125–126
city targeting, 196
click fraud, 109
click throughs, 94
   (see also CTR)
clicks, 108, 181
   Ad Campaigns, displaying for, 226
   Ad Groups, displaying for, 227
   displaying, 177
   (see also CPC; CTR)
click-through rate (see CTR)
client manager accounts, 222
client objects, creating, 291–296, 303, 307,
      333
cloak pages, 78

custom channels, 163, 168
    generating reports and, 180
customer conversion (see converting
        prospects)
customers, targeting via AdWords, 193–198
customizing
    AdWords reports, 251
    channels, 163, 168
    colors, 166
    geographic targeting, 195, 197
    Google home page, 150
    Search Results page, 173
CyberAge, 126
CyberSitter, 125

D

date ranges, choosing for reports, 179
Debian Social Contract, 35
deceptive techniques, 79
Description lines, 198
descriptive information, meta tag for, 63
design, 15
    search engine optimization and, 56
    separating from content, 18–20
    web site optimization and, 66
Destination URLs, 199
developer token, obtaining, 282–286
diagnostics, Ads Diagnostic Tool
        for, 231–234
directories, 32
    vs. indexes, 34
    working with, 34–40
Disallow line (robots.txt file), 61
discussion threads, 45
Display URLs, 199
document literal web services, 288
domain name registrars, 44
domain names, prohibitions and, 79
domain spamming, 79
doorway pages, 78
double quoting, 143
Download CSV file link (AdSense), 182, 184
Dreamweaver (Macromedia), conversion
        tracking and, 256
DynamiContext, 114

E

e-commerce sites, 8
earnings
    displaying, 176, 177, 181
    monitoring, 183

Earnings link (AdSense), 184
earnings per click (EPC), 94
eBay, 9, 10
eCPM (effective CPM), 109, 181, 182
Edit Campaign Settings window
        (AdWords), 213
editing tools, for Ad Campaigns, 239
Editorial Guidelines (Google), 201
effective CPM (eCPM), 109, 181, 182
elevator pitch, 30
    meta tags and, 64
email lists, 52
email management, 53
email newsletters, 53
entry pages (see opening pages)
EPC (earnings per click), 94
error-handling, 299–311
estimating traffic, 237
ETrade, 9
exact matches, 237
Excel (Microsoft), importing report files
        into, 182, 184
exclusion operator (-), 143
exit pages, 186
expulsion, 80

F

Fastclick, 114, 115
FeedForAll, 51
file formats, bot searches and, 57
filtering competitors' ads, 169
filtering, collaborative, 203
Find and Edit Keyword tools, 242
Find and Edit Keywords window
        (AdWords), 242
Find and Edit Max CPCs window
        (AdWords), 239
Find and Edit Text window (AdWords), 240
Findwhat, cross-channel tracking and, 266
First Amendment (United States
        Constitution), 123
focused traffic, 3
frames, placing ads on, 164
framesets, 164
FreePressRelease.com, 45
FrontPage (Microsoft), conversion tracking
        and, 256
Froogle, 149

national targeting, 195
navigability, web site optimization and, 66
negative keywords
    ad exclusions and, 212
    search exclusions and, 237
Net Nanny, 125
NetMechanic, 34
NetTracker tool, 185
Network Solutions, 44
newsletters, 53
newspapers, 6
nichology, for adult content, 130
NuSOAP, 290
NuSOAP libraries, 333, 335

O

obscenity, legal issues and, 123
ODP (Open Directory Project), 34, 35–37
    Google Directory and, 149
ODP-Adult, 134
Open Directory Project (see ODP)
opening pages
    adult content and, 122, 125
    splash pages and, 15
operators, Google searches and, 142
optimizing
    Ad Groups, 235–238
    ads, 214
    keywords, 71–77, 235–238
    links, 69, 70
    pages, 70
    search engines, 55–80
    web sites, 66, 67
OR operator, 142, 144
Org.com, domain spamming and, 79
outbound links, 68
    optimizing, 69
Overture, 114
    cross-channel tracking and, 266

P

Page CTR (Page click-through rate), 109,
    177
page design (see design)
page eCPM, 109
page impressions, 94, 109, 181
page size, 16
    optimizing, 70
page width, 17
PageRank, 55, 69, 144
    prohibitions and, 78

pages
    cloak, 78
    duplicating, prohibitions and, 78
    optimizing, 70
    positioning ads and, 20–22, 110, 166
    tracking users to specific, 263
parental control software, 125
PartnerCentric, 92
pay per sale, adult sponsors and, 132
Pay Per Sign-up (PPS), adult sponsors
    and, 132
Payment History link (AdSense), 183
payment history, reviewing, 157
PayPal, conversion tracking and, 256,
    256–263
people, highlighting on web site, 31
pay-for-click, 9
performance
    Ads Diagnostic Tool for, 231–234
    improving for Ad Campaigns/Ad
        Groups, 225–243
    keywords and, 327–337
    monitoring with AdSense, 176–189
Persian Kitty, 129, 135
Personalize Your Home Page, 150
PHP (Hypertext Preprocessor)
    conversion tracking and, 256
    using AdWords API with, 288–291
.php files, 24
PHP includes, 24, 26
PHP programing, 19
PHPList tool, 53
phrase matches, 237
PIDs, 94
pipe character (|), 142
plus (+) operator, 142
popularity
    Alexa rankings and, 10–13
    celebrities and, 31
    enhancing, 40–44
pornography (see adult content)
positioning ads, 20–22, 166
    average position and, 228
    contextual advertising and, 110
PPC, 267
PPS (Pay Per Sign-up), adult sponsors
    and, 132
press releases, 31, 44–48
    adult industry and, 137
    preparing, 47
pricing, for ads, 203
products, linking to, 87

W

W3C, 276
W-9 tax form, 116, 157
WCM (Web Content Management), 19
web analytic software, 189
web applications, AdWords API and, 287
web browsers, 58
Web Content Management (WCM), 19
web hosting, adult content and, 126
web log analysis programs, 185
web log data, 185–188
web methods, 276
web metrics, 14, 17
Web Nymph, 137
web pages (see pages)
web references, adding to web
    services, 316–319
web search boxes, 171
web services, 276–280
    authentication information for,
        creating, 319
    client for, creating, 291–296
    document literal, 288
    request headers and, 277
    working with, 314–319
Web Services Description Language
    (WSDL), 276
web site advertising, ix
    Alexa and, 10–13
    drawing traffic and, zero-cost ways
        of, 29–54
    elements of success and, 4
    excluding sites from Ad Campaigns
        and, 211
    naming your site and, 30
    optimizing web sites and, 66, 67
    shallow-site/broad-site approaches
        and, 113
    Site / Keyword Report and, 245, 246
    submitting sites to search engines
        and, 31–34
    types of, 82
web sites
    AdSense, 114
    AdWords API Center, 282
    Amazon.com Associate program, 104
    Braintique.com, 15, 288
    Content Match, 114
    Google Directory, 36
    Googlefight, 4
    Open Directory Project, 35
    RSS Compendium, 5
    Yahoo! Directory, 38
Web spammers, 78
Web Trend Analytics tool (Microsoft), 185
Webalizer tool, 185
weblogging software, email list functionality
    and, 53
weblogs (see blogs)
webmaster programs, adult sites and, 132
webmasters, finding email address for, 42
WebTrends tool, 185, 189
Whois service, 44
Whois.net, 44
wide skyscrapers, 161, 166
wire services, 44
Woods, Linda, 92
WordPress, 7
WSDL (Web Services Description
    Language), 276
WSDL files, 276–282
    creating client objects and, 295

X

XBiz
    adult web hosts and, 126
    press releases and, 137
    sponsors, finding through, 134
    Traffic/Marketing section of, 135
XBiz Directory
    adult content legal issues and, 123
    purchasing adult content and, 122
XML wrappers, 291, 298, 302
Xml.com site, 50

Y

Yahoo! Stores, conversion tracking and, 256
Yahoo!, 32
Yahoo! Directory, 34, 37–40
Yellow Pages data, Google Local and, 149
YNOT.COM, 137

About the Author

Harold Davis is a strategic technology consultant, hands-on programmer, and author of many well-known books. He's also a popular speaker at trade shows and conventions, giving presentations on topics ranging from digital photography to wireless networking, web services, and programming methodologies. His books include: *Building Research Tools for Google for Dummies* (Wiley), *Learn How to Program Using Any Web Browser* (Apress), *Red Hat Linux 9: Visual QuickPro Guide*, and *Visual Basic .NET: Visual QuickStart Guide* (both Peachpit Press). Harold has served as a consultant for investment funds, technology companies, and Fortune 500 corporations. In recent years, he has been Vice President of Strategic Development at YellowGiant Corporation, a company providing infrastructure for Internet marketing; Chief Technology Officer at a CRM analytics startup; Technical Director at Vignette Corporation and a leader in customer-centric content management; and a Principal in the enterprise consulting practice at Informix Software.

Colophon

The animal on the cover of *Google Advertising Tools* is a white-headed capuchin monkey (*Cebus capucinus*). The capuchin monkey is named after an order of monks, the Capuchins, because the color of the monkey's head is said to resemble a cowl worn by these monks. Native to parts of Central and South America, capuchin monkeys can be found in a range of habitats, including rain forests, mangrove forests, and wooded areas.

Traveling in groups of 6 to 20 monkeys, capuchins spend much of their day foraging for food. While they prefer fruit, capuchins will also eat leaves, nuts, flowers, insects, spiders, and sometimes small birds and lizards. Because food can be scarce, capuchins have to come up with creative ways to feed themselves. For example, they have been observed using tools to crack open the tough nuts of shells and teaching their offspring how to use these tools.

Scientists postulate that the challenges that the monkeys face in procuring food has helped develop their intelligence. Capuchins' small size and high intelligence make them good pets, and they are sometimes trained to act as assistants to paraplegic people. Most famously, perhaps, the capuchin monkey is the traditional companion of the organ grinder.

The cover image is from *Wood's Illustrated Natural History*. The cover font is Adobe ITC Garamond font. The text font is Linotype Birka; the heading font is Adobe Myriad Condensed; and the code font is LucasFont's TheSans Mono Condensed.